FARMHOUSE FARE

FARMHOUSE FARE

New and Enlarged Edition

Country Recipes collected by
FARMERS WEEKLY

COUNTRYWISE BOOKS

© Copyright Countrywise Books 1973
First published by Agricultural Press Ltd., 1935

Published for Countrywise Books by
Hamlyn Publishing, a division of
The Hamlyn Publishing Group Limited
Bridge House, London Road, Twickenham, Middlesex, England
First published 1973

Thirteenth impression 1986

ISBN 0 600 33509 7

Line drawings by Brian Walker
Cover photograph by John Lee

Printed in Portugal by Resopal

CONTENTS

FOREWORD

EVERY year since Farmers Weekly was first published in 1934, farmers' wives have been sending us their recipes for the kind of cooking which is traditional in their own corner of the British countryside, or for new dishes which they have invented to provide hardworking, hungry families with three square meals a day.

It was the idea of Mary Day, the first editor of Farmers Weekly's Home Section, that these recipes would find a wider appreciation in book form. Mary was a tremendous enthusiast, but even she could not have foreseen that Farmhouse Fare would reach more than half a million other homes in Britain and everywhere else in the world where good British cooking is appreciated.

In this, our seventh edition, we have brought the whole book up to date again, and in addition to the recently-contributed recipes you will also find a chapter on that most useful modern aid to country cooking—the deep freezer. We hope, as farmers ourselves, that more and more townspeople will be able to enjoy fresh, unprocessed food which they have selected and frozen for later use, either from their own gardens or from the increasing number of farms which offer meat, fruit and vegetables on direct sale to those who really appreciate freshness and flavour.

British farmers have a tremendous part to play in providing the nation with good, wholesome food and they do so at prices which are still well below those anywhere else in Europe. We at Farmers Weekly like to feel that through this little book, their wives, too, can help to uphold the tradition that the best of British cooking cannot be bettered anywhere else in the world.

TRAVERS LEGGE
Editor, Farmers Weekly.

SOUPS

CHEESE SOUP

A little butter or margarine.
1 tablespoonful finely-chopped onion.
½ pint hot water.
1 pint milk.
2 tablespoonfuls flour.
Seasoning.
2 tablespoonfuls finely-grated cheese.

FRY the onion, without browning, in the butter or margarine. When soft add the hot water. When the fragments of the onion are fully cooked, add the milk to increase the measure to about a quart, and as soon as it boils stir in the flour mixed smooth with milk. Season to taste, stir, and simmer till it thickens. A moment or so before serving, mix in the cheese.

From Miss Agnes S. Robertson, Lanarkshire.

CHESTNUT SOUP

¾ lb. chestnuts.
Seasoning.
1 quart stock.

CUT tops of chestnuts, bake until both skins come away easily, peel them and put them into a saucepan. Cover with the stock and simmer gently until the nuts are thoroughly cooked. Strain and pass through a sieve.

7

At this point there are alternatives:

(a) If the sweetness is liked, the sieved chestnuts can go back into the stock in which they were boiled, together with salt and a little cayenne pepper. Bring to the boil.

(b) Add the sieved nuts to fresh stock and counteract the sweetness by adding mace to the seasoning.

A third method is to simmer the nuts in milk, sieve them and add both stock and the reduced milk in which they were cooked. Bring to the boil.

From Mrs. C. I. Chell, Essex

CHUCKIE SOUP

1 quart stock in which fowl or knuckle of veal has been cooked.
Bunch of sweet herbs (thyme, marjoram, a few peppercorns and mace).
1 leek, finely sliced.
1 medium carrot cut into dice.
1 onion, finely sliced.
1 oz. beef dripping or butter.
1 tablespoonful flour.
1 gill milk.
Pepper, salt and 1 tablespoonful parsley cut into small snippets with scissors.

FRY the carrot, onion and leek in fat made smoking hot in a saucepan but do not brown. Season with pepper and salt, add the stock and cook for 30 minutes.

Thicken with flour mixed with milk and cook over a gentle heat for another 5 minutes. Add the parsley snippets just before serving.

A tablespoonful of cream greatly improves this soup if added with the parsley just before serving.

Sufficient for four good servings.

From Mrs. E. C. Webb, Shropshire.

COCKIE LEEKIE

An old hen.
2 tablespoonfuls vinegar.
½ cupful rice.
4 large leeks.
¼ lb. prunes.
A good tablespoonful chopped parsley.

CLEAN the hen, put in cold water with the vinegar, and let it stand overnight. Wash well, and put on to boil; afterwards allowing to simmer until fairly tender (about 2½ hours). Add the rice and leeks, cook until tender: add the prunes (previously stewed and stoned) without the syrup. Add the parsley. Take out the hen, but put a few pieces of the breast back into the soup. Skim the fat off, and serve.

The remainder of the meat may be removed from the bones, reheated, and sent to table covered with egg sauce and it will serve as a separate dish.

From Mrs. H. Nelson, Pembrokeshire.

CREAM OF CHICKEN SOUP

1 spring chicken.	3 large carrots.
1 onion.	Small piece turnip.
Heaped tablespoonful cornflour.	$\frac{1}{2}$ teacupful cream.
1 heaped tablespoonful chopped parsley.	Salt and pepper to taste.

PREPARE chicken and put in stock pot with 5 pints of cold water. Bring very slowly to the boil. Have ready carrots, onion and turnip, and add. Simmer gently for $3\frac{1}{2}$ hours. Lift chicken, remove skin and bones, and either cut flesh finely or put through the mincer.

Strain stock, add chicken along with a heaped tablespoonful of cornflour blended smoothly with $\frac{1}{2}$ teacupful of cream. Bring to the boil, add chopped parsley, pepper and salt to taste, and serve piping hot in well-warmed tureen.

From Miss Christian Milne, Aberdeenshire.

FISH SOUP

BOIL 1 lb. of fresh cod in salted water, to which a dash of vinegar has been added, until tender. Remove skin and bones and flake finely. Put 3 pints of sweet milk into a saucepan add flaked fish and simmer gently for 1 hour. Then add a tablespoonful of cornflour blended with a little cold milk and salt and pepper to taste. Just before lifting add a piece of butter the size of a walnut and a heaped tablespoonful of finely-chopped parsley. Serve piping hot in a well-warmed tureen.

From Miss Christian Milne, Aberdeenshire.

GREEN SOUP

DON'T throw away pea pods. Wash them thoroughly in salt water. Put into a pan with water, salt, an onion, carrot and a bunch of herbs. Boil until tender (on the back of the stove all the afternoon), then pass through a sieve. Thicken with a little cornflour and butter.

From Miss R. Overington, Surrey.

HARE SOUP

PREPARE hare, cut into joints, being careful to retain the blood. Wash thoroughly in salted water. Then place in a stock pot and cover with cold water. Add 4 large carrots, 2 pieces of turnip, 2 onions, and a large, well-scrubbed potato in its jacket.

Simmer gently for 4 hours. Then remove hare from pot and put the flesh, heart, kidneys and liver through the finest cutter of the mincer. Strain stock, return to pot and add minced hare. Strain blood through a gravy strainer, add 1 tablespoonful cold water and blend smoothly with a heaped tablespoonful of cornflour. Bring very slowly *to the boil*. The idea of adding water to the blood is to prevent it curdling. Be careful to see that the soup does not boil after the blood is added, or curdling may result despite the precaution.

Mushroom ketchup is the perfect seasoning for hare soup, but should be added to individual taste after the soup is in the plates.

From Miss Christian Milne, Aberdeenshire.

IMITATION HARE SOUP

1 lb. shin beef.	1 oz. flour.
1 onion.	1 quart stock.
1 carrot.	4 peppercorns.
1 turnip.	2 teaspoonfuls Worcester sauce.
1 oz. dripping.	

MELT dripping and fry the onion. Cut the meat very small and remove the fat. Brown the flour in the pan when the onion is taken out. Cut the vegetables very small. Add cold liquid, and put everything in saucepan. Bring to the boil, and simmer for 1½ hours. Make forcemeat balls as below, and toss them in flour. Strain the soup and cook the balls in it for ½ hour.

Forcemeat balls :

1 tablespoonful breadcrumbs.	A little grated nutmeg.
½ tablespoonful chopped suet.	A little grated lemon rind.
1 teaspoonful mixed herbs.	Salt and cayenne pepper.
1 egg.	

Put all in a basin and mix to a stiff paste with the beaten egg. Make 6 balls.

From Miss F. Hopkins, Caernarvonshire.

HARICOT BEAN SOUP

1 lb. haricot beans.	2 Spanish onions.
1 peeled turnip: 1 stick celery.	2 quarts water: 1 pint milk.
2 ozs. dripping.	Pinch ground mace.
Sprig parsley: 2 tomatoes.	Salt and pepper.

SOAK beans in cold water overnight. Next day drain and add to water with mace, diced vegetables, pepper and dripping. Bring to boil and simmer for 3 hours, adding the sliced tomatoes 30 minutes before the soup is ready. When ready, rub through a wire sieve and add milk, minced parsley, and salt to taste. Reheat and serve. For 6 or 8 people.

From Mrs. J. R. Robinson, Cumberland.

MULLIGATAWNY SOUP

1 rabbit.	1 turnip.
A few good gravy bones.	A little salt.
4 pints water.	⎰ 6 tablespoonfuls flour.
6 onions.	⎬ 1 tablespoonful curry powder.
1 carrot.	⎱ $\frac{1}{2}$ pint water.

PREPARE the rabbit, boil in water till quite tender, take all the meat off, and put in a basin by itself. Put the gravy bones in the water the rabbit was boiled in, and boil for two hours. Strain through a sieve. Put back in saucepan. Mix the flour and curry powder with the $\frac{1}{2}$ pint of water, and add to stock. Let it boil 15 minutes. Add the rabbit, and it is ready for serving.

A glass of port wine is an improvement.

From E. C. Pratt, Bedfordshire.

OAT SOUP WITH CREAM (OR MILK)

1 cupful rolled oats.	1 little bayleaf.
4 teacupfuls white stock.	Seasoning.
3 cloves.	1 teacupful scalded thin cream or
1 teaspoonful sugar.	milk.
2 sliced onions.	

PUT the ingredients, except sugar and cream, in a saucepan and simmer for 1 hour. Strain through a cheese-cloth, put again into a saucepan, and add the sugar and cream (or milk). Pour into a tureen which contains a lump of butter, a little salt and cayenne, and serve.

From Miss J. Harle, Durham.

11

PEA SOUP WITHOUT MEAT

1 pint dried whole peas.	4 onions.
3 quarts water.	4 carrots.
3 medium-sized turnips.	Oatmeal. Pepper and salt.

SOAK the peas all night; next day put them into 3 quarts of boiling water, boiling them till tender. Take them out, mash them together so as to form a paste, put them back into the water with the turnips and carrots (cut into dice) and the sliced onions. Let the soup simmer gently for 2 hours, then thicken with oatmeal and season with pepper and salt.

From Mrs. S. A. Ladd, Pembrokeshire.

POTATO SOUP

1 lb. potatoes.	1 oz. margarine.
2 small onions.	1 pint water.
1 dessertspoonful sago.	Salt and pepper.

PEEL potatoes and onions, and cut in slices. Put them into a saucepan with the margarine, put on the lid and let them cook together for 5 minutes or so. Shake the pan from time to time. Add water and simmer gently for about an hour. Then add the milk and the sago, and cook until the sago is transparent. Season, and serve hot.

From Joyce Mustill, Cambridgeshire.

RICH HARE SOUP

A large hare.	1 large wine-glassful port wine.
¾ lb. ham or bacon.	3 quarts beef stock.
2 onions.	A little salt and cayenne.
2 blades mace.	¼ lb. breadcrumbs.
A bunch of thyme, parsley and sweet marjoram.	

CUT the hare into pieces, and the ham or bacon into slices. Put into a stewpan with the beef stock, onions, bunch of herbs and mace. Stew all together for about 2½ hours. Take out the bacon and pound all the inferior parts of the hare with it in a mortar. Strain the soup back into the stewpan, add the pounded meat and the breadcrumbs and the port wine. Simmer for nearly ½ hour. Rub through a sieve, season with a little salt and cayenne. Make it very hot, but do not let it boil, and serve it up quickly.

From Mrs. Rose H. Dancer, Northamptonshire.

SCOTCH BROTH (1)

1 lb. neck of mutton.	1 quart water.
1 turnip.	1 grated carrot.
1 onion.	1 tablespoonful rice.
½ teaspoonful chopped parsley.	Potatoes.
Seasoning.	

WIPE the meat and cut into neat joints. Put in a pan with the water, and season to taste. Bring slowly to the boil, and skim. Cut the vegetables into small pieces, wash the rice and put it all into the pan. Let it simmer for 2 hours. Add the chopped parsley to the broth and serve at once.

From Miss Sarah Lund, Lancashire.

SCOTCH BROTH (2)

1 fowl or piece fat boiling meat.	4 ozs. barley.
8 ozs. split peas.	1 oz. whole peas.
2 leeks.	3 carrots.
2 pieces turnip.	4 brussels sprouts.
1 onion.	2 blades of kale.
Few sprigs parsley.	Few turnip tops.

PUT 7 pints of water in a soup pot. Bring to the boil, then add salt to taste, vegetables cut in dice and fowl (stuffed with oatmeal stuffing and securely tied) or meat if no fowl is available. Boil for 3½ hours. Then serve piping hot in a well-warmed tureen. This is ample for 6 persons.

N.B.—The parsley should be very finely chopped and added just before serving.

From Miss Christian Milne, Aberdeenshire.

SHEEP'S HEAD BROTH

and a Potted Meat recipe for use with the same sheep's head

SOAK a sheep's head overnight in cold, salted water. Pour off the next morning, wash well and place the head in a good-sized pan. Cover the head with water and put on to boil. Simmer for 30 minutes, skimming all the time, then add a good handful of peas, and the same quantity of barley; both having previously been steeped. Add 2 carrots, 1 small turnip and 2 onions, all cut up into dice; then 1 firm white heart of cabbage cut up. Simmer for 1 hour, then throw in a suet ball for each person. Simmer for another hour, taking the scum off as it appears. Remove from the fire and take the sheep's head out on to a plate. Serve the soup with squares of bread. For the suet balls, mix 2 ozs. suet, 3 ozs. flour, a little salt and water. Roll into balls in a little flour. See that the soup is boiling when the balls are put in.

After the sheep's head has cooled, remove all the meat from the bone and put it through the mincing machine. Add salt, pepper and a good scrape of nutmeg, and stir it together with three tablespoonfuls of the clear liquor it has been boiled in. Press into small jars and run melted butter over the top.

From Mrs. M. Scott, Durham.

SPRING SOUP

1 large lettuce.	1 tablespoonful cornflour.
12 spring onions.	Parsley.
1 pint milk.	Salt.
1 pint stock, or water.	Nutmeg.
Crusts of bread.	Sugar.

Watercress, endive or sorrel may be used either with or in place of, the lettuce for a change.

WASH lettuce and onions, shred lettuce, and slice onions thinly. Melt dripping in saucepan, and fry lettuce and onions for about 5 minutes. Add stock and part of milk, and let simmer gently for 10 minutes. Mix cornflour with remainder of milk, pour into soup, and stir until it boils, allowing to simmer for another 10 minutes. Season to taste with pepper, salt, sugar and a little nutmeg. Cut crust of bread into thin strips, dry quite crisp in oven, put into tureen with parsley picked small, and pour soup over.

From Miss F. Hughes, Denbighshire.

TATTIE HUSHLE

3 fair-sized potatoes.	Skimmed milk.
Small leek or onion.	A little sauce.
1 heaped tablespoonful oatmeal.	Salt and pepper.
Nut of margarine.	

PUT potatoes and leek in a pan. Season and cover with water. Boil till tender, mash and add the margarine. Soak the oatmeal in a little of the milk, then pour off the liquid into the soup and add the rest of the milk (about 1 pint).

Bring to a good boil and add a teaspoonful of sauce. If you wish to keep some until the next day do not add the sauce until required. I can thoroughly recommend this soup for it is economical, quick and delicious.

From Mrs. E. Grant, Surrey.

TOMATO SOUP

6 tablespoonfuls tinned tomatoes.
1 pint milk.
1 oz. butter.

Pepper and salt to taste.
1 teaspoonful sugar.
Pinch bicarbonate of soda.

PUT the tomatoes into a saucepan with the bicarbonate of soda; when they present a frothy appearance, add butter, sugar, pepper and salt, boil the milk and pour it over the tomatoes and stir until it boils. The soup is now ready for use. If preferred it may be strained. Serve with a little paprika.

From Mrs. Burton, Melton Mowbray.

VEGETABLE MARROW SOUP

1 large onion.
1 large marrow.
2 ozs. dripping.
1 pint milk.

2 pints white stock.
2 ozs. flour.
Salt and pepper.

MINCE the onion finely. Peel and cut up the marrow and remove seeds. Melt 1 oz. of dripping in a pan, add the marrow and onion, and steam for 20 minutes. Add the milk and stock, and cook until marrow is tender. Then rub through a sieve, melt the second ounce of dripping, add it to the soup, together with the flour and seasoning; and stir until it boils.

From Mrs. H. Cobley, Leicestershire.

VELVET SOUP

1 large tablespoonful butter.
1 teaspoonful curry powder.
Salt and pepper to taste.

1½ large tablespoonfuls flour.
1½ pints milk and a little cream.

MELT the butter in a pan, add the flour and curry powder and mix to a smooth paste. Then add the milk and bring to the boil. Cook ½ tablespoonful of rice and put it into the soup tureen before pouring in the soup. Serve hot.

From Miss M. Holliday, Yorkshire.

WHITE SOUP

THIS is a nourishing soup in the warmer weather. Get an old fowl and after preparing it, put it on to boil with 3 quarts water, to which have been added a few pieces of turnip, 2 carrots and 2 onions. Let all simmer gently for 3 hours or until the fowl is cooked. Next add 2 pints sweet milk to which

4 tablespoonfuls ground rice have been stirred in. Let all simmer again for 10 minutes; then add a tablespoonful chopped parsley, and salt and pepper to taste.

From Mrs. Cromar, Aberdeenshire.

WHITE VEGETABLE SOUP

2 lbs. potatoes.
2 lbs. carrots.
2 lbs. onions.
2 lbs. turnips.
1 level tablespoonful margarine.
Salt and pepper.

1 rounded tablespoonful chopped parsley.
1 rounded teaspoonful sugar.
1 rounded teaspoonful fine sago.
6 breakfastcupfuls water.
1 breakfastcupful milk.

PREPARE the carrots, turnips, onions and potatoes, and cut them into fine dice. Melt the margarine, and sweat the vegetables in it for 20 minutes. Add the water, sugar and seasoning, and bring to boiling-point. Remove any scum caused by vegetables. Simmer from 1 to 1½ hours until vegetables are tender. Then wash sago, mix with a little water, add, and allow to simmer till sago is clear, which will take 20 minutes. Add milk and reheat. Place the chopped parsley in a tureen, and add the soup.

From Mrs. G. Neaves, Kent.

FISH

ANCHOVY POTATOES

TAKE two cups of mashed potatoes and add a small jarful of anchovy paste (or any other paste preferred). Mix well together, make into flat cakes. Dip in milk and breadcrumbs, fry in a little fat. These make delightful fish cakes and are very quickly prepared.

From Mrs. M. Callard, Kent.

COD AND MACARONI CASSEROLE

2 ozs. macaroni.
1½ lbs. cod.
Salt, pepper: 1 egg.
Dried herbs.

3 ozs. white breadcrumbs.
½ pint milk.
½ teaspoonful chopped parsley
Margarine.

BREAK macaroni into pieces, put in boiling salted water and boil for 10 minutes. Strain. Put cod into a casserole. Season, add parsley and herbs. Arrange macaroni and breadcrumbs in layers round the cod. Heat milk until nearly boiling, pour on beaten egg.

Pour over macaroni, put margarine dabs on top, cover with lid and bake for 1 hour. Remove lid when almost done to brown crumbs.

From Mrs. Rogers, Wrexham.

COD PANCAKES

½ lb. cooked cod.	Salt and pepper.
1 level tablespoonful chopped parsley.	Pinch of mixed herbs.
6 ozs. mashed carrot or parsnip.	

For the batter you require:

4 ozs. flour	Pinch of salt.
1 egg.	½ pint of water.

MAKE the batter by mixing the flour, salt, and egg together. Mix to a stiff batter with about half the water. Beat well. Add the rest of the water and beat again. Flake the fish and add to the batter. Then add the mashed carrot or parsnip, parsley, herbs and seasoning.

Melt a little fat in a frying-pan and when smoking hot, drop large spoonfuls of the mixture in and fry until golden brown on both sides.

From Mrs. Rogers, Wrexham.

COD'S ROE PASTE

SCRAPE all the cooked cod's roe away from the skin, add to taste pepper, salt, mustard (made with vinegar) and a little butter, then heat all well together and pound into a smooth paste. Press it into small basins or glass jars and allow to get cold, then pour over the top some oiled butter, which when set will form a protective covering and the paste will keep for several weeks. This paste can be used as a sandwich filling or as a savoury piled on hot buttered toast, or on bread and butter or toast at tea-time.

From Miss I. Turner, Somerset.

FISH AND BACON HOT-POT

6 ozs. boned, smoked fillets.	2 ozs. bacon.
½ oz. margarine.	6 ozs. tomatoes.

GREASE the bottom of an oven dish. Cut the fish in neat portions for serving and place in dish. Sprinkle with pepper and dot with margarine. Add a tablespoonful of water, then the sliced tomatoes (peeled), and lastly the bacon. Cover dish and cook in a moderate oven for 20 minutes. Remove lid and allow bacon to brown and crisp. This is sufficient for 2 persons.

From Mrs. Rogers, Wrexham.

FISH LOAF

1 breakfastcupful cooked fish.	1 tablespoonful anchovy essence.
¾ breakfastcupful breadcrumbs.	1 teaspoonful piccalilli.
Salt and pepper.	1 egg.

FLAKE the fish finely, removing skin and bone, mix well with the breadcrumbs, seasonings and anchovy essence. Take a good teaspoonful of piccalilli, add the liquid to the fish mixture, and chop the vegetable part finely; then add to the other ingredients. Bind with the beaten egg. Put into a greased basin; cover with greased paper, and steam for about 1 hour. Turn out and serve with sauce.

From Mrs. M. Bridges, Kent.

FISH PIE

1½ lbs. fresh filleted haddock.	Chopped parsley.
½ lb. soaked bread-crusts.	Seasoning to taste.
1 large cupful grated suet.	1 egg.

WASH the haddock and put in a fireproof pie-dish. Make a forcemeat of the other ingredients, binding together with the egg. Cover the fish with forcemeat and bake in a hot oven.

This can be prepared beforehand, and a hot tea or supper served without any trouble.

From Mrs. W. Woodcock, Yorkshire.

FISH PUDDING

1 lb cod.	1 beaten egg.
1 gill milk.	Breadcrumbs.
Margarine: mustard.	Pepper and salt.

BOIL cod in salted water, then remove the bones and skin and flake. Grease a mould and place alternate layers of fish and breadcrumbs. Season with a pinch of mustard, pepper, and salt. Pour over the milk and beaten egg, dot the top with bits of margarine and bake in a good oven until lightly browned. Turn out and serve very hot.

From Mrs. Rogers, Wrexham.

FISH RAMEKINS

1 lb. cold cooked fish.
Milk.
2 ozs. grated cheese.

1½ cups white sauce.
2 teaspoonfuls of Worcester or other sauce.

FLAKE fish into basin. Add a little milk and thick, white sauce mixed with the cheese. Season to taste with Worcester sauce. Mix well and pile into buttered ramekins. Sprinkle with stale breadcrumbs and grated cheese. Bake in the top of a moderate oven for ¼ hour.

From Mrs. Rogers, Wrexham.

FISH ROLL

½ lb. cooked fish.
¼ lb. oatmeal.
1 teaspoonful baking powder.
Seasoning.

¼ lb. flour.
2 ozs. shredded suet.
A little anchovy essence.

REMOVE all skin and bone, flake and season fish with pepper, salt and a little anchovy essence. Mix the flour, suet, oatmeal and baking powder into a firm paste with a little water. Roll out to an oblong shape. Spread fish mixture on to it and roll up, pressing the edges together. Tie in a cloth and boil gently for 2 hours. Turn out and serve with parsley sauce.

From Mrs. Rogers, Wrexham.

FISH ROLL

1 lb. boiled cod.
2 ozs. grated cheese.
1 dessertspoonful chopped parsley.
1 egg.

2 breakfastcupfuls mashed potatoes.
Pepper and salt.
A little milk and browned breadcrumbs.

FREE the fish from skin and bone and flake with a fork. Mix with the potatoes, cheese, parsley, and seasoning. Bind with the egg and a little milk if necessary. Form into a thick roll and coat with browned crumbs. Put into a well-greased baking tin and bake for about ½ hour. Serve cut in slices with cheese sauce.

From Mrs. Rogers, Wrexham.

FISH SOUFFLE

1 lb. codfish (any other kind of fish will do—Finnan Haddock makes a very good savoury).
Pepper and salt to taste.

1 large tablespoonful flour.
2 ozs. butter.
2 eggs.
½ pint of milk.

PUT flour, milk and butter into a saucepan and stir until boiling. Pick all the bones from the fish, which should then be broken into pieces—not too small. Add fish to sauce and draw pan to side of fire, beating in the yolks of two eggs. Then whisk the whites well into the mixture. Fill a dish three parts full with the mixture, and bake in a moderate oven for ½ hour. Serve at once.

From Miss M. Holliday, Yorkshire.

FISH TOAST

The remains of any kind of boiled fish.	Margarine.
	Chopped parsley.
A little milk and seasoning.	1 onion, if possible.

POUND the fish with a little margarine, chopped parsley, chopped onion, seasoning, and enough milk to moisten to a paste. Cook under griller or in oven for 10 minutes and spread on very hot toast. Sprinkle with fried breadcrumbs or fried parsley.

From Mrs. Rogers, Wrexham.

FRIED HERRINGS
(As generally served in Buchan)

6 fresh herrings.	Salt and pepper.
2 heaped tablespoonfuls of oatmeal.	Dripping.

CLEAN herrings in usual way and dry well. Dip in seasoned oatmeal. Make dripping smoking hot and fry herrings slowly in this until firm and golden brown on each side. Serve on hot ashet. Vinegar and oatcakes are the perfect complement to this dish.

From Miss Christian Milne, Aberdeenshire.

HADDOCK PUFFS

½ lb. cooked haddock.	Salt and cayenne to taste.
Liquor in which haddock was boiled.	½ oz. finely chopped parsley.
2 ozs. self-raising flour.	2 eggs.
	Milk.

21

FLAKE the haddock with a little of the liquor it was boiled in, add the flour, seasoning and eggs, and add sufficient milk to make the mixture of a soft consistency like sponge sandwich dough. Have ready some very hot fat, and drop in tablespoonfuls of the mixture. Fry until golden brown. They will puff up beautifully.

Serve very hot, with mashed potatoes.

From D. G. Peard, Devonshire.

HADDOCK SURPRISE

1 lb. filleted haddock or ling.
A little milk and a small piece of margarine.

½ lb. tomatoes.
¼ lb. sausages.

WASH and dry fish, then roll one sausage in each fillet and place in an oven dish, so that each fillet roll is standing upright. Place one slice of tomato on top of each fillet, add milk and the small piece of margarine and cook in oven for 1½ hours. (Tinned or bottled tomatoes can be used.)

From Mrs. Rogers, Wrexham.

HADDOCK WITH SAVOURY BALLS

2 lbs. fresh haddock.

3 slices of fat bacon.

Stuffing :

2 ozs. breadcrumbs.
2 teaspoonfuls chopped parsley.
1 boiled, chopped onion.

2 ozs. chopped bacon.
½ teaspoonful mixed herbs.
Pepper and salt, and egg to bind.

WASH and dry fish well. Put two slices of the fat bacon into a baking-dish, place the fish on top and cover with the third slice of bacon. Mix all the stuffing ingredients together, form the mixture into balls and place these round the fish in the baking-dish. Cover with greased paper and bake in a moderate oven for about 20 minutes.

From Mrs. Rogers, Wrexham.

KROMESKIES

(This is a very good way of using up herring roes)

6 croûtons of bread.
6 soft roes.

3 rashers of bacon.
2 tomatoes.

SKIN tomatoes, cut into slices, and bake on a greased baking-sheet in a moderate oven. Cut rashers in half, wash roes, and roll each roe in a piece of bacon. Dip in the following batter and fry. Fry croûtons of bread first, and keep tomatoes and croûtons hot while frying roes.

Batter:

2 ozs. flour.	½ gill tepid water.
1 white of egg.	1 dessertspoonful salad oil.

Mix flour into a smooth dough with water and salad oil. Beat up white of egg stiffly and fold into batter.

Lay the cooked tomato slices on the fried croûtons, and the roes on top of the tomatoes. Serve hot.

From Miss H. Butler, Hertfordshire.

PILCHARD HOT-POT

LIFT out the pilchards from their tin, taking care not to break them. Slit them open to remove the bones, fold together again, and place side by side in a greased shallow pie-dish. Make a creamy sauce with margarine, flour and milk, adding seasoning and the liquid in which the pilchards were packed. Pour the sauce over the pilchards; cover each from head to tail with partly boiled potatoes overlapping each other. Place a greased paper on top, and bake for 15 to 20 minutes in a moderate oven; brown for a couple of minutes under the grill before serving.

From Mrs. F. Haynes, Warwickshire.

SALMON IN CUSTARD

1 small tin of salmon.	½ pint milk.
2 eggs.	Seasoning.

FLAKE the salmon with a fork and season well. Place in a greased fireproof dish. Pour over a custard made with 2 eggs beaten in the milk, and bake in the oven for about 30 minutes till set. To prevent the custard boiling, stand the dish in a shallow tin with a little water in it. Serve either hot or cold. This quickly-prepared dish is excellent for the summer supper-table.

From Mrs. R. Duckett, Somerset.

SALMON PIE

MASH the cooked fish well with a fork, and place a layer in a buttered pie-dish. Cover with mashed potatoes, well seasoned with salt and pepper, and then with a layer of finely-shredded onions. Repeat until the dish is nearly full, covering with a thick layer of white sauce. Put the dish in a moderate oven, and bake for about an hour. This is almost equally good made with tinned salmon.

From Mrs. G. M. Harris, Shropshire.

SARDINE ROLLS

1 small tin sardines or small pilchards.
Pepper and salt.

8 ozs. cold mashed potatoes.
Short-crust pastry or potato-crust
pastry (less fat being needed
for the latter).

MIX mashed potatoes, fish, and seasoning. Roll out pastry, cut into squares or rounds, and fill with a spoonful of mixture. Bake in a hot oven. These pasties are delicious cold, and very suitable for meals out of doors.

From Miss L. Thomas, Carmarthenshire.

SAVOURY BAKED COD

1 lb. cod.
1 tin celery soup, medium size.

Water.

WASH fish and cut into neat pieces. Put into a fireproof dish and season lightly. Pour over the soup mixed with enough water to cover the fish. Cover with greased paper and bake for 40 minutes in a moderate oven.

From Mrs. Rogers, Wrexham.

SAVOURY FILLETS OF FISH

1 fresh filleted haddock, or any
other fish.
1 packet celery soup powder.

1 pint hot water
4 ozs. forcemeat.

WIPE the fillets and place in each 1 oz. forcemeat. Roll up and tie with thread. Crumble the soup into a stew-pan, add the water slowly, stirring until smooth and bring to the boil. Place the fillets very gently in the soup and simmer for 20 minutes. Serve the rolls on a hot dish (after removing threads) with the soup poured round and over.

From Mrs. Rogers, Wrexham.

24

SAVOURY FISH CUTLETS

Cutlets of hake or cod.   Tomatoes.
Small lump of butter.   Flour.

WELL grease a baking-dish. Slice tomatoes and arrange them in a layer with fish cutlets on top. Add another layer of tomatoes, cover with water and small dabs of butter, and bake in a quick oven for 25 minutes. Strain stock and thicken with flour to make a sauce.

 Serve with potatoes or thin slices of toast.

From Margaret Brooke, Worcestershire.

SCALLOPED ROES

PLACE ½ lb. of herrings' roes in a saucepan; cover with water to which a little salt and vinegar has been added; boil until firm. Then butter a pie-dish, put a layer of brown breadcrumbs and a layer of the cooked roes alternately in the dish, sprinkle with salt and pepper; finish with breadcrumbs, and add a few knobs of butter on the top. Bake in a moderate oven until brown and serve very hot.

From Mrs. M. G. Ann, S. Walse.

SMOKED HADDOCK

LINE a flan-case with short pastry and add the following filling. Make a white sauce with ½ oz. margarine and ¾ oz. flour. Cook for 2 or 3 minutes, add 1 gill of milk or water. Flake the cooked haddock, removing all bones. Add to the sauce. Fill the flan and grate some cheese on top. Cook in a hot oven.

From Mrs. Rogers, Wrexham.

SMOKED HADDOCK WITH SPAGHETTI

1lb. haddock.   ½ lb. spaghetti.
2 slices of bacon.   Cheese sauce (with a little grated
            nutmeg).

BOIL, skin and flake the haddock. Boil and strain spaghetti and dice and fry bacon. Fry onions. Mix all together in a large pie-dish, season well. Pour cheese sauce over all and stir in. Cover with crumbs. Dot with fat and brown in the oven.

 N.B.—Use a fairly thin sauce.

From Mrs. R. Brown, Oxfordshire.

SOUSED HERRINGS

4 or more herrings.   Seasoning to taste.
1 onion.   Vinegar.

WASH and scale the herrings, cut off the heads and take out the backbones. Slice the onion finely, season with salt and pepper, and lay in a pie-dish. Roll up fish tightly, and place over the onions. Cover with vinegar and a little water, and bake in a slow oven for about an hour.

From Mrs. A. Darnell, Derbyshire.

STUFFED HADDOCK

CLEAN a medium-sized haddock, keeping it whole. Dry it, and rub a little salt down the backbone. Make a stuffing with 2 teacupfuls breadcrumbs, 2 teaspoonfuls chopped parsley, 1 oz. chopped suet, pepper and salt to taste, and a little milk to bind: stuff the fish, and sew or tie up with tape, and lay in a greased dish. Shake some flour over the fish, dot with butter or dripping, and bake for 20 minutes. Serve, garnished with slices of lemon, and sprigs of parsley.

From Mrs. E. Symes, Northumberland.

STUFFED HERRINGS

WASH and dry four fresh herrings. Remove heads, split herrings open, and take out backbone. Cook the roes gently in boiling water and then chop them. Mix with them 1½ tablespoonfuls of breadcrumbs, 1 tablespoonful melted butter, 1 teaspoonful anchovy essence, ½ teaspoonful chopped onion; season with salt and pepper. Close them, brush over with warm butter, and bake in moderate oven for 20 minutes. Serve with mustard butter; which is made as follows: Mix 1 oz. of butter with 1 teaspoonful dry mustard and 1 teaspoonful lemon juice. When thoroughly mixed together form into little pats and put one on top of each herring.

From Miss G. Beck, Sunbury Co., N.B.

26

SALADS

BROCCOLI SALAD

BOIL one fair-sized broccoli and place in centre of a dish; pour over a fairly thick mayonnaise dressing; garnish with a mixture of chopped cooked vegetables, including diced carrots and canned peas.

Do not pour any sauce over this as the colour contrasts with the broccoli, which may also be sprinkled with a little chopped parsley. A few lettuce leaves finish this substantial dish.

From Mrs. Eva Milner, Staffordshire.

GOOSEBERRY SALAD

SHRED ½ lb. young turnip tops and arrange in a bowl. Mix 1 breakfastcupful of diced, cooked potatoes, and 1 break-fastcupful of diced cooked beetroot. Arrange in small mounds alternately round the edge. In the centre, put 1 lb. of goose-berries, that have been cooked in sweetened water until tender, but not broken.

Strain off the syrup and use it for sweetening a thick mayonnaise to serve with this salad. Before serving, sprinkle some coarsely chopped parsley over all.

From Miss Dorothy Lakin, Leicestershire.

GREEN SALAD

WASH, drain and dry a large crisp lettuce. Tear into small pieces, add ½ dozen finely chopped spring onions and a handful each of well-washed mustard and cress. Mix and season.

Have ready one or two eggs, boiled till firm, and allowed to cool. Crumble with a fork, and, after mixing with salad dressing and seasoning, sprinkle over the salad.

From Mrs. M. Johnstone, Northumberland.

LETTUCE SALAD

RINSE some cabbage lettuce; drain and dry thoroughly; then break into convenient pieces. Have ready three hard-boiled eggs. Rub the salad bowl with a spring onion, arrange a layer of lettuce, then a few slices of egg. Repeat until the bowl is full.

Put 2 tablespoonfuls of sugar in a bowl, add a pinch of salt, a ¼ teaspoonful of mustard. Blend with a cup of cream. Then drop in, very carefully, sufficient white vinegar to make the dressing thick. Pour over the salad and serve immediately.

From Miss Christian Milne, Aberdeenshire.

MAYTIME SALAD

PREPARE some cabbage lettuce, drain and dry thoroughly. Have ready some finely-grated carrot, some grated turnip or radish, some finely-chopped spring onions and some cooked beetroot cut into dice. Pile some lettuce on plates, arrange a small pile of each kind of vegetable round. Pour over some salad dressing and serve immediately.

From Miss Christian Milne, Aberdeenshire.

POTATO SALAD

TAKE about 1 lb. potatoes, boiled (with salt) and cold, cut into small dice; put into the salad bowl and mix with ½ doz. washed and grated radishes.

Immediately before serving mix with dressing and sprinkle with a handful of finely-chopped chives. My economy dressing is 2 or 3 tablespoonfuls skimmed condensed milk; a small teaspoonful made mustard and vinegar added gradually and stirred all the time till a creamy mixture results.

From Mrs. M. Johnstone, Northumberland.

SPRING SALAD

Lettuce.
Chives.
Chopped sprouts (only the hearts).

Carrots.
Boiled beetroot.
Grated cheese.

LINE a shallow circular dish with crisp lettuce leaves. In the centre make a pile of grated cheese. Put a ring of beetroot slices round the cheese, then an outer ring of alternate heaps of grated carrot and chopped sprouts. Sprinkle chopped chives over the cheese.

From Mrs. Birkett, Cumberland.

TOMATO AND CHEESE SALAD

CHOOSE large firm tomatoes, allowing one to each person. Cut in half and scoop out a small part of the centre; fill in with scrambled egg and cheese (cooked together); and lay in large square entrée dish. Garnish all round edge with small pieces of lettuce hearts, and arrange cooked peas, carrots and beetroot in alternate heaps down the centre of the dish.

Serve with a good, well-seasoned salad dressing. This makes a delicious salad or supper dish.

From Mrs. Bennett, Lancashire.

JELLIED VEGETABLE SALAD

For this you will need:

The heart of a young cabbage.
½ oz. powdered gelatine.
¼ cupful cold water.
¼ teaspoonful salt.
1 dessertspoonful sugar.
1 dessertspoonful chopped parsley.

¼ cupful diced cooked carrot or beetroot.
Watercress or lettuce.
¾ cupful cooked peas.
1 cupful boiling water.
1 tablespoonful vinegar.

WASH and dry the cabbage well. Shred finely. Add the peas and diced carrot or beetroot. Add the cold water to the gelatine and then dissolve it in the boiling water, stirring well. Next add the sugar, vinegar, parsley and salt. Leave till it cools.

Now stir in the vegetables and pour into a wetted mould. Stand in a cold place to set. Turn out and garnish with lettuce or watercress leaves.

From Mrs. King, Kent.

POULTRY and GAME

BOILED DUCK

WHEN table ducks are plentiful, here is a recipe for boiling them.

Take a nice plump duck, and salt it for 24 hours by placing it in an earthenware vessel, and sprinkling a handful of salt over it. Take it out next day, wash it, and let it stand in cold water for about ½ hour. Tie it in a cloth and put into a saucepan of boiling water; to which add 2 tablespoonfuls of chopped sage and mint, and 3 medium-sized onions. Boil slowly until tender, about 2 hours. Serve with onion sauce and green peas.

From Mrs. O. Done, Shropshire.

CHICKEN GALANTINE

1 fairly large fowl.	1 teaspoonful chopped parsley.
1 egg.	Glaze.
1 lb. sausage meat.	Aspic jelly.
6 ozs. ham or tongue.	Grated rind of ½ a lemon.
1½ pints white stock.	2 ozs. breadcrumbs.
2 hard-boiled eggs.	A pinch of herbs.
Pepper and salt.	

BONE the fowl. Make a stuffing with the sausage meat, breadcrumbs, seasonings and beaten egg. Cut the ham into square pieces. Place this inside the fowl, with the hard-boiled eggs cut in quarters. Sew up with fine string, and roll in a clean cloth. Bring the stock to boiling-point, put in the fowl, and simmer gently for 2 to 2½ hours. When cold remove the cloth, glaze all over and dish up on a border of lettuce and cress, and garnish with chopped aspic jelly.

From Miss M. Ramage, Cheshire.

CHICKEN IN BATTER

1 chicken.	1 teacupful flour.
2 eggs.	Cupful cold water.
1 tablespoonful salad oil.	1 onion.
A little gravy.	3 sprigs of parsley.
2 tomatoes.	Salt.

PARBOIL the chicken, sprinkle with salt, and let it cool a little. Beat the yolks of 2 eggs with a pinch of salt. Stir in the salad oil and the gravy. Mix in the flour, then pour in the water. Stand this on one side to set. Take the onion, parsley, tomatoes, chop them finely and stir into the batter. Add the whipped whites of 2 eggs. Cut the chicken into neat pieces. Dredge with flour. Dip in batter and fry. Serve with rolls of fried bacon.

From Miss A. E. Parry, Flintshire.

CHICKEN AND PORK BRAWN

1 old fowl.	Seasoning.
2 pigs' feet and hocks.	

SKIN and clean fowl and cut up into joints. Clean feet and hocks. Put all in saucepan and cover with cold water, bringing to boil and simmering gently for 4 hours. Strain and remove bones, cut up meat finely and season highly with pepper and salt. Boil again for 10 minutes. Press into a mould and allow to set.

From Miss C. Provan, Middlesex.

CREAM OF CHICKEN MOULDS

1½ oz. rice.	Pepper and salt.
1 pint milk.	1 teaspoon chopped parsley.
½ lb. cold, cooked chicken.	Paprika and parsley to garnish.

USE a double saucepan and cook the rice in the milk until all the milk is absorbed. Cut the chicken into neat, small pieces, removing all the skin and add it to the rice with the seasoning and the parsley. Stir well together and fill small ramekin cases. Decorate with chopped parsley and paprika. Alternatively the mixture can be moulded into small cones, which should be egged, breadcrumbed and fried. When cold, decorate the top of each cone with paprika and chopped parsley, and garnish with mustard and cress.

From Kathleen Thomas.

CURRIED RABBIT

1 rabbit.	2 ozs. butter.
½ lb. cooked rice.	A little flour.
1 lb. onions.	Juice of ½ a lemon.
1 teaspoonful curry powder.	

CUT the rabbit into joints, dust with flour, and fry each in fat until a nice brown. Cut up the onions and fry these, then dust in the curry powder and the rest of the flour. Put the rabbit into a saucepan, and cover with stock or water. Boil up, then add the onions, etc., and simmer for 1½ hours, or till the meat seems quite done. Heat the rice, squeeze the lemon juice over the rabbit, then pile the rabbit and curry in the centre of the dish with a wall of boiled rice around. Serve hot.

From Mrs. A. M. Helliar, Somerset.

BOILED FOWL AND DUMPLINGS

THE prepared boiling fowl is placed in a pan or pot with a lid, covered with water to an inch above the bird, brought to the boil and continued to simmer, either on a stove or better in the oven (the top oven in an Aga). If the bird is to be just a boiled fowl it will need 2½ hours simmering, but if a more tasty dish is required, take the bird out of the boiling pan at 2 hours, put into roasting tin with a little liquor out of the pan, garnish with sausages, bacon rashers and stuff with a mixture of bread, onions and herbs mixed with an egg or just water, cover with brown paper and roast in the oven until tender and brown (it usually takes ¾ hour in an Aga oven, depending on the age of the bird).

During the boiling process prepare vegetables for the soup— one or several kinds can be used. I use onions, carrots, turnips and diced celery, and put in the pan after the first hour. Potatoes or any other main vegetables can be cooked separately in the usual way. About 30 minutes before serving I put into the pan the dumplings to boil for 20 minutes (1 lb. self-raising flour mixed with 4 oz. shredded suet or dripping or any other fat and a little salt, then add cold water until it can be mixed into little floury balls).

The soup can be served just as it is or thickened, but if the latter is preferred, take the dumplings out of the pan first and keep hot, then add thickening and boil for 2 minutes.

From Mrs. F. M. Willingham, Nr. Boston, Lincs.

BOILED FOWL WITH RICE

1 large fowl.	1 slice fat salt pork.
Bouquet garni, tied in muslin.	1 clove.
Salt and a few peppercorns.	½ lb. rice.
3 onions.	

PLACE the fowl in a deep saucepan and cover with hot water. Add all ingredients, except the rice. Cook gently for 1½ hours, then sprinkle the rice into the broth, laying the fowl on top. Reduce heat and gently simmer until rice is done. Some French cooks brown the fowl in butter before boiling to give a nice colour to the rice. Remove bouquet garni before serving.

From Kathleen Thomas.

FOWL PIE

1 old fowl.	A blade of mace, a few pepper-
2 chopped onions.	corns, a little thyme, tied in
1 stick of celery.	muslin bag.
¼ lb. ham, cut small.	3 hard-boiled eggs.
	Some chopped parsley.

PREPARE the fowl and cut into neat pieces, and put into a saucepan with the onions, celery, and ham and seasoning bag; salt, of course, should be added. Cover with cold water, bring to the boil and simmer till quite tender. Turn out and leave till cold; then remove the fat, and seasoning bag. Have ready 3 hard-boiled eggs and some chopped parsley. Put a layer of fowl in a pie-dish, with some of the gravy, and a layer of eggs and parsley alternately with the meat until the dish is filled. Cover with a good pastry crust and bake in a brisk oven till the pastry is nicely browned.

From Miss C. Ball, Bedfordshire.

GAME OR CHICKEN PIE
(*Cold—no crust*)

TAKE meat off raw bird (put aside) and boil carcase for about 5 hours to make a good jelly.

Put layers of chicken (or game meat) into a casserole with

a layer of hard-boiled egg slices, and raw sausage meat and a little fat bacon or streaky pork cut into strips (if chicken add the liver), sprinkle a little finely chopped parsley, pepper and salt and continue until the dish is three-quarters full. Pour strained stock in to just cover (retain the rest till later), and simmer slowly in the oven for an hour. When cold, remove fat from the top and pour in the remaining stock to fill with a lot of very finely chopped parsley and herbs (chervil especially) in it. Leave for top to set. Serve cold with separate salad. Jelly should be just wobbly when cut.

From Mrs. E. A. Cox, Herts

GAME SALADS

6 oz. cooked game (pheasant, hare, etc.).
2 oz. cooked ham.
Beetroot.

Potatoes.
White of 1 hard-boiled egg.
Stuffed olives.
Watercress.

For the dressing—
Yolk of 1 hard-boiled egg.
Black pepper and salt.
½ teaspoon made mustard.

2 tablespoons olive oil.
1 tablespoon white vinegar.

TO make the dressing, remove the yolk from the hard-boiled egg, beat in a basin with the seasonings, stir in the oil and the vinegar. Mince the game and ham, moisten with 1 tablespoonful of dressing, turn into small moulds or patty tins and press down. Dice the beetroot, potatoes and egg white. Toss in the dressing and arrange on individual dishes. Turn the game moulds carefully on to the bed of vegetables. Garnish each with a slice of olive and arrange watercress round the edge.

From Kathleen Thomas.

GLAZED PIGEON

2 pigeons.
½ lb. liver.
¼ lb. fat bacon.
½ a small onion.

1 bay leaf.
1 sprig of thyme.
1 sprig marjoram.
2 cloves.
A little meat glaze.

34

BONE the pigeons carefully without breaking the skin. Cut the liver and bacon into small pieces and chop the onion. Put the bacon into a frying-pan and fry a little then add liver, onion, bay leaf, thyme, marjoram and cloves and cook all together stirring well for about 12 minutes, then remove the bay leaf, pound all in a mortar, rub through a sieve and season well with salt and pepper. Stuff the pigeons with this mixture and braise them for about ¾ of an hour. Remove any grease with kitchen paper and allow to get cold, then cut each one in quarters, glaze them well and dish with a good salad and some chopped aspic jelly in little paper cases or on a bed of salad. Serve cold.

From Mrs. C. Frampton, Somerset.

GIPSY PIE

1 tender rabbit.	¼ lb. cooked ham or pork sausages.
½ lb. beef steak.	Salt, pepper and nutmeg.
2 teaspoonfuls chopped parsley.	Stock.

SOAK rabbit in cold salted water for 1½ hours. Wipe dry, joint; slice ham, or skin sausages, and with floured hands make meat into round balls. Cut steak in small pieces. Arrange rabbit, ham or balls, and beef in pie-dish. Sprinkle over the parsley, grated nutmeg, pepper, salt to taste. Add stock, cover with pastry, and bake slowly for 1½ hours after the pastry has risen.

From Mrs. M. Stockes, Caernarvonshire.

HAM AND CHICKEN BRAWN

1 chicken.	Pepper and salt.
1 lb. ham or streaky bacon.	Bunch of herbs tied in muslin.

KILL and pick chicken, remove inside, joint and simmer for 3 hours in just enough water to cover. Put in any flavouring cared for such as nutmeg, pepper and salt and herbs. Cook the ham or bacon with the bird. When cooked cut all up in very small pieces. Rinse out a very large cake tin with water and pack pieces in it and then strain enough of the gravy over to make it jelly between. This makes a good brawn and does not need any pressing.

From Mrs. C. Frampton, Somerset.

HARVEST RABBIT

Allow 1 small rabbit to every two
 persons.
Dripping.
3 prunes to each rabbit.
A bunch of fresh herbs to each
 rabbit.

Seasoned flour.
Onions (large, or salad onions).
1 thin slice of fat bacon to each
 rabbit.
Stock.

Forcemeat balls:

Chopped bacon (or suet).
Chives (or young onion tops).
Sweet marjoram.
Parsley.

Seasoning.
Breadcrumbs.
1 or 2 eggs.

SKIN, draw and cut off the heads, scuts and feet of the
rabbits. Wash well, leave in salt water for 15 minutes, then
dry and fry whole in dripping until a pale golden brown all over.
Drain, and stuff under the ribs of each 3 well-soaked prunes
and a bunch of fresh herbs. Coat thickly with well-seasoned
flour. Cover the bottom of a large deep baking-dish with thinly
sliced onions, or the bulbs of salad onions, lay the floured
rabbits on them, with a thin slice of fat bacon over each, and
just cover with stock. Bake slowly for 2 hours.

Serve on a hot dish, garnished with the onions and plenty
of large forcemeat balls, made of the ingredients above bound
with the egg, or 2 eggs if as many as 3 rabbits are cooked.

Fry a deep brown, and be sure that plenty of fresh herb is
used, as they must cut a bright green. Strain the gravy, and
serve separately.

From Mrs. Jennifer Dane, Buckinghamshire.

PIGEONS

Some pigeons—halved.
A few thin slices of bacon.
A sweetbread.
5 or 6 asparagus tops.
A few mushrooms.

2 cockscombs.
1 tongue.
Yolks of 4 eggs.
Some savoury forcemeat.
A little good gravy.

LINE a well-buttered dish with some savoury forcemeat;
put in a layer of thin slices of bacon, then the pigeons,
and on them a sweetbread cut into slices, 5 or 6 asparagus
tops, a few mushrooms, 2 cockscombs, a tongue boiled tender
and cut into small pieces, and the yolks of 4 hard-boiled eggs,
lay some forcemeat over the whole, like a pie-crust. Bake it,
and when done, turn it out on a hot dish and pour some good
gravy round it. Time, about 2 hours.

From Mrs. Ritter, Derbyshire.

JUGGED PIGEONS

4 pigeons.
2 hard-boiled eggs.
1 raw egg.
A sprig of parsley.
1 lemon.
A little suet.
A little flour.
Breadcrumbs.
Pepper and salt.

Nutmeg.
A little fresh butter.
1 head of celery, or a little celery salt.
A bunch of sweet herbs.
4 cloves.
A little mace.
A glass of white wine.

PICK and draw the pigeons, wiping very dry. Boil the livers a minute or two, and mince fine. Bruise with a spoon and mix with the yolks of the hard-boiled eggs, a sprig of parsley, chopped lemon peel, suet, breadcrumbs, pepper, salt and nutmeg. Mix in the raw egg and the butter. Stuff pigeons (including crops), dip them into warm water, dredge with pepper and salt, and put them into a jar with the celery or celery salt, sweet herbs, cloves, mace and white wine. Cover jar closely, and set it in a pan of boiling water for 3 hours. When pigeons are done, strain gravy into a stew-pan, stir in a knob of butter rolled in flour, cook until thick, then pour over pigeons. Garnish with slices of lemon.

From Mrs. George Marchant, Somerset.

OLD DEVONSHIRE RABBIT BRAWN

1 large rabbit.
2 pig's trotters.
Salt.

Pepper
Spice.
Water.

PUT 2 pig's feet in a saucepan with cold water to cover and boil gently for 1½ hours. Then put in with them a rabbit which has been prepared and soaked in salted water for ½ hour to whiten the flesh. Boil all together for 2 hours, or until the flesh is tender and leaves the bones easily; adding more water in the meantime if needed. Remove from the fire, and when cool enough, take out all the bones, cut the meat in small pieces, and season with salt, pepper and spice to suit taste. Boil all up together, then put into 2 moulds or pudding basins previously rinsed with cold water. Let it stand overnight, turn out, and serve with a dish of lettuce and tomatoes.

This makes a very good meat course for luncheon or supper, and is fit to put before any one—as the saying is.

From Mrs. B. Heal, Devonshire.

MARINATED PIGEONS

CUT up your pigeons and put them in a large earthenware pot, covered with a mixture of two-thirds red wine (the cheapest you can buy) and one-third vinegar. Leave for at least three weeks, but the pigeons will keep indefinitely provided they are completely covered by the liquid and pigeons can be added and taken away according to supply and demand. After three weeks or more remove pigeons.

Fry some sliced onions and with these line a casserole dish. Lightly fry the pieces of pigeon and place on top of the onion. Use the fat, a little flour and some of the red wine mixture to make a fairly thick sauce and pour this over the pigeons. Put the lid on the casserole and cook for a long time in a very slow oven.

From G. R. Marsh, Esq., Hants.

OLD NORFOLK PARTRIDGE STEW

Brace of partridges.
Oil, lard, butter or dripping.
1 or 2 slices lean ham.
Clove of garlic.
1 tomato.
6 small mushrooms.
4 cloves.
6 peppercorns.
Salt water or stock.

CUT up the birds into joints or halves, fry in a little oil or dripping, then put them into a stew-pan with the slices of ham, clove of garlic, tomato, mushrooms, cloves, peppercorns, salt, and enough water or stock to cover them. A glass of port may be added if you wish. Simmer the birds very slowly for 2 hours; when they will be tender enough to melt in the mouth, yet not in the least stringy or overdone. Serve them on a dish, heaped up, surrounded by the gravy; which has been freed from fat, thickened and made very hot. Garnish the dish with triangles of toast.

From Mrs. W. Gibbons, Norfolk.

PARTRIDGE CASSEROLE

Brace of birds.
4 onions.
2 rashers of bacon.
2 carrots.
2 ozs. diced bacon.
Pepper and salt.
Sprinkling of chopped parsley and thyme.
1 savoy cabbage.
Stock made from "trimmings."

TRUSS the birds and place an onion inside each one and a rasher of bacon over each. Put them in a casserole with sliced carrots and onions cut into rings, the diced bacon, pepper and salt, and the parsley and thyme. Parboil the cabbage, drain it and cut into four. Pack this round the birds in the casserole, cover with boiling stock, and simmer gently for 3 hours. Serve in the casserole.

From Mrs. K. Porter, Leicestershire.

PIGEON POT

Pigeons as required, 4–6 for amounts below—
¼ pint cider.
¾ oz. butter.
1 small apple.
Bouquet garni.

¾ pint stock.
1–2 oz. sliced onion.
½ oz. flour.
To garnish—
2 apples.
2 rashers bacon

WASH breasts, dry in cloth, roll in seasoned flour. Brown in butter in a frying-pan, or in a casserole in the oven. Remove and brown sliced onion and apple. Sprinkle in flour, cook for a few minutes (or thicken after adding the stock). Bring to the boil and season with salt, pepper and bouquet garni. Add cider. Replace pigeon breasts. Cover tightly in casserole and cook for 1½–2 hours. Serve in casserole after adding the garnish of fried browned apple rings, and diced bacon, or place pigeon on a dish with apple rings and bacon.

From Mrs. Mary H. Arney, Wilts.

POTTED PIGEON

3 pigeons.
Pepper and salt.

A dash of Worcester sauce, if liked.
A little melted butter.

SKIN and clean the pigeons. Place them in a pan, cover with water and boil until the meat is leaving the bones. Remove from fire, and, when cool enough to handle, carefully take away all bones and mince meat finely. Put the bones back into the saucepan and boil until the water has reduced to about 1 cupful. Season and add the Worcester sauce, if liked. Moisten the mince with stock from bones and a little melted butter. Press into jars and run a little melted butter on the top to seal each jar.

From Mrs. Stanley White, Cheshire.

RABBIT PASTE

1 rabbit.
Lump of butter size of egg.
1 lump sugar.
12 allspice.

6 peppercorns.
3 blades mace.
1 onion stuck with 12 cloves.

CUT rabbit into small joints, and put into casserole or jar with butter and other ingredients. Cover closely and cook slowly until the meat will leave the bones easily. When cold put the meat through a mincer 2 or 3 times, then beat together with ½ lb. margarine, 1 dessertspoonful Worcester sauce and a little cayenne pepper and a teaspoonful more sugar. Put into small pots, and pour over a little melted butter.

From Mrs. M. R. Slade, Hampshire.

RABBIT PIE

SKIN and wash well a rabbit. Then boil it in a little water with one or two onions, pepper and salt, until tender. When cooked, remove all bones and chop up the meat. Then mix it all well together with ½ lb. of sausage-meat and a little sage. Put into a pie-dish with a cupful of stock and cover with pastry made with 3 ozs. lard and 8 ozs. of self-raising flour. Bake in a good oven for ¾ hour to 1 hour.

This is a very tasty supper dish served either hot or cold.

From Mrs. Letch, Essex.

RABBIT PUDDING WITH MUSHROOMS

2 young rabbits cut up in joints.	Pepper and salt to taste.
A few slices of fat bacon.	¼ lb. suet.
4 large sage leaves chopped fine.	½ lb. flour.
Tablespoonful chopped onion.	Good plate of mushrooms.

LINE a good-sized pudding basin with a suet crust, put in a layer of rabbit, chopped sage and onion, then a layer of peeled mushrooms, and continue until the basin is filled. Sprinkle plenty of flour between each layer, as that makes good thick gravy. The slices of bacon should be cut up in thin strips and put in each layer. Nearly fill the basin with water, cover with suet crust, and steam for about 3 hours. This is a very tasty and nourishing dish.

From Mrs. E. Arthur Hurst, Buckinghamshire.

ROOK PIE

PLUCK and dress rooks, chop off wings, head and feet, skin and throw away all but the breast and legs, nothing else is any good. Put pieces in a large saucepan of cold water with a bunch of thyme, marjoram and sage and an onion. Cook slowly until meat comes off bones. Take all meat off breast and legs and put in layers in a pyrex dish, putting rings of hard-boiled eggs between. Heat enough of the liquor to cover meat and egg, add ½ oz. powdered gelatine to 1 pint liquor and cover all. Cover the pie with any kind of pastry preferred and bake until brown. Leave till next day until quite cold, cut in wedges and serve with a green salad.

From Mrs. D. M. Harris, Dorset.

SOMERSET ROOK PIE WITH FIGGY PASTRY

6 rooks.	Pieces of fat bacon cut in chunks
Weak stock.	Pepper and salt to taste.

For the paste:

1 lb. flour.	4 ozs. raisins stoned.
½ lb. fat.	Pepper and salt to taste.
4 ozs. currants.	

TAKE the rooks, which must have been skinned: using only the legs and breast, as all other parts are bitter. They should be left soaking in salt and water overnight. In the morning drain away the brine and put the legs and breast in a good-sized pie-dish, adding the fat bacon. Cover with the stock, and season well with the pepper and salt.

For the paste: Rub the fat well into the flour, adding pepper and salt, then add the currants and raisins. Mix well, and add sufficient water to make a stiff paste. Roll out to about ¾ in. thick, then place right over the pie, letting it come well over the sides. Cover the pie with a piece of greaseproof paper, and then put the pudding cloth on top. Tie well down and see that the water has no chance of getting in. There must be sufficient water in your boiler to cover it. Do not put the pie in until the water is boiling. The pie takes a good 3 hours to cook, and is delicious served with gooseberry jelly.

From Miss G. M. Dinham, Wiltshire.

SUFFOLK JUGGED HARE

1 hare.	A strip of lemon peel.
A bunch of sweet herbs.	Thickening of butter and flour.
2 onions (each stuck with 3 cloves).	2 tablespoonfuls ketchup.
6 whole allspice.	Little port wine if liked.
½ teaspoonful black pepper.	

WASH hare and cut into small joints, flouring each piece. Put these into a stew-pan with herbs, onions, cloves, allspice, pepper and lemon peel. Cover with hot water, and let it simmer until tender. Take out pieces of hare, thicken the gravy with the butter and flour, and add ketchup and port

41

wine. Let this boil for 10 minutes, then strain through a sieve over the hare and serve very hot.

Do not omit to serve red-currant jelly with it. It is seasonable from September to the end of February. Rabbit cooked in a similar fashion is equally tasty.

From Miss O. M. Fincham, Suffolk.

A TASTY HOT-POT

A boiling fowl.
Flour.
2 onions.
2 carrots: 1 small parsnip.

3 sprays each of parsley and thyme.
Water or stock, seasoned.
A few fresh cooked green peas, or
a tin of peas.

SEPARATE all the joints of the fowl, as you would a rabbit. Flour well and put in a stew-jar with onions, carrots and parsnip (sliced up), and the parsley and thyme, tied in muslin. Cover with water or stock, seasoned. Cook gently for about 2½ hours. Thicken with a little flour and water, if necessary, about ½ hour before it is done. For the last ¼ hour, add the peas.

From Mrs. C. H., Staffordshire.

TURKEY LOAF

CAREFULLY remove the bones from the remains of the turkey, and pass the flesh through a fine mincer, with a little onion, Season well with salt, pepper, and a little gravy and beaten egg. Roll tightly in a cloth, and boil for 1½ hours in boiling water, to which an onion and carrot have been added. Remove the cloth and serve hot. If wanted cold, glaze later.

From Miss Jerrams, Buckinghamshire.

TO COOK AN OLD DUCK

DUCKS up to the age of 5 years may be cooked in this way. Truss and stuff as for roasting. Melt ¼ lb. of dripping in a saucepan. When hot, put in the duck and braise for about 15 minutes, turning twice. Add a breakfastcupful of cold water, cover closely and simmer for 4 hours.

From Mrs. Montgomery, Gloucestershire.

TWO DISHES FROM ONE FOWL

PREPARE chicken or boiling fowl, removing both legs. Boil the giblets, 1 small onion, 2 or 3 slices of carrot, a little celery in water to cover for 1 hour, adding a few peppercorns and salt to taste. Strain and replace in the pan. Put in the trussed chicken; add sufficient water or stock just to cover the chicken. Simmer gently till tender; when cool, cut into pieces, removing any protruding bone.

Meanwhile, boil the stock, with any trimmings, for 1 hour or till reduced to 1 pint. Pour in a dish to make a layer of 1 in. Melt 2 ozs. of butter, blend in 2 ozs. of flour, stir in 1 pint of milk; cook, stirring over gentle heat till thick. Coat each piece of chicken separately; place the pieces on the layer of jelly. Decorate with cooked pieces of turnip and carrot, cut in pretty shapes, add slices of tomato and cucumber. Serve cold.

S*TUFFED Legs of Fowl.*—Remove the bone without breaking the skin. For each leg allow ¼ lb. of sausage meat or veal passed through a mincer. Season to taste, add any flavouring liked; with sausage meat, a little chopped ham or tongue. Or add to the veal a few breadcrumbs. Press the forcemeat inside the legs, form them into plump rolls, tie in muslin, simmer gently with the fowl for 1 hour or till tender. Serve cut in thick slices with a good brown gravy.

From Miss E. Fulton, Northumberland.

WOOD PIGEONS

2 wood pigeons.
Seasoned flour.
2 slices of fat raw bacon.
2 large Spanish onions (or their equivalent bulk in home-grown ones).

About 6 large leaves of sage.
Good beef dripping or lard.
Hot water.
Seasoning.
1 meat cube.
Cornflour.

P*ICK* and clean the wood pigeons, cut them through lengthwise and cover with seasoned flour. Cut the bacon in dice and fry to extract the fat. Place the bacon in a stewpan, leaving the fat in the frying pan, into which put the onions and sage leaves. Fry together till onions are tender; then add them to the bacon already in stewpan, still leaving the liquor in frying-pan and adding to it the dripping or lard in which to fry the birds till browned all over. Lay the pigeons on the onions and pour over them all the liquor from the frying-pan. Add hot water just to cover the bed of onions: cover closely, and allow to simmer till the birds are tender—about 1½ hours. When nearly done, season and add the meat cube. If necessary add a little more hot water, then thicken with cornflour. Serve with onion sauce and green peas.

From Mrs. Sara Wilson, Hampshire.

SAVOURY DISHES

APPLE MARIGOLD

3 large cooking apples.
2 eggs.
1 teacupful milk.
1 teaspoonful marigold petals.
1 teaspoonful sweet thyme.

1 teaspoonful sage.
1 small peppercorn crushed to powder.
Butter.

PEEL and core the apples and cut in rings. Beat the eggs in the milk, season with the marigold, thyme, sage and peppercorn. Put mixture in a shallow dish, carefully place apple rings on top with 1 or 2 pieces of butter. Bake in a good oven from 20 to 25 minutes.

From Mrs. J. Preston, Oxfordshire.

ARTICHOKE PIE

CLEAN and peel about 2 lbs. of artichokes; boil with a teaspoonful of salt until tender, then drain and keep the water. Melt 1 oz. margarine in a saucepan; stir in 1 tablespoonful of flour and gradually add enough of the boiling artichoke water to make a creamy sauce. Line a 1½-pint piedish with mashed potato, put in the artichoke, pour the sauce over, adding pepper and more salt if needed. Grate as much cheese as can be spared over the top, and put in a hot oven to brown.

From Mrs. W. Madgwick, E. Sussex.

BAKED BACON DISH

CHOP four rashers of bacon into small portions, together with four medium-sized onions chopped finely.

Make the batter to the consistency of a Yorkshire pudding with 1 pint milk, 2 eggs and flour, salt, pepper to taste.

Well grease a pie-dish and line with bacon, onion and pour over them the batter. Bake in a good oven for half an hour.

From Mrs. D. Thomas, Warwickshire.

BAKED CELERY CUSTARD

BOIL 2 heads of celery for 10 minutes; drain, place in stew-pan with ½ pint milk and small piece margarine; salt and pepper to taste. Simmer until celery is quite tender, then let it cool. Beat up one egg with the cool liquor, then pour over celery placed in a pie-dish; bake until custard turns light brown. Grate a little cheese over top and serve hot.

From Mrs. Scarlet, Suffolk.

BEETROOT MOUSSE

1 onion.
1 oz. margarine.

2 small beetroots.
Pepper and salt.

BOIL beetroots and put through mincer. While still hot, add the onion (finely chopped), the margarine and pepper and salt. Place in a buttered basin, cover with greased paper, and steam for 1 hour. Serve with meat and potatoes.

From Miss Christian Milne, Aberdeenshire.

BEAN PIE

EMPTY a tin of beans in a pie-dish, add a layer of crumbs, pepper and salt and a little mustard. Add a little of the bean liquor. Cover with grated cheese, then with a thick layer of mashed, seasoned potatoes. Bake for ¾ of an hour in a moderate oven until nicely browned. Serve piping hot.

From Mrs. Rogers, Wrexham.

BAKED CHEESE POTATOES

6 baked potatoes.
A little salt.
¾ cupful grated cheese.

1 gill hot milk.
1¼ tablespoonfuls butter.

WHEN the potatoes are cooked, cut them in halves length-wise. Scoop out the inside, and mash it. Mix in the butter, salt, cheese, milk and a little pepper. Pile this mixture

45

into the shells. Sprinkle with cheese. Put in a greased dish, and bake in a moderate oven until crisp and brown on top.

From Mrs. Skelton, Tallantire.

BEETROOT AND POTATO PIE

1 lb. boiled or steamed potatoes.	¾ lb. beetroot.
1 large onion.	1 oz. margarine.
½ oz. flour.	½ pint milk.
2 tablespoonfuls grated cheese.	Pepper and salt.

GREASE a pie-dish. Place in it alternate layers of sliced cooked potatoes and beetroot, having potatoes on top. Pour over the onion sauce made as follows:—

Melt fat. Fry in it the onion, previously skinned and chopped; but do not allow it to brown. Stir in the flour. Add milk, and let sauce cook undisturbed until it nearly reaches boiling-point. Then beat until quite smooth. Season with pepper and salt.

Sprinkle grated cheese over the top of the pie-dish, and bake till a golden colour in the oven.

From Miss Christian Milne, Aberdeenshir

BIRD NESTS

TAKE the required number of hard-boiled eggs, cover them with smoothly mashed potatoes in which ½ teaspoonful of curry powder has been mixed. Roll in egg and breadcrumbs and fry to a golden brown. Cut in half and serve each half on buttered toast.

From Mrs. C. Davenhill, Shropshire.

"BOXSTY"

THIS is a dish that I have enjoyed during holidays in the West of Ireland. It has a name which I do not know how to spell, but it sounds like "Boxsty."

Peel and wash large potatoes, grate them into a basin, drain them lightly; and to each cupful of grated potatoes add 1 level teaspoonful of salt, ½ cupful flour and enough milk to make a fairly stiff batter. Leave to stand for 1 hour, then fry like pancakes in bacon dripping. Serve hot with butter.

For boiled "Boxsty" prepare the grated potatoes in the same way, but then strain them tightly through muslin. Mix each cupful with $\frac{1}{2}$ cupful of flour and 1 level teaspoonful of salt. Mix to a dough with milk, place in a floured cloth and boil the dumplings rapidly for $1\frac{1}{2}$ to 2 hours. Serve hot with butter or cut up cold and fry with bacon.

From Mrs. K. Martlew, Lancashire.

CARROTS STUFFED

8 medium-sized carrots.	1 tablespoonful salt.
$\frac{3}{4}$ breakfastcupful grated cheese.	A pinch of pepper.
$\frac{1}{4}$ breakfastcupful brown bread-crumbs.	$1\frac{1}{2}$ teacupfuls cooked rice.
	Margarine.

2 large-sized tomatoes.

SCRAPE the carrots and cook in boiling salted water till tender. Hollow out one side of carrots, and remove a thin slice from the other side; so that they will lie flat in a tin. Add cheese, crumbs, tomato, milk and seasoning to the rice. Stuff the carrots with the mixture and place in a greased baking-tin. Place a few dabs of margarine on top, and bake in a hot oven for about 20 minutes.

From Mrs. H. Betteridge, Herefordshire.

CARROTS AND RICE

$1\frac{1}{2}$ lbs. carrots.	1 onion or leek.
1 teacupful rice.	1 oz. margarine.
1 teacupful milk.	1 tablespoonful grated cheese.

Seasoning.

FIRST scrape the carrots and cut into cubes. Peel and chop the onion or leek; put vegetables and rice into a pan and cover with plenty of boiling salted water. Boil until rice and vegetables are tender (30 to 35 minutes). Drain. Save the liquid for adding to soup.

Put vegetables and rice back into the pan; season to taste. Stir in the margarine and milk. Stir over gentle heat until the milk is absorbed. Serve sprinkled with grated cheese, in a hot dish.

From Mrs. H. Handy, Leicestershire.

CASSEROLE OF CARROTS

PUT the raw carrots through a mincer (coarsest cutter), then into a casserole with a little pepper and salt, 3 or 4 small knobs of butter and 2 tablespoonfuls of hot water. Cover and put into the oven.

Carrots take less time to cook this way, are ready chopped to serve, and all the flavour is in the vegetable and not lost in the water.

From Mrs. A. C. Thomas, Montgomeryshire.

CAULIFLOWER FRITTERS

1 cauliflower.
Fat for frying

Batter
Grated cheese.

CLEAN and boil the cauliflower until tender. When cold, divide into sprigs, dip each one in batter then fry in boiling fat. Drain and sprinkle with grated cheese and serve.

From Mrs. E. Holland, Cheshire.

CAULIFLOWER SAVOURY

1 medium cauliflower.
Cauliflower leaves or any other greens.
¼ cup mayonnaise.

1 tablespoon coarsely chopped pimento.
1 tablespoon chopped green pepper.
3 slices crisp, cooked bacon.

COVER whole cauliflower with salted water, cook until just tender, drain. If cauliflower leaves are green, mash, drain and arrange on a plate. Place cauliflower on leaves. Spread with mayonnaise, sprinkle with pimento and green pepper. Lay strips of bacon on top. Serve hot.

From Kathleen Thomas.

CELERY CHEESE

1 head of celery.
A little milk.
4 ozs. grated cheese.

1 egg.
Breadcrumbs.
Salt to taste.

WASH celery, grate on a fine grater, place in a saucepan with a little milk and simmer till almost cooked. Allow to cool. Now mix in cheese, salt and beaten egg. Place in a greased pie-dish, cover with breadcrumbs and bake till brown in a moderate oven.

From Mrs. Rogers, Northumberland.

CHAMP

OLD potatoes, when cooked this way, are beautifully white and floury—much nicer even than new potatoes similarly treated until the latter have really come into season.

Pick as large potatoes as possible and wash thoroughly. Peel and place in a vessel containing cold water, to prevent potatoes changing colour until enough are peeled. Then boil in the usual way. Get ready a generous handful of chives, cut short with a pair of scissors; add salt, as required, also sweet milk, but not enough to make the champ sloppy. When the potatoes are sufficiently tender, drain, set the pot firmly on the ground, and pound thoroughly with a beetle, after adding the chives and salt. Heat the milk to boiling-point, pour over all, and stir well.

The usual way of serving is to lift each helping on to a plate, make a well in the centre, and quickly add a chunk of butter. Then lift each spoonful round the outer edge of the champ, dip it in the melted butter to eat.

From Miss Mary Stevenson, Co. Down.

CHEESE BALLS

2 ozs. cheese (grated).	1 oz. flour.
1 egg.	Salt and pepper.
Cayenne.	Frying fat.

MIX cheese, flour, salt and pepper to taste. Beat the egg, well and fold into the cheese and flour mixture. Have ready a pan with hot fat, drop the mixture in, in teaspoonfuls, fry a golden brown. Drain well and serve very hot.

From Mrs. McClennan, Argyllshire.

CHEESE BATTER PUDDING

6 ozs. flour.	1 pint milk.
2 eggs.	$\frac{1}{2}$ lb. cheese.
Pinch salt.	

MAKE a batter of the milk, eggs and flour. Leave to stand for one hour. Grate the cheese and add half of it to the batter. Bake until risen and lightly browned.

Sprinkle the rest of the grated cheese over it. Return to the oven until the cheese is crisply browned. If you are short of cheese, omit it from the batter and just sprinkle an ounce of cheese on top.

From Mrs. C. P. Rowan, Cornwall.

CHEESE AND CARROT FLAN

6 ozs. pastry.	$\frac{1}{2}$ egg.
4 ozs. carrot.	1 tablespoonful water.
2 ozs. cheese.	3 tablespoonfuls milk.
Seasonings.	

49

ROLL out the pastry and use it to line an enamel plate or flan ring. Grate the carrot finely and the cheese coarsely. Mix together with the egg and milk; add seasonings.

Spread this mixture in the pastry case and bake for about ½ hour in a hot oven.

From Mrs. Rogers, Wrexham.

CHEESE CRESS

Watercress.
½ oz. butter or margarine.
2 ozs. grated cheese.

1 hard-boiled egg.
Salt and pepper.
6 rounds toast (spread lightly with margarine or butter).

PICK, wash, dry and chop the watercress. Melt the butter or margarine in a small pan, stir in the cheese and when it is melted, stir in the watercress. Season with pepper and salt.

Have the toast and egg, both quite hot, pile the watercress and cheese mixture on the toast and place a slice of hard-boiled egg on each.

From Mrs. J. B. Lindsay, Dunbartonshire.

CHEESE CRUNCH

¾ lb. short-crust pastry.
½ lb. rolled oats.
4 ozs. cheese.
¾ oz. margarine.

1 dessertspoonful made mustard.
1 tablespoonful water.
Salt.
Pepper.

DIVIDE the pastry into two parts, roll out thinly and line a shallow tin with it. Grate the cheese and mix with the oats, the tablespoonful of water, the mustard, pepper and salt. Melt the margarine and mix in.

Spread the mixture over the pastry; roll out the rest of the pastry to cover the whole. Nip up the edges and bake in a moderate oven for about half-an-hour.

From Mrs. Haynes, Warwickshire.

CHEESE MOULDS

1 breakfastcupful breadcrumbs.
1 tablespoonful custard powder.
½ teaspoonful made mustard.
Beetroot.

1 pint milk.
4 ozs. grated cheese.
Pepper and salt.
Parsley.

MAKE a custard with the milk and custard powder in the usual way without sweetening, and sprinkle in the breadcrumbs. Grate the cheese and blend into the mixture and season with pepper, salt and mustard. Pour into small wetted moulds and leave to set. Turn out on to individual plates and garnish with slices of beetroot and little mounds of potato salad sprinkled with chopped parsley.

From Mrs. Rogers, Wrexham.

CHEESE SANDWICH LOAF
(*A dish which needs no cooking*)

CUT 8 slices of bread. Spread the top piece on both sides, and the bottom piece on the inner side only, with 2 ozs. melted margarine and 2½ ozs. soft cheese, adding a pinch of salt and pepper. Add to alternate pieces of spread bread a sprinkling of chopped parsley and a few sultanas. Place slices on top of one another to form a "loaf." Press firmly together. Draw a fork in pattern across the top, thickly-spread layer of cheese. Sprinkle a few pieces of chopped parsley on the centre.

From Miss E. H. Hughes, Buckinghamshire.

CHEESE SAVOURY

1 lb. onions.	3 ozs. cheese.
¼ lb. spaghetti.	1½ ozs. butter.

BOIL onions, then chop into slices. Put spaghetti into salted water and cook until soft, and grate cheese. Butter a pie-dish, put a layer of spaghetti, then onions, then cheese. Season to taste. Add alternately until dish is full. Sprinkle a little cheese on top, dot with lumps of butter and bake in moderate oven until nicely browned.

From Miss W. L. Wedd, Hertfordshire.

CHEESE TARTLETS

Short pastry or flaky pastry.	1½ ozs. of grated cheese.
1 egg.	1 oz. butter.
1 oz. flour.	1 teacupful milk.
Pepper and salt.	

LINE patty tins with pastry. Melt butter in a saucepan. Stir in flour. Add milk and stir until mixture thickens as for white sauce. Boil for 2 minutes. Cool. Add grated cheese, egg, pepper and salt. Half fill lined patty-tins. Cook for 20 minutes in a quick oven. These can all be prepared the day before.

From Mrs. Birkett, Cumberland.

CHEESE AND TOMATO PIE

WELL grease a pie-dish and put in it a thick layer of stale breadcrumbs (which have previously been soaked in milk to a pulp), then a layer of grated cheese with a little grated suet: then a good thick, layer of sliced tomatoes (or just halved tomatoes), pepper and salt, and a few little knobs of butter on the tomatoes. Add another layer of the soaked breadcrumbs. Cover with a little butter and bake in a moderate oven. Serve hot.

From Miss B. Higgs, Buckinghamshire.

CHEESE AND TOMATO SAVOURY

1 large grated onion.	4 grated tomatoes.
3 ozs. grated cheese.	2 eggs.
3 ozs. margarine.	½ cupful white breadcrumbs.
Tomato sauce.	

PREPARE the day before. Simmer onion in water. Add margarine and chopped-up tomatoes. Simmer until tender. Draw pan from fire. Cool. Add cheese and stir well. Beat eggs. When cool, add eggs, sauce and bread crumbs. Stir over low fire until mixture thickens. Grease pie-dish. Set in a moderate oven until top is slightly browned. This will heat up beautifully. Serve hot with buttered brown bread and coffee.

From Mrs. Birkett, Cumberland.

CHEESE WUNDY

1 pint 2nd milking beestings.	2½ oz. grated cheese.
3 tablespoons ordinary milk.	Salt.
1 level dessertspoon cornflour.	

MAKE cheese sauce with cornflour, ordinary milk and cheese. Add to beestings when cool and bake in a slow to moderate oven for half an hour. (If beestings is thick dilute with ordinary milk.)

From Mrs. V. Berkley, Somerset.

COLCANNON

Boiled cabbage.	Cooked potatoes.
A little dripping.	Pepper and salt.

REMAINS of cabbage and potatoes can be used for this dish. The cabbage is better to be green—or green kale can be used. The potatoes should be very well boiled, and dry.

Have about equal quantities of each vegetable. Chop cabbage finely; mash potatoes. Put a piece of dripping in a frying-pan in proportion to the quantity of vegetables you have. Melt it; add cabbage, potatoes, pepper and salt to taste. Stir over fire until perfectly hot. Then dish up neatly in a pyramid, making the sides smooth and marking with a fork. This is a nourishing and tasty dish, and very satisfying instead of meat.

From Miss Christian Milne, Aberdeenshire.

CORNISH POTATO CAKE

½ lb. boiled potato.   2 ozs. flour.
½ oz. butter.   A pinch of salt.

MASH the boiled potatoes, while hot, with the butter, and mix well together; add salt, sprinkle in flour, mix evenly. Roll out very thin on a floured board. Cut out in rounds about the size of a saucer, and place on a hot girdle or greased frying-pan; prick with a fork and cook 3 minutes on each side. Serve hot.

From Miss B. Olver, Cornwall.

COTSWOLD DUMPLINGS

2 eggs.   4 ozs. grated cheese.
2 ozs. butter.

STIR grated cheese and creamed butter together, add beaten egg and pepper and salt to taste, and enough white bread-crumbs to make into a stiff mixture. Form into dumplings, roll in breadcrumbs and fry in hot fat a biscuit brown. Serve with vegetable purée, preferably tomato, broccoli or onion.

From Miss K. M. Chappell, Gloucestershire.

COTTAGE CHEESE ROLL—BAKED

2 cups dry cottage cheese.   a small onion (chopped).
1 cup dry breadcrumbs.   1 cup chopped peanuts.
1 cup cold cooked oatmeal.   Salt and pepper to taste.

MIX well. Form into a roll about 2 inches in diameter. Bake in a greased tin until brown. Serve with tomato sauce.

From Mrs. E. Taylor, Lincs.

CREAMED CELERY

Good head of celery.   1 oz. butter.
1 pint milk.   1 oz. flour.
Level teaspoonful salt.   4 ozs. finely-grated cheese.
Breadcrumbs.   Pepper.

WASH and clean the celery, and cut into dice enough to fill a pint measure. Put in a saucepan with the milk and salt. Cook gently till tender, then drain off the milk. In another saucepan melt the butter and mix in the flour. When quite smooth gradually add the milk in which the celery has been cooked, keeping well-stirred until it boils. It should then be thick and smooth. Let it boil for a few minutes, then add the grated cheese, a dash of pepper, and the cooked celery. Bring to the boil again, and serve with buttered breadcrumbs, i.e., breadcrumbs fried in butter until golden brown.

From Mrs. Webb, Oxfordshire.

A DELICIOUS WAY OF COOKING LEEKS

Leeks.	Seasoning to taste.
Milk.	A little cream or an egg-yolk,
Butter.	if liked.
Flour.	Small rashers of bacon.

SCALD the leeks for a few minutes in boiling water and then stew them slowly in milk. Drain when tender, and make a sauce with a little butter and flour and the milk in which the leeks were cooked. A little cream or an egg-yolk may be added to the sauce if stirred in after removing from the stove. Before serving, pour the sauce over the leeks and decorate the top with tiny rolled rashers of bacon, crisply grilled.

From Miss K. L. Siddall, Yorkshire.

DISHED ONION CRISPS

12 small onions.	½ pint milk.
2 cupfuls cooked peas.	3 ozs. margarine.
2 tablespoonfuls self-raising flour.	1 cupful breadcrumbs.

PEEL the onions. Boil them in milk, together with the same amount of water; and when tender, remove from saucepan, taking care not to break them. Grease a large baking-tin, put in the onions, covering them with the peas. Next make a sauce with the milk and water the onions were boiled in, the margarine, flour, and salt to taste. When quite smooth, pour over the onions and peas, adding a pinch of cayenne. Bind the breadcrumbs with enough melted margarine to make a nice stiff mixture and spread this over. Bake in a hot oven until golden brown.

From Mrs. H. Betteridge, Herefordshire.

EGG CUTLETS

1 egg and fine breadcrumbs to coat.	Pepper and salt.
4 eggs.	Pinch curry powder *or*
1 oz. butter.	Chopped parsley, for flavouring.
1 oz. flour.	Fat to fry.
Little milk, about a gill.	

BOIL eggs until hard, put into cold water, shell and chop very finely. Melt butter in a pan, add flour and stir until smooth, then add enough cold milk to make a good thick binding sauce, about a gill, bring this to the boil stirring all the time, cook for a few minutes. When cool mix with chopped egg, add pepper and salt to taste and one or other of the flavourings. Make into small shapes, lightly flour, then coat with beaten egg and breadcrumbs. Fry in hot fat for a few minutes until golden brown. Drain on kitchen paper.

From Mrs. McDonald, Glos.

EGG PIE

GREASE a pie-dish, line it with fine crumbs, season with pepper and salt. Cover with a layer of tomatoes, then a thin layer of mashed potatoes. On to this break 4 or 5 eggs, according to the size of your dish. Scatter chopped gherkins or capers lightly over; then add some breadcrumbs, another layer of tomatoes, and so on until the dish is full. Let the last layer be breadcrumbs. Place a few bits of butter on top and bake about 20 minutes.

From Mrs. Rogers, Wrexham.

EGG PUFFS

HALVE some hard-boiled eggs lengthwise. Dip them in melted butter on a plate, and sprinkle them with a mixture of finely chopped parsley, a little lemon thyme, grated lemon rind, a few chopped capers, a pinch of nutmeg, pepper and salt. Then roll out some scraps of pastry very thinly and cut out two ovals for each half egg. Place one under and one over each piece, and pinch the edges together.

Brush the puffs over with a little milk or beaten egg, and sprinkle them with finely-grated cheese. Bake in a good oven until brown and crisp. These are good for high tea or supper.

From Mrs. Roberts, Montgomeryshire.

EGG TOAST

BEAT up the eggs with a little milk and salt, as if for scrambled eggs. Cut the bread as if for toast and soak both sides in the egg till the bread is saturated. Fry in hot fat till a golden brown on both sides. Serve plain or with either jam or sugar to taste.

From Miss O. M. Montgomery, Somerset.

FARMHOUSE LOAF

BOIL 2 lbs. of potatoes and mash them. Mix in 3 ozs. margarine and 2 teacupfuls flour. Bind with milk and line bottom and sides of a large loaf tin, making walls about an inch thick, and reserving some for the top.

Chop up any cooked vegetables you may have, add ¼ lb. sausage meat, mix well, moisten with a little gravy and pack into tin. Place remainder of potato crust on top, brush over with egg, and bake in a moderate oven until nicely browned.

From Miss E. Rutherford, Northumberland.

FLAKED RICE CHEESE PUDDING

1 cup shredded cheese.　　　　　1 small onion chopped finely.
1 cup flaked rice.　　　　　　　Pepper and salt.
1 cup breadcrumbs.　　　　　　2 ozs. butter.

MIX well with milk to the thickness of batter, and turn into a greased pudding basin. Steam or boil for ¾ hour and serve hot. This is a savoury pudding easily made and quickly cooked and makes a light tasty dish for invalids.

From Mrs. W. Wagstaff, Nottinghamshire.

FRIED MARROW WITH POACHED EGGS

CUT a marrow into slices, about ½ in. thick. Pare off the rind and remove the seeds, etc. Flour each slice and brush over lightly with beaten egg. Dip into breadcrumbs, and fry in hot fat until a golden brown. Keep hot while the eggs are poached. Allow 3 or 4 slices of marrow to each egg.

The marrow slices may be dipped into batter instead.

From Miss Ruth Jones, Hampshire.

GROATS

I HAVE never come across this recipe anywhere but in one part of Herefordshire; nor have I read it anywhere. But all the members of my family had the recipe and used it.

Soak the groats for at least 12 hours in water. To 2 lbs. groats add about ¼ lb. fat cut up fine (we used to put the fat left after straining lard as well, as it may need a little extra fat.) Chop heads of leeks, or onions, and a little origany (origany was the word always used, but it is better known as marjoram), pepper and salt. Boil all together till quite tender and the mixture is getting stiff. Stir frequently, as it will be apt to burn.

If it is intended to put this in skins, a little milk must be added to moisten it, but not if it is intended to fry it in pieces. A little cooked rice and chopped thyme are good added, and stirred well in. If they are put in skins, and are floured, they will keep some time.

From Miss M. Joan Parry, Buckinghamshire.

HARICOT BEAN BALLS

1 lb. haricot beans.	1 large grated onion.
1 dessertspoonful chopped parsley.	Salt and pepper.
Egg : breadcrumbs.	½ teacupful milk.

MASH beans thoroughly, add onion, parsley, salt, pepper, milk and breadcrumbs to make the mixture firm. Flour your hands and shape the mixture into balls; dip in egg and breadcrumbs, and fry in boiling fat.

From Miss Christian Milne, Aberdeenshire.

LEEK PIE

THIS is one of the most appetising and nourishing ways of serving one of the best of vegetables.

Take 2 lbs. of leeks, clean them and cut into lengths about ½ in.; put in saucepan and boil until tender, then strain and put in pie-dish, adding 2 ozs. of streaked bacon cut finely, ¼ lb. cream, 2 eggs well beaten, pepper and salt to taste. Cover with a good pastry and bake in the oven for ½ hour. This would be sufficient for 4 persons; more cream may be added, when serving, if available.

From Mrs. C. Tremayne, Cornwall.

57

LIVER PUDDING

GRATE or chop finely 1 lb. liver and ¼ lb. scraps of bacon, mix with ¼ lb. stale breadcrumbs, season and moisten with 4 tablespoonfuls milk. Put mixture into greased cups or basin, cover with greased paper and steam for 1½ hours. Serve with brown sauce.

From Mrs. Rogers, Wrexham.

MACARONI, CURRIED

½ lb. macaroni.	1 tablespoonful curry powder.
2 onions.	2 tablespoonfuls sugar.
1 apple (sliced).	1 tablespoonful vinegar.
1 oz. margarine.	2 pints boiling water.

MAKE the margarine hot in a pan, put in sliced onions and apple, and fry for 5 minutes. Add the curry powder mixed with vinegar and sugar. Bring to the boil, then pour in boiling water and salt to taste. Put in the macaroni, broken into small pieces. Cook for ½ hour, and serve very hot. Slices of hard-boiled eggs make a tasty addition to this dish.

From Miss Louie Fitzpatrick, Co. Down.

MACARONI AND ONION FRITTERS

COOK 2 ozs. of macaroni and 2 large onions, peeled and sliced, in boiling water till macaroni is soft. Drain well, then chop finely. Add 4 ozs. fine breadcrumbs, 1 teaspoonful baking powder and season with salt and pepper. Take 1 egg, beat well, then use to bind mixture; add a few drops of milk if required. Form into small round cakes, fry in boiling hot fat till nicely browned on both sides. They should be served very hot with a good sprinkling of grated cheese on top.

From Mrs. Haynes, Warwickshire.

MALTESE CABBAGE

BARELY cover the bottom of a saucepan with lard (or dripping). In this fry 1 small clove of garlic till brown. Having washed and soaked the cabbage in the usual way, chop it finely as for pickling, and add to fat in saucepan. Add enough water to prevent burning and a pinch of salt. Cook for 10 minutes. Cabbage cooked this way is delicious. "Bubble and Squeak" is also much improved by browning a clove of garlic in the fat in which it is cooked.

From Mrs. L. J. Harper, Calcara, Malta.

MASHED CHESTNUTS

1 lb. of sweet chestnuts.
2 ozs. butter.
3 ozs. breadcrumbs.

Milk.
Pepper and salt.

TO shell the chestnuts, put them into a saucepan, with just enough water to cover them; having first made a cut in the skin of each. Bring to the boil, cook for 2 minutes, remove from stove, and you will find that the outer shell and inner skin will come off quite easily. After skinning, put them into another saucepan, with enough milk to cover them. Simmer gently until quite tender, then rub through a sieve, or mash until quite smooth. Return to the saucepan, add the butter and breadcrumbs, and season with pepper and salt. Stir well and serve hot.

From Mrs. F. L. Saunders, Berkshire.

MASHED POTATOES AND CHIVES

BOIL the potatoes carefully, shaking in the wind to make white and floury. Mash well. Heat some creamy milk in a saucepan, along with a half cupful of finely cut chives. When boiling, add to the potatoes and stir until creamy and fluffy. The chives add pep to the potatoes and zest to the appetite.

From Miss Christian Milne Aberdeenshire.

MEAT AND BACON ROLL

THIS is an excellent way of utilising left-overs, and makes an appetising main dish for a busy day dinner.

Mince ½ lb. cold meat or chicken and ½ lb. of bacon. Add 1 cupful of fine breadcrumbs and pepper and salt. Beat up an egg lightly and add, along with sufficient gravy to make a fairly firm mixture.

Place in a buttered mould, cover with buttered paper and steam for 1½ hours. Allow to cool in mould, putting a plate and weight on top to press. Turn out carefully and serve with mashed potatoes.

From Miss Christian Milne, Aberdeenshire.

MINT AND EGG PIE

THIS pie is very simple to make, very good to eat and quite practical on a farm where fresh eggs are plentiful.

Line a shallow baking-tin with short-crust pastry. Break

into this whole, unbeaten eggs to cover, and sprinkle with chopped mint, salt and pepper.

Place pastry lid on top, trim and bake in a hot oven until brown and crisp. Serve hot or cold. It is excellent cold with salad for high tea.

From Mrs. Rankin, Midlothian.

MOCK MACARONI

¼ lb. flour.
½ pint of milk.
2 ozs. butter or margarine.

2 eggs.
1 oz. cheese.
Salt and pepper.

BRING milk to boil, sieve flour and stir into milk, beating vigorously until mixture leaves side of pan. Beat eggs in after flour has been stirred in milk.

Season with pepper and salt, and turn on to plate to cool.

When cold divide into small flattened squares, roll in flour and fry in margarine or butter. Sprinkle with cheese after they are dished up to serve.

From Mrs. Andrew Arthur, Cornwall.

MUSHROOM PANCAKES

Batter:

6 ozs. flour.
½ pint milk.
2 tablespoonfuls water.
2 ozs. grated cheese.

2 eggs.
A little salt and pepper to taste
Lard for frying.

Filling:

¼ lb. peeled and chopped mushrooms.
2 ozs. grated cheese.
1 small finely-grated onion.

1 teaspoonful chopped parsley.
1 egg.
Butter for frying.

MAKE a batter with the flour, eggs, milk and water; and beat until smooth. Leave for an hour. Then add the cheese, and season to taste with salt and pepper. Put a little lard into the frying-pan; when smoking hot, pour in a little of the batter. Cook on both sides till brown, then spread with a thick layer of the filling. To make the filling, mix the mushrooms, cheese, onion and parsley together; season and fry in the butter. When sufficiently cooked, stir in the beaten egg to bind the mixture. Roll up and serve hot. This quantity is sufficient for 6 pancakes.

From Mrs. E. Cruse, Worcestershire.

MUSHROOM PIE

Shortcrust pastry—to line and top a 9-in. pie plate about 3 in. deep.
2 eggs, beaten.
2 rashers bacon, chopped.
¾ lb. mushrooms—more or less according to size of plate.
Salt and pepper and a little dried sage.

LINE a pie plate with the pastry reserving enough for the top. Cut the bacon small and cover the bottom, fill up with the sliced mushrooms and season. Pour over the beaten eggs, reserving a little to brush the top. Brown in a hot oven and reduce heat for about ¾ hour after browning to cook mushrooms.

From Mrs. Joan Oldfield, Bucks.

MUSHROOM PUDDING

8 ozs. flour.
3 ozs. suet (cooking fat or margarine) or 2 ozs. fat and 2 ozs. grated potato.
Mushrooms, peeled and sliced.
Seasoning.
½ teaspoonful salt.
1 teaspoonful baking powder (optional).
1 or 2 rashers of bacon, cut up in small pieces, or a piece of butter or margarine the size of a walnut.

LINE a basin with pastry made with flour, suet, etc.; fill with prepared mushrooms, and bacon or butter. Season, and add a small cupful of water. Cover with crust and steam for about 2 hours. Serve with potatoes and a second vegetable.

From Mrs. K. P. Aldred, Suffolk.

MUSHROOM PATTIES

CUT up into dice, and then stew, ½ lb. mushrooms; and stir in about 2 tablespoonfuls of plain white sauce. Line some patty tins with puff paste and fill them with the mushroom mixture, placing a cover of pastry on the top. Bake them in a moderate oven for about ½ hour.

From Mrs. Rogers, Wrexham.

MEAT "DUCKS"

¼ lb. sausage meat.
3 boiled onions (minced).
Pepper, salt and mustard.
3 tablespoonfuls breadcrumbs.
A little powdered sage.

MIX quite stiff, form into round cakes, dust with flour and fry brown in fat. Peel, core and slice apple into rings and fry. Place apple rings on toast and "ducks" on top. Serve hot.

From Mrs. Rogers, Wrexham.

OATMEAL AND HERB "SAUSAGES"

¾ pint salted water.
1 cupful flaked oatmeal.
1 medium-sized onion, chopped finely.
1 teaspoonful mixed herbs.

Salt and pepper to taste.
A little tomato sauce, if liked.
1 egg.
Some breadcrumbs.
Some chopped parsley.

BRING the water to the boil, stir in the oatmeal, and cook for ½ hour, stirring frequently. Pour the oatmeal mixture over the onion, herbs, parsley, salt and pepper and tomato sauce. Then add a well-beaten egg and enough fine breadcrumbs to make a stiff dough, flour the hands and roll the mixture into sausage shapes. Dip the "sausages" into flour, egg and breadcrumbs, and fry a golden brown. Serve with hot sauce.

From Mrs. V. Cantwell, Hampshire.

ONION CAKE

HAVE ready a nice bright cake tin and butter it well. Peel some potatoes and slice them, laying them at the bottom of the tin. On this sprinkle some finely-chopped onion and some tiny bits of butter. Sprinkle with pepper and salt. Repeat these layers until the cake tin is full, pressing each potato layer firmly down, and a potato layer with bits of butter on it must be the last. Cover with a plate and bake in a moderate oven for 1 hour. This is delicious with hot or cold meat.

From Mrs. Rogers, Wrexham.

ONION CHARLOTTE

COOK some fairly large onions until half done. Then drain off the liquor for soup and fill pan up with one-third water and two-thirds milk. Finish cooking. Thicken liquor with cornflour, add some grated nutmeg, a pinch of cinnamon, salt and pepper to taste. Pour over the onions and simmer with a good piece of butter (or margarine).

Take enough bread to line a baking dish, fry it golden brown in margarine, line the dish and pour in the onion. Top with a mixture of 1 tablespoonful grated cheese to 2 of fine breadcrumbs, pour ½ oz. melted margarine over this, and bake in a quick oven until the breadcrumbs are brown. Serve hot with green salad.

From Mrs. C. Gibbons, Cheshire.

OATMEAL PUDDING

Take ½ lb. oatmeal.
2 onions, chopped fine.
½ teaspoonful pepper.

¼ lb. suet, chopped fine.
1 teaspoonful salt.

MIX well together without water. Pour the mixture into a floured cloth and boil for 3 hours. This is a favourite Scotch pudding and can be taken with bread or potatoes.

It is also an excellent accompaniment to braised liver, or rissoles made with sausage meat.

From Miss E. Walker, Lanarkshire.

ONION FLAN

LINE a sandwich tin with short-crust pastry. Make a filling as follows:—

Make ¾ pint of thick white sauce, add a cupful of chopped, boiled onions, 2 tablespoonfuls grated cheese, 1 tablespoonful chopped parsley. Season well.

Garnish with slices of tomato and a little grated cheese. Bake ½ hour in a moderate oven. It can be made beforehand and warmed up when required.

From Mrs. Willis, Salop.

ONION PANCAKES

FRY chopped onions in a little fat till golden brown. Mix into a thick pancake batter. Drop mixture in spoonfuls into a slightly greased, hot frying-pan. Cook on one side, turn and finish.

Serve with chopped, corned beef and mashed swedes.

From Mrs. Rogers, Northumberland.

ONION TOAST

Spanish onions.
Hot buttered toast.
Salt and pepper.

Cheese.
Mustard.

FRY some sliced Spanish onions a nice brown and spread thickly over rounds of hot buttered toast. Season. Cover with thin slices of cheese spread with a little mustard. Put into a hot oven or before a fire until the cheese is melted. Serve at once.

From Mrs. T. Cole, Hampshire.

63

PARSNIP FRITTERS

1 or 2 large parsnips.   2 tablespoonfuls flour.
½ oz. margarine.   Salt and pepper.

BOIL and mash parsnips, rub fat into flour. Add seasoning and mashed parsnips. Beat well. Drop in spoonfuls and fry golden brown. Nice for a breakfast dish.

From Mrs. Rogers, Wrexham.

POTATO AND CHEESE SAUCE

4 to 6 cooked potatoes.   1 oz. butter: ½ pint milk.
3 ozs. grated cheese.   1 tablespoonful breadcrumbs.

CUT the potatoes into slices. Melt the butter in a saucepan, add the milk and bring slowly to the boil. Add 2 ozs. of the cheese; simmer for a few minutes. Arrange the sliced potatoes in a pie-dish; pour over the sauce; mix the breadcrumbs and the remaining 1 oz. of cheese together. Sprinkle over top of pie, and brown in the oven.

From Mrs. Skelton, Tallantire.

POTATO AND CHEESE SAVOURY

HERE is a recipe of which our family is very fond. It is cheap and nourishing and very appetising.

For 6 people you will require: 3 lbs. potatoes, 1 pint milk, 1 oz. butter, salt, pepper and grated nutmeg to taste, 3 ozs. grated cheese and some chopped parsley. Boil the milk with seasoning and butter and cut the peeled potatoes in ⅛ in. slices. Place in a pan and pour the boiling milk over and let cook very slowly for 1 hour; just before serving add the grated cheese and parsley.

From Mrs. E. Gordon, Montgomeryshire.

POTATO AND CARROT MOULD

½ lb. mashed potatoes.   ½ cupful mashed carrots.
1 oz. margarine.   1 teacupful milk.
1 dessertspoonful chopped parsley.   Salt and pepper.

RUB vegetables together through a sieve; add milk, margarine, seasonings, parsley. Put into a well-greased mould, bake in a hot oven for 15 minutes, turn out on a dish and return to the oven until nicely browned.

From Miss Christian Milne, Aberdeenshire.

POTATO OMELETTES

3 cupfuls mashed potatoes.	½ cupful hot milk.
½ teaspoonful salt.	¼ teaspoonful pepper.
1 egg.	

MIX all the ingredients together, and season to taste. Cook a tablespoonful at a time on a hot, greased girdle, or in a small frying-pan; turn each omelette when brown, and brown also on the other side. Serve with grilled chops.

From Mrs. Skelton, Tallantire.

POTATO PASTIES

½ lb. mashed potatoes, cold.	Tomato sauce.
2 teaspoonfuls baking powder.	A little cooked meat.
6 ozs. butter.	½ lb. flour.

SIFT the flour, rub in the butter. Add the baking powder and stir in the sieved potatoes with cold water to make stiff dough. Roll out and cut in suitable lengths. Set out seasoned meat, slightly moisten with tomato sauce, on one half. Fold other half over. Press edges together, prick and bake light brown.

From Mrs. J. R. Robinson, Cumberland.

POTATO PICK-UPS

SERVE mashed potatoes, topped with pieces of bacon dipped first in beaten egg, then into fine oatmeal and finally fried until crisp. This makes the perfect quick lunch.

From Mrs. Rogers, Wrexham.

POTATO SCONES

10 ozs. flour.	2 ozs. fat.
6 ozs. cooked mashed potatoes (cold).	Milk to mix.
½ teaspoonful salt.	

RUB fat into flour, add potatoes and salt and mix to soft dough with milk. Roll out on floured board about ½ inch thick and cut into scone rounds. Bake in very hot oven for 20 to 30 minutes. Split and serve hot with dripping or margarine spread between: good with stuffed marrow instead of bread.

From Mrs. F. J. Sparey, Herefordshire.

QUICK MEAT PANCAKES

MAKE a pancake batter, leave standing in a jug for at least 1 hour. Make pancakes and fill up with heated mince, parsley, chopped onion; or, while pancakes are cooking, heat up some cooked, diced beetroot. Put a spoonful in the centre of each pancake and roll up. Serve at once with a dish of fried potatoes.

From Mrs. Rogers, Wrexham.

SAGE AND ONION PUDDING

6 ozs. breadcrumbs.
2 ozs. oatmeal.
2 tablespoonfuls chopped onion.
2 ozs. chopped suet.

1 teaspoonful sage.
Seasoning.
Milk to mix.

MIX all the ingredients together; add sufficient milk to form a soft mixture. Turn into a greased tin and bake in a moderate oven about 1 hour. Cut into squares and serve with roast pork, mutton or rabbit: or it is excellent without meat if a thick brown gravy is served with it.

From Mrs. W. Bratt, Derbyshire.

SANDWICH PIE

THIS is a good way to use up a tough piece of beef that no one can eat as it is. Put it in a small saucepan with a small diced carrot and a finely-chopped shallot. Just cover with water or stock and stew until it is tender.

Make "rough puff" pastry. I use about ½ lb. of S.R. flour and make do with 2 ozs. margarine. Shave up the latter and add to the flour with a little salt, use milk for mixing to the usual consistency, then push it out with the fingers and fold in three and repeat this two or three times, handling it very quickly and lightly. Now, reserving about one-third for the cover, roll out the remaining two-thirds to line an ordinary jam sandwich tin.

Take the meat from the saucepan and chop small. Put it in the pastry-lined tin, fortify the liquid with meat extract, and well moisten the meat with it. Then roll out the pastry cover and put it on, pinching the edges in the usual way.

I aim to put it in the fairly hot oven about ½ hour before it is required, as it is important not to overbake it. The whole thing should be done very quickly to get the best results from the pastry. This will do for 4 persons, with a little extra gravy, potatoes and a second vegetable—or it is quite good cold as a carried meal; or again, carried straight from the oven makes a welcome hot snack for hungry workers in the field. Any odd bits of meat can be used—two or three kinds mixed if necessary.

From Mrs. A. Adlem, Dorsetshire.

SAUSAGE PUFFS

2 ozs. flour.
½ teaspoonful baking powder.
Pepper and salt.

1 egg.
Add a little water if necessary to make a stiff batter.

STIR 4 ozs. sausage meat into the batter, mix well and drop in small spoonfuls into hot fat, when they will puff up into little balls. Cook until golden brown.

From Miss E. Rutherford, Tweedmouth.

SAUSAGES IN POTATO CASES

½ lb. sausages.
¼ pint milk.
A little margarine.

2 lbs. potatoes.
Pepper and salt.

BOIL the potatoes, then mash while warm, add milk (which has been heated), also salt, pepper and margarine. Beat until very light.

Prick the sausages with a fork, then simmer them in a little water for 20 minutes. Take a spoonful of potatoes and place a piece of sausage upon it, cover with more potatoes, rough up the surface with a fork. Put all the cases on a greased baking-tin and bake for 20 minutes or until lightly browned. Serve with tomato sauce.

From Mrs. Lingard, Lincolnshire.

SAVOURY BACON OLIVES

6 ozs. bacon rashers.
3 ozs. sausage meat.
1½ ozs. breadcrumbs.
¾ level teaspoonful mixed herbs.
1 slice bread.

1½ level teaspoonfuls chopped parsley.
Salt and pepper.
2 or 3 dessertspoonfuls milk.
Some mashed potatoes.

REMOVE the rind from the bacon rashers and spread them out with a knife to make them as thin as possible. If they are very narrow this will also widen them. Then cut each rasher into halves. Mix the sausage meat with the breadcrumbs, herbs and parsley, season with pepper and salt, then add sufficient milk to moisten.

Divide the stuffing into equal portions, allowing one portion for each half rasher, and form them into small rolls. Roll up a portion in each piece of bacon. Run a skewer through the rolls, place them on a tin and bake them till they are tender.

Cut a slice of bread, not too thick, into 1 in. strips, then cut it into squares and again into triangles. When the stuffed bacon rolls are cooked, take them up and keep warm for a few minutes whilst you toast the bread, toasting them in a tin with the bacon fat. Have some potatoes ready boiled and mashed, then heap them along the centre of the dish. Arrange the rolls on the top and the snippets round them, and serve hot.

From Miss M. Scott, Yorkshire.

SAVOURY BACON PIE

AT the bottom of pie-dish lay a few pieces of uncooked bacon; next slice a layer of onions, then a layer of tomatoes, covering the top with a thick layer of grated cheese. Repeat these layers. Put a few dabs of margarine on the top, and bake in moderate oven on middle shelf for about an hour.

From Mrs. Patricia Capon, Kent.

SAVOURY CUCUMBER

1 cucumber.	Pepper and salt.
Small piece of butter.	Dash of cayenne.
1 tablespoonful cream or top milk.	Some slices of fried bread.

PEEL the cucumber and cut into 2 in. lengths. Throw into boiling salted water, and cook until soft enough to break up. Drain well, and put in a bowl; mash with butter, pepper and cream; dust with a little flour. Then put into small saucepan, and simmer for a few minutes. Serve on slices of fried bread, with a little minced parsley on top.

From Miss D. Hemus, Worcestershire.

SAVOURY DUCKS

1 lb. liver.	2 lb. cooked potatoes.
½ pint stock.	2 ozs. bacon.
1 large onion.	Pepper, salt and sage.

PUT a layer of sliced potatoes in a baking-tin, then slices of liver, onions, seasonings and sage until all are used. Have a layer of potatoes on top. Pour in the stock or water and put a few dabs of dripping on top. Cook for 1½ hours in moderate oven until nicely browned.

From Mrs. Rogers, Wrexham.

A SAVOURY FROM BREAD SAUCE

IF by any chance you have some bread sauce left over, try using it up like this. Put it into a basin, add a very little milk, if necessary, and some grated cheese. Mix well, put into buttered cocotte dishes, scatter a very little grated cheese on top and put a tiny piece of butter on each, bake in a moderate oven till brown.

From Mrs. H. Handy, Leicestershire.

SAVOURY MARROW

PEEL and steam a medium-sized marrow until it is tender. Cut into 1 in. cubes and put into a glass dish. Make a junket with 1 pint of lukewarm milk, a beaten egg, required amount of rennet and seasoning. Pour over the marrow and leave to set. Sprinkle with 1 tablespoonful of grated cheese and serve with crisp, dry toast.

From Mrs. Rogers, Wrexham.

SAVOURY NUT PUDDING

3 large potatoes.
2 ozs. mixed nuts.
1 oz. butter.
1 egg.

1 tablespoonful grated cheese.
½ cupful milk.
Pepper, salt and nutmeg.

WASH the potatoes and bake in a moderate oven until tender. Remove the skins and press potatoes through a sieve. Melt butter in a saucepan, add the sieved potato, stir in the milk, and season. Add the nuts, chopped small, and the yolk of the egg; mixing with beaten white of egg. Put in a buttered pie-dish, sprinkle the grated cheese over the top, stand in a moderate oven and bake until brown.

From Mrs. M. E. Taylor Buckinghamshire.

SAVOURY PANCAKES

4 tablespoonfuls flour.	Small bunch parsley.
1 egg.	2 ozs. margarine.
1 teacupful milk.	2 ozs. minced ham.

WASH and chop the parsley, fry it in the margarine for a few minutes, then add the ham and gently cook for about 10 minutes. Beat the egg well, together with a little salt, gradually mix with the flour, lastly adding the milk.

Have ready some hot fat in the frying-pan and put the mixture into it, 4 tablespoonfuls at a time. Fry to a golden brown on both sides and when ready spread with the ham mixture (which should be moistened with a little milk, if necessary). Sprinkle with pepper and salt and serve very hot, decorated with sprigs of parsley.

From Mrs. Betteridge, Herefordshire.

SAVOURY PIE

2 lbs. diced turnips and carrots.	1 large onion (diced).
1 cupful stock.	½ teaspoonful grated nutmeg (or
4 ozs. dry mashed potato.	mixed herbs).
2 ozs cooking fat.	4 ozs. flour.
1 teaspoonful salt.	½ teaspoonful baking powder.
2 ozs. grated cheese.	

WASH vegetables thoroughly, slice them and boil till tender. Mix in the nutmeg, and put all into a pie-dish with the stock. Now make crust as follows:—

Mix flour, baking powder and salt; rub in fat until all lumps are out. Mash potatoes finely and lightly mix in. Add the grated cheese and mix all well together. Mix to smooth, dry dough by adding a little water. Roll out and put on top of vegetables in dish. Bake in a moderate oven for 20 minutes. If any margarine to spare, put dabs on top before adding crust.

From Miss Lessie Powell, Suffolk.

SAVOURY RICE

4 eggs.	1 tablespoonful chopped raisins.
2 ozs. rice.	1 oz. grated Parmesan cheese.
1 ozs. butter.	2 tablespoonfuls tomato sauce.
1 pint stock.	Salt, pepper and paprika.
4 teaspoonful lemon juice.	1 teaspoonful chopped parsley.
3 shallots.	

MELT the butter in a stew-pan, add well-washed rice and finely-chopped shallots. Fry for a few minutes, then gradually pour in the stock. Bring slowly to boiling-point, and continue to cook gently until the stock has been absorbed by the rice. Season with salt and pepper to taste. Stir in most of the grated cheese, the chopped raisins and the tomato sauce. Cook again for a minute or two. Arrange the savoury rice in an entrée dish and keep hot. Carefully poach the eggs in boiling water to which the lemon juice has been added. Take up, drain well and arrange on the rice: sprinkle with the remainder of the grated cheese and a pinch of paprika, finishing off with the chopped parsley. Pearl barley can substitute for rice.

From Miss Hannah Morgan, Herefordshire.

SAVOURY ROLL AND BATTER

MINCE or cut up any remains of cold meat and mix with breadcrumbs, herbs and parsley, pepper and salt. Mix together with beaten egg, and a little meat extract to form a roll (not too moist). Melt a little dripping in baking-tin and cook in oven for about ½ hour.

Make a batter with 4 tablespoonfuls flour, pinch salt, 2 tablespoonfuls dried egg, ½ pint water. Add half the water and beat well, then the remainder and beat again.

Pour each side of roll and bake in good oven about 25 minutes. If there is any left over, cut into strips and fry with rashers for breakfast.

From Mrs. A. G. Mussell, Hampshire.

SAVOURY SCRAMBLED EGGS

Butter.   Onion.
3 eggs.   Chopped parsley.
Pepper and salt.

MELT a piece of butter in a pan, pour into it 3 well-beaten eggs seasoned with pepper and salt; also a little braised onion and chopped parsley. Cook, stirring all the time with a fork, until set. Serve on hot buttered toast. A little mushroom sauce may be sprinkled on top.

From Mrs. A. E. Clamp, Nottinghamshire.

SCALLOPED BEANS

1 lb. cooked beans (either French   2 hard-boiled eggs.
    or runner).   ½ pint of white sauce.
1 oz. grated cheese.   1 oz. breadcrumbs.
1 oz. margarine or cooking fat.

71

GREASE a fireproof dish, Put in a layer of beans and then a layer of egg slices, repeating the alternate layers and finishing with a layer of beans.

Pour the white sauce over the beans. Mix the grated cheese and breadcrumbs, and sprinkle over the top. Then dot the fat over, and bake for 20 minutes in a hot oven.

From Mrs. Rogers, Wrexham.

SKIRLIE-MIRLIE

2 teacupfuls cooked turnips.　　2 teacupfuls cooked potatoes.
1 tablespoonful margarine.　　$\frac{1}{4}$ teacupful milk.
Salt and pepper.　　Fried or toasted bread.

MASH vegetables very thoroughly. Melt margarine in pan, and add milk. Heat. Add vegetables and whisk over fire till light and creamy. Add salt and pepper to taste. Serve in hot vegetable dish with croûtons to decorate.

From Miss Christian Milne, Aberdeenshire.

TWO WELSH RECIPES FROM THE HUNGRY 'FORTIES

SIOT

$\frac{1}{2}$ cupful oat bread.　　1 pint buttermilk.

CRUSH the bread (made of equal parts of oatmeal and flour), and put into a basin. Pour in the buttermilk, and let the bread soak for 1 hour: when it will be ready to serve with bread and butter.

From Mrs. Williams, Caernarvonshire.

BRYWES

2 tablespoonfuls breadcrumbs.　　Salt and pepper to taste.
1 tablespoonful crushed oatmeal.　　$\frac{1}{2}$ pint boiling water.
1 teaspoonful butter or dripping.

PUT the breadcrumbs and oatmeal into a basin, add salt and pepper to flavour, break in the dripping or butter. Pour the boiling water over it, and stand for 5 minutes before serving.

From Mrs. Williams, Caernarvonshire.

SOMERSET RABBIT

PUT alternate layers of grated cheese and chopped onions in a pie-dish, topping with cheese and breadcrumbs. Bake in a medium oven till the onion is cooked.

From Miss E. M. Ball, Somerset.

STELK
(*An Irish recipe*)

2 doz. of the later spring onions. Those which are almost too coarse to use otherwise are best for this dish.

Potatoes.
Milk.

CHOP the onions into small lengths and simmer in milk until tender. Meanwhile, boil or steam a good dish of potatoes. When cooked, mash them with a little milk. Strain the onions and add these to the potatoes, mixing well. Serve very hot.

The correct Irish way is to add a large piece of fresh butter to each plate of stelk after serving. This makes a delicious and warming supper dish for the cool evenings. Chives may be used in place of spring onions if preferred, and make an equally appetizing dish.

From Mrs. M. Cheshire, Gloucestershire.

STEWED ONIONS AND CHEESE

1 or 2 large onions.
1 dessertspoonful flour.
Pinch each of salt and pepper.

1 teacupful milk.
1 or 2 tablespoonfuls grated cheese.

SKIN the onions and put into a pan with water and boil till tender, 1 to 1½ hours, depending on size; drain off water and, if no milk available, use some of it for the sauce. Make the flour smooth with a little water, add the milk and seasonings; stir till it boils; put in the onion and cook for 5 minutes. Cool slightly, stir in the cheese, then turn into a hot dish and serve.

If the water in which the onions were cooked is not required to make sauce, keep it till next day and use in stew or soup. This is an excellent supper dish.

From Mrs. McLennan, Argyllshire.

STUFFED MARROW RINGS

YOU will need marrow, tomatoes, bacon, breadcrumbs, egg, seasoning and chopped mint.

First prepare your baking-dish. Cover the bottom with lukewarm water, to which add 2 tablespoonfuls of liquid dripping: then stir in 1 heaped tablespoonful of seasoned flour (pepper and salt seasoning) previously mixed into a paste with water. Stir all together and keep warm whilst preparing the marrow.

Peel and core the marrow, cut into rings about 1 in. thick (allowing 1 ring per person), lay in the baking-pan. Next take tomatoes (large enough for one to go inside the marrow ring). Cut the top off each and scoop out the inside, mix in a basin with 2 ozs. of breadcrumbs, pepper, salt and a little mustard, pour over 1 gill of boiling milk, add 2 rashers of chopped bacon (lean preferred), and beat together with a small egg. Fill the tomato cases with this mixture, give a good sprinkling of finely-chopped mint, and put inside the marrow rings.

Dot the marrow rings with knobs of dripping, cover with greaseproof and bake in a moderate oven for about 40 minutes. After 20 minutes take away greaseproof and baste the marrow rings. Serve with brown gravy made from stock in the baking-tin.

If the marrow is old, bake it about 20 minutes before putting the tomatoes in and have an extra cup of water in the baking-tin.

From Mrs. F. A. Foden, Gloucestershire.

STUFFED MUSHROOMS

WASH 1 dozen large mushrooms. Remove stems and chop them finely. Peel the caps. Melt 3 tablespoonfuls of butter or mild-flavoured fat, add $\frac{1}{2}$ tablespoonful of finely chopped shallot and the chopped stems of mushrooms. Cook for ten minutes then add $1\frac{1}{2}$ tablespoonfuls flour, some chicken stock or milk to moisten, a slight grating of nutmeg, $\frac{1}{2}$ teaspoonful finely chopped parsley and salt and pepper to taste.

Cool the mixture and fill the caps, rounding well over the tops. Cover with slightly buttered cracker crumbs and bake for $\frac{1}{4}$ hour in a hot oven.

From Mrs. Rogers, Northumberland.

SURPRISE LOAF

Young vegetables.   Lemon.
A sandwich loaf.   Eggs.
Butter.

THIS may be made with fresh or tinned vegetables according to the season.

Chop up as many young vegetables as you want. If fresh, fry them lightly in butter, frying potatoes separately and other vegetables together according to the time that each takes to cook. Take a small sandwich loaf and scoop out the crumb, keeping the top crust for a lid. Fill the hollow loaf with the fried vegetables (or with tinned ones, strained from their liquor), and over them pour the following sauce:

Melt 2 ozs. butter and stir in 1 tablespoonful of flour; when smooth add about 1 gill milk and stir over gentle heat for 15 minutes. Beat the yolk of 1 egg into a tea-cup of cold milk and stir it into the sauce without letting it boil.

Pour it into the loaf over the vegetables, adding a squeeze of lemon. Put on the crust lid, butter it lightly, and bake in a moderate oven for about 20 minutes.

From Miss E. M. Dyer, Gloucestershire.

SWEET STEWED ONIONS

PEEL and slice finely three or four nice sized onions. Put into stew jar or pudding basin and almost cover the onions with equal parts of vinegar and water. Add a pinch of salt, 1 tablespoonful of sugar. Cover the basin with lid or old plate and cook in the oven for about 1½ hours. This is delicious with the roast meat or served cold with any cold dish.

From Mrs. F. Gott, Lancashire.

SWISS EGGS

INTO a shallow baking dish pour a little milk to about ½ inch in depth. Break as many eggs as you need, one at a time, round the dish into the milk and season with pepper and salt and then grate over all a generous sprinkling of cheese. Bake gently in the oven for about ten minutes and serve hot.

A little finely chopped parsley can be added as a garnish and variant when cooked.

From Mrs. C. R. Harrison, Bedfordshire.

TUESDAY HOT-POT

Remains of the joint.
2 medium-sized onions or few leeks.
1 small cabbage or savoy.

Pepper and salt.
Flour or gravy salt for thickening

CUT the lean and fat into fairly thick slices and arrange at the bottom of a large pan so that the fat is evenly distributed. Fry for a few minutes in the saucepan, shaking occasionally to prevent burning. Meanwhile, cut up the onions or leeks, and shred the cabbage or savoy finely; place on top of meat; add seasoning and sufficient water to barely cover, see that the lid fits closely.

Simmer for 1 hour, then remove meat and vegetables on to a hot dish and pour on the gravy, thickened with flour or gravy salt. Much of the fat will have been absorbed in the cooking and the whole takes on a delicious flavour.

From Mrs. N. Wright, Monmouthshire.

TOMATO SAVOURY

1 lb. tomatoes.
1 lb. breadcrumbs.
1 onion.

1 egg.
A little milk.
2 teaspoonfuls margarine.
Pepper and salt.

SKIN the tomatoes and stew until soft in $\frac{1}{2}$ pint of water. Leave to cool. Put breadcrumbs, chopped onion and pepper and salt into a basin. Beat the egg, add milk and melted margarine to the beaten egg and pour on to the breadcrumbs. Mix in the tomatoes and bake in a good oven in a buttered dish until nicely set.

From Miss M. Scott, Yorkshire.

TURNIP BROSE

WASH and pare 6 Swedish turnips. Cut into small dice. Place in pot with enough water just to cover, a marrow bone, and a little salt. Boil gently until the turnips are soft and richly yellow.

Put 3 tablespoonfuls oatmeal in a bowl. Add a knob of margarine and a little salt and pepper. Strain the liquid from the turnips into a small saucepan, and bring to the boil. Pour a little of the liquid into the prepared oatmeal, and stir until the brose forms into small knots. Add a little more liquid and serve piping hot.

Mash the turnips well. Add a little creamy milk, a knot of margarine and salt and pepper to taste. Stir over the fire until boiling; then serve at once in a hot dish.

From Miss Christian Milne, Aberdeenshire.

TURNIP AU GRATIN

1 turnip.
1 tablespoonful grated cheese.
1 teacupful breadcrumbs.

1 small teacupful milk.
2 tablespoonfuls cream.
Margarine.

PEEL the turnip and cut into squares. Put in salted water and parboil for 10 minutes. Strain and cut the turnip into slices. Put into a greased pie-dish, season to taste, dot with pieces of margarine. Pour over the milk and cream, cover with breadcrumbs, sprinkle the cheese over all. Bake for $\frac{1}{2}$ an hour in a hot oven.

From Mrs. Kemp. Orkney.

TURNIP PIE

(Here is an unusual and delicious way of serving turnips)

WASH 4 new turnips, and put into plenty of boiling water slightly salted. Allow to boil for about $\frac{1}{2}$ hour, or till they are almost cooked. Take them out of the water, peel and cut them into thin slices. Put into a pie-dish, and sprinkle a little salt and pepper over them. Add a teacupful of milk, and cover with breadcrumbs and a little grated cheese. Put the dish in an oven or in front of the fire until nicely browned on top.

Anon.

VEGETABLE HOT-POT

VEGETABLES such as carrots, swede turnips, sliced parsnips, the white part of leeks, Jerusalem artichokes and onions make a very tasty hot-pot. Fry the vegetables lightly in good fat and put them into a deep stone pot of any kind. Season well with pepper and salt, especially pepper. Mix a little flour smoothly with enough water just to moisten the vegetables, pour the mixture in, put on the lid and cook slowly either in the oven or on the side of the stove for 2 hours.

From Mrs. E. G. Thomas, Pembrokeshire.

VEGETABLE MARROW STEW

1 fair sized marrow.
6 medium sized tomatoes.
2 onions.

A good sized lump of butter.
1 teaspoonful of Demerara sugar.
Salt and pepper to taste.

PEEL and remove seeds from marrow; cut into small cubes. Skin tomatoes, peel and cut up onions. Put these together in an enamel saucepan with enough water to cover the bottom of the saucepan (no more, as the marrow will provide enough moisture). Add butter, sugar, salt and pepper to taste. Stew slowly for 1½ to 2 hours. Serve with toast or brown bread and butter. And here you will have a meal fit for the most fastidious.

From Mrs. Garrett, Sussex.

VEGETABLE PIE

2 medium sized carrots.
1 small swede.
Chopped parsley.
2 tablespoonfuls rice.

1 large turnip.
1 onion.
½ pint white sauce.
Small tin baked beans.

PREPARE vegetables. Slice onion and fry in fat left over from bacon. Cube carrots, swedes and turnips, and cook till tender in salted water; steam rice over this pan, or boil in muslin bag in vegetable pan. Mix all vegetables together with rice and baked beans.

Place in pie-dish. Add enough white sauce and parsley to bind. Cover with short-crust pastry, and bake for 20 minutes. Serve with jacket potatoes.

From Mr. A. C. Hilton, Sussex.

VEGETABLE ROLY-POLY

3 carrots.
3 parsnips.
1 small turnip.
Pepper and salt to taste.

3 potatoes (sliced).
3 tomatoes.
A little gravy powder.
Suet crust.

ROLL out the suet crust fairly thinly, sprinkle over with gravy powder. Over the crust lay the grated carrots, parsnips, turnip and sliced potatoes. Cover with a layer of sliced tomatoes, then pepper and salt to taste. Roll up in a cloth, and boil for 2½ hours. Serve steaming hot with a little good gravy.

From Miss E. J. Watson, Somersetshire.

WATER LILIES

SCRUB and trim ½ dozen even-sized white turnips, and boil in salted water for about 20 minutes. Drain, and when cool enough to handle, cut three deep incisions with a sharp knife across each turnip, so that they will open like six white petals. Put ½ oz. of cheese inside each one, and press together a little. Arrange in an oven dish, and pour a little fat over each. Cook until thoroughly heated and slightly browned. This makes a very attractive dish for lunch or supper.

From Miss E. Rutherford, Northumberland.

YORKSHIRE OLD WIVES' SOD

5 good sized eggs.
3 gills new milk.
Pepper and salt.

Butter.
2 thin oatcakes.

BREAK the eggs into a basin and beat for 2 minutes. Add the milk and seasoning, mixing well. Have ready a baking-pan nicely greased with fresh butter. Pour in the beaten eggs and milk mixture. Next break the oatcakes into pieces about ½ in. square. Sprinkle them on top of the sod. Add a few nuts of butter and place in a moderate oven. Bake for 20 minutes. If the oatcakes are lightly toasted and buttered before breaking up they make the sod a tastier dish.

From the late Mrs. Ellen Cowking, Lancashire

MEAT DISHES

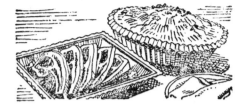

BACON AND EGG PIE

Cooked ham or bacon.   Flaky pastry
Eggs.

LINE a shallow dish with flaky pastry. Spread a layer of cooked ham or bacon on it, and then break the eggs over the meat, so that the whites of the eggs run together, and the yolks are placed evenly apart. Cover the whole with another thin layer of pastry, and bake in a moderate oven for about ½ hour.

From Marjorie H. Bosley, Berkshire.

BACON IN CIDER

IN Sussex I was shown the following way of cooking bacon. It is delicious.

You will want 1 corner bacon (6 lbs.), 1 pint cider, 1 bunch sweet herbs, 1 dozen cloves, 1 teacupful brown breadcrumbs and 2 ozs. brown sugar.

Soak bacon overnight. Then bring to the boil, pour off water and add fresh. Add herbs and simmer slowly, allowing 20 minutes to each pound, and pouring in the cider 1 hour before it is done. When cooked, let bacon cool and remove skin; cover with sugar and breadcrumbs, and stick with cloves. Bake till brown.

From Miss Nellie Richmond, Co. Antrim.

BALMORAL TRIPE

CUT 1 lb. uncooked tripe into 4 inch squares, cover each with a thin slice of lean bacon and sprinkle finely-chopped onion over. Roll up tightly, bind each roll with thread dip in seasoned flour and fry pale brown in fat. Drain well.

Into a saucepan put sufficient sliced onions and carrots to cover the bottom, put rolls on top, and a little water and cook gently till tender. Remove rolls, add generous lump of butter and enough milk to make a sauce, then thicken with a little flour. Add chopped parsley and serve hot with green vegetables.

From Mrs. J. B. Lindsay, Kirkintilloch.

BRISKET OF BEEF—PICKLED

6 lbs. salted brisket of beef.
3 slices of bacon.
2 carrots.
1 onion.

Bunch of savoury herbs.
Salt, pepper, cloves.
Allspice, mace.

PUT the beef in a stew-jar, together with the rest of the ingredients, and cover all with water. Stew gently in oven for 4 hours. When cooked leave to cool, then remove from the liquid and press between two plates under a weight.

From Alice Kilding, Yorkshire.

BUCKINGHAMSHIRE DUMPLING

1 lb. flour.
6 ozs. suet.
½ lb. fat bacon cut into thin strips.
½ lb. liver cut small.

2 large onions, grated.
1 dessertspoonful chopped sage.
Salt and pepper to taste.

MIX the flour and suet into a stiff dough, adding a little salt; roll out on a floured paste-board. Cover the dough with the cut-up bacon. Now cover the bacon with the small pieces of liver, spread over with the grated onion and chopped sage; add pepper and salt. Roll up tightly in a floured cloth and boil about 2½ hours.

Serve with a good brown gravy made from a pint of stock and a little beef extract: thicken with a tablespoonful of corn-flour, stirring all the time for 5 minutes to keep it smooth.

From Mrs. E. A. Hurst, Buckinghamshire.

CALF'S HEAD PIE

BOIL a calf's head till tender, then cut off the meat in thin slices. Make some good stock of the bones, skimming it carefully and flavouring with vegetables, herbs, etc. Next day make the pie.

Take some slices of hard-boiled eggs and lay them in the bottom of a greased pie-dish, and on these put alternate layers of meat and jelly, more eggs, and so on. Flavour all delicately till the dish is full.

Cover with some good puff paste and bake till the pastry is quite done. When cold, carefully remove the pastry and turn it upside-down on a cold dish and turn the contents of the pie on to it. This makes quite a pretty mould, and is very tasty.

From Miss A. Harrison, Derbyshire.

STUFFED CHINE

Chine.
Parsley.
Leeks (or chives).

Marjoram.
Mace.
Salt.

SOAK the chine one night in water, having first weighed it. Wipe dry, then cut well into the bone, across both sides. Mix up stuffing made of the other ingredients, press it well into each split: tie in a clean cloth and boil, allowing $\frac{1}{2}$ hour for the first pound and $\frac{1}{4}$ hour for each other pound.

This was always prepared for suppers, and was called "the sheep-shearing chine." It was taken from the back of a big fat pig. My grandmother used this recipe when she was young. She has been dead about thirty-five years, and she was nearly 75 when she died.

From Mrs. M. Bloxham, Warwickshire.

CORNED BEEF SAVOURY

1 cupful flour.
Salt and pepper to taste.
$\frac{3}{4}$ cupful milk.
Corned beef.

1 teaspoonful baking powder.
1 egg.
$\frac{1}{2}$ teaspoonful mustard.

MIX flour, baking powder, pepper and salt together. Mix mustard into milk. Beat up egg, add to milk, and mix to a smooth batter with dry ingredients.

Cut meat into slices, dip into batter, and fry in hot fat.

From Mrs. W. Morley, Lincolnshire.

82

TINNED CORNED BEEF HASH

8 ozs. corned beef.	1 carrot thinly sliced.
4 ozs. large or haricot beans (soaked overnight).	2 ozs. turnip or swede cut into 1-in. cubes.
2 dessertspoonfuls pearl barley.	½ bay leaf (optional).
1 beef cube (crushed).	Salt and pepper to taste, prefer-
2 onions, cut small.	ably gravy salt.

R INSE the beans and place in pan along with all the other items except the corned beef. Well cover them with heated stock or boiling water, and boil slowly until the beans are cooked, stirring occasionally. Then add the beef cut into small pieces, and thicken the hash with a little flour; heat through.

This recipe can be varied by adding soaked peas in place of beans and pearl barley, and using dried mint to flavour in place of bay leaf. The following vegetables boiled or steamed together make an unusual but tasty accompaniment to the above-mentioned dishes: 1 medium-sized onion, 2 carrots, ½ a small swede or 2 turnips, all sliced small, put in a pan with 4 large potatoes left whole. When cooked, drain well and dry a little, add seasoning to taste and a little butter, and mash well together. Sufficient for 4 persons.

From Mrs. E. W. Anderson, Yorkshire.

CORNED BEEF AND TOMATO PIE

8 ozs. self-raising flour.	Pinch of salt.
2 or 3 ozs. fat.	Water to mix.

Filling:

½ lb. corned beef.	2 large tomatoes.
2 tablespoonfuls beaten egg.	Pepper and salt to taste.

R UB fat into flour with pinch of salt and mix to a firm paste with water. Roll out and line a tin or dish, leaving suffic-ient paste for the crust.

Cover the pastry in the tin with corned beef, then slices of tomato. Beat the egg, add seasoning and pour over beef and tomato. Cover with the remaining pastry and brush over with a little of the egg. Bake quickly for 15 minutes, then at a lower temperature for 10 minutes.

From Mrs. Julia Kirby, Bedfordshire.

CORNISH PASTY

½ lb. flour.
½ lb. steak.
¼ lb. butter.
2 medium-sized potatoes.

1 small onion.
Salt and pepper.
A little cold water.

RUB the fat into the flour, add the salt and mix into a stiff dough with the water. Divide into two parts and roll each piece out thinly into a round. Season the chopped potatoes, onion and sliced meat, mix and place a layer on one half of each piece of pastry. Fold over the other half and pinch together. Bake in a moderate oven for ¾ hour. This is sufficient for 2 pasties.

From Miss V. Newton, Cornwall.

"DRESSMAKER" TRIPE

TAKE a piece of prepared tripe large enough to fold over. Make a stuffing of onions (boil these first), breadcrumbs, pepper, salt and herbs.

Spread thick layer of this in half the tripe, fold the other piece on to it and sew the edges together. Place in a greased tin with a few slices of bacon on top. Bake for 1 hour. Pour over a good brown gravy.

From Mrs. W. Morley, Lincolnshire.

EXMOOR LAMB STEW

4 lean chops.
1 oz. butter.
8 small potatoes.
4 small onions.
4 tablespoonfuls white breadcrumbs.
4 oz. mushrooms.

½ cup white wine.
½ cup stock (or ½ chicken cube).
½ cup thick cream.
Little thyme, parsley, bay leaf.
Sprig of lovage (or bunch celery tops).

TRIM chops, fry gently in butter. Take out and put into the fat the potatoes, cut in half, the whole onions and the chopped mushrooms. Cook for 5 minutes. Remove the vegetables and drain off any fat, add wine, stock, breadcrumbs and cream. Add seasoning and stir well, add chopped herbs and the bay leaf, put back the vegetables with the chops, cover the pan closely and simmer until meat is tender. Remove bay leaf. Garnish with chopped parsley. Serve hot.

From Mrs. J. Weatherlake, The Croft, Wargrave, Berks.

FAVOURITE ROLL

½ lb. cold meat.
1 thick slice stale bread.
¼ pint gravy or milk.
Salt.

¼ lb. mashed potatoes.
1 teaspoonful chopped onion.
Browned breadcrumbs.
Pepper.

BREAK the bread into small pieces, soak them in the gravy or milk, beat out all the lumps with a fork, and add the finely-chopped meat. Add the potato, onion and salt and pepper to taste, and mix all well together. Grease a basin or mould, coat it thickly with browned breadcrumbs, and pour in the mixture. Press it down firmly with a greased paper, and either steam or bake gently for about 1 hour.

From Mrs. Smith, Worcestershire.

FRICO

THIS is a very excellent and savoury dish. Take 2 lbs. of lean beef, fillet or any other juicy part, 2 lbs. of potatoes, and 1 lb. of Spanish onions, seasoning, butter, stock and claret as below. Cut the meat into thick pieces of 2 in. square, parboil the potatoes and slice thickly; slice the onions and fry a yellow colour in butter for 10 minutes or so; then put all into a jar, with onions top and bottom, together with the butter they were cooked in; add pepper but no salt, add a pint of stock and a glass of claret. Tie down with greased paper, and cover the jar with the lid.

Cook in a gentle oven, setting the jar in a pan with the hot water half the depth of the jar, the contents of which must not reach boiling-point. In 2 to 3 hours the meat will be tender; then add salt to taste (nothing else, unless more pepper is needed) and serve in a hot, deep dish. If the meat is cooked slowly enough, there will be plenty of gravy.

From Mrs. F. Walker, Essex.

GAMMON AND APRICOT PIE

1 gammon rasher 1 in. thick.
½ lb. dried apricots.
Pepper.

1 oz. sultanas.
6 potatoes.
A little gravy.

LIGHTLY brown the rasher on both sides in a frying-pan. Lay in a large pie-dish. Place apricots—which have been in water 12 hours previously—on top. Sprinkle a little pepper over, add the sultanas, pour a little gravy over, cover with sliced potatoes. Put a piece of greaseproof paper over all and bake in a moderate oven for 1 hour. Serve hot.

From Miss E. Hughes, Buckinghamshire.

COOKING A HAM
(*An Economical Method*)

PUT your ham in the copper, well cover with cold water, and slowly bring to boil. Boil for 20 minutes, if ham is 15 lbs. or under; for 20 lbs. or more, 1 hour is sufficient. Then take away all fire from underneath and well cover the copper with old coats, bags or anything to keep in the heat. Leave for about 12 hours (if cooked overnight leave until next morning). Lift off coats, etc., also cover, and if water is cold enough, lift ham on dish. You will have a well-cooked but not over-cooked ham with a minimum amount of fuel.

From Mrs. M. Francis, Somersetshire.

HARICOT OX TAIL

1 ox tail.	½ lb. turnips.
½ lb. onions.	Salt and pepper.
1 dessertspoonful flour.	3 cloves.
1 oz. butter.	6 peppercorns.
½ lb. carrots.	1 teaspoonful chopped parsley.

JOINT ox tail and cut in pieces. Stick one onion with cloves and put in pan with parsley, peppercorns, seasoning, meat and enough water to cover. Bring to boil and simmer gently for 1 hour. Strain off gravy, and skim off the fat. Put gravy in the pan again with meat, and remainder of onions, peeled and sliced; cut up carrots and turnips small. Simmer until vegetables are tender. Mix butter and flour and stir into the stew. Simmer for 10 minutes. Turn on to a hot dish and give a border of boiled haricot beans.

From Mrs. J. R. Robinson, Cumberland.

HUNTINGDON FIDGET PIE

1 lb. cooking apples.	Seasoning.
½ lb. onions.	Pastry crust.
¾ lb. streaky home-cured bacon.	

PUT 1 layer of apples at the bottom of a pie-dish, on top of this place a layer of sliced onions, followed by a layer of bacon cut into dice. Repeat until dish is full adding to each layer a sprinkling of pepper and salt. Add a very little water, cover with a good pastry crust, and bake in a moderate oven for 2 hours.

From Mrs. D. Berry, Huntingdonshire.

JARRETT STEAK

1½ lbs. stewing steak.	1 cupful water.
A few sticks of celery.	1 tablespoonful Worcester sauce.
6 small rolls of bacon.	2 tablespoonfuls tomato sauce.
	A little flour.

CUT the steak up into pieces 1 in. square, rolling each piece in flour, put in a casserole dish and add the celery, finely cut, and the bacon. Over this pour the water into which has been mixed the Worcester and tomato sauce. The meat should now be covered. Put in oven, boil up, and then allow to simmer 2 hours. Turn meat occasionally, and if too dry add a little water. If very mild bacon has been used, add a little salt.

From Mrs. T. H. Robinson, Gloucestershire.

JELLIED EGG AND SAUSAGE MEAT

1 egg.	1 teaspoonful dried herbs.
1 teaspoonful gelatine.	¼ lb. cooked sausage meat.
1 gill gravy.	Pinch of dry mustard and salt.
	Few sultanas.

BOIL egg till hard. Shell when cold. Slice, and place in a shallow tin. Dissolve gelatine in gravy; add to sausage meat, with dried herbs and seasonings. Pour into tin. Place sultanas singly on top. Next day—when set—cut into suitable pieces. Wrapped in paper, they carry easily.

From Miss E. Hughes, Buckinghamshire.

IMITATION JUGGED HARE
(*The Surrey Way*)

A GOOD imitation of jugged hare can be made with shin of beef. Cut the meat into slices about the size of the joints of a hare, flour well and just fry brown in a little dripping. Place in a casserole with an onion stuck with four cloves, a strip of lemon rind, a teaspoonful of mixed herbs and seasoning. Cook slowly for 3 hours. When finished, strain the gravy and thicken with 1 teaspoonful of flour mixed with a little ketchup. Put meat on hot dish and pour gravy over. If served with red-currant jelly and forcemeat balls, the illusion is complete.

For forcemeat balls, mix 2 tablespoonfuls breadcrumbs, ½ oz. butter or chopped suet, ½ teaspoonful parsley and herbs, ¼ teaspoonful grated lemon rind, seasoning, 1 beaten egg to mix. Roll into balls and "poach" in boiling water 10 minutes. These are much more wholesome than fried, and should be laid round the dish.

From Mrs. A. E. Godfrey, Surrey.

JUGGED STEAK
(*A Berkshire Method*)

A thick piece of steak.	2 onions.
Cloves.	1 teaspoonful mushroom ketchup.
Celery.	Pepper and salt.

CUT the steak into pieces about 1 in. square, and put into a stone jar. Add the onions stuck with cloves, the celery, mushroom ketchup, pepper and salt. Cover the jar closely and place in a pan of boiling water. Let it simmer until the meat is tender: or it can be placed in the oven and left to stew for a couple of hours. Add no water or grease. When done it is like jugged hare.

From Mrs. P. Horsell, Berkshire.

LAMB MOULD

DISSOLVE ½ oz. gelatine in ½ pint of hot water, add 1 teaspoonful lemon juice, 2 dessertspoonfuls of castor sugar, 1 teaspoonful of salt, and ½ gill of vinegar. Strain, and allow to cool. As soon as it begins to set add 1¼ cupfuls finely-shredded cabbage, 1 tablespoonful cooked peas, 1 sliced hard-boiled egg, and diced or sliced lamb to taste.

Turn into a wet mould and leave until set. Serve turned out on a bed of lettuce leaves, accompanied by mayonnaise and tomatoes.

From Mrs. A. M. Duckett, Somerset.

LAMB-TAIL PIE

ON some farms it is the custom to cut off lambs' tails when the lambs are very young; the tails then are small and not of much use. When left to get to a fair size, they make a delicious pie. When the tails are severed instruct the shepherd to keep them warm by covering with a sack.

Cut off the longest of the wool with scissors. Prepare the scald by putting 1 part cold to 3 parts of boiling water, and immerse the tails for a few minutes: then the wool will come off easily. Stew the tails in water with a carrot and onion, or in veal stock; they will want to stew for some time if they are fairly big—some farmers' wives roll each tail in chopped parsley before putting into the pie-dish. Hard-boiled eggs may —or may not—be added. Cover with short crust, and bake. Brush with beaten egg when partly baked.

From Miss V. Grey, Oxfordshire.

LITTLE PIGS FROM ROTHES

4 veal steaks.	1 tablespoonful mixed herbs.
¼ lb. butter.	½ pint white wine.
¼ lb. breadcrumbs.	2 oz. porridge oats.
¼ lb. sausage meat.	Seasoning to taste.

BEAT the steaks until they are paper thin. Mix the breadcrumbs, the sausage meat and butter to a paste, season and add the herbs. Spread this mixture over each veal steak, roll up and secure with a cocktail stick. Grease a shallow fireproof dish, put the "little pigs" in and add the wine. Cook in a moderate oven, 350 deg. F., Mark 5, for about 45 minutes. Take out, sprinkle porridge oats over the top and put back to brown for a further 15 minutes.

From Mrs. Rowntree, Yorks.

LIVER AND BACON HOT-POT

1 lb. pig's liver.	Breadcrumbs.
Salt and pepper.	Onions.
½ lb. streaky bacon.	Chopped parsley and marjoram.
Apples.	

CHOP the apples and onions, cut bacon in very thin slices and liver in thin pieces. Place a layer of liver in a greased casserole or pie-dish, cover with bacon, sprinkle with breadcrumbs, parsley, onions, marjoram, salt and pepper. Add one thick layer of chopped, sharp apples. Repeat these layers until dish is full, the last layer being breadcrumbs; fill dish right up with lukewarm water. Bake in a moderately hot oven for 2 hours, covering the dish. Add a little more water if it gets too dry. ½ hour before the cooking is finished, remove the cover to brown top. Serve very hot.

From Mrs. Doris Vincent, Devonshire.

LIVER IN BATTER

LIVER cooked in this way becomes as tender as chicken. Take about ½ lb. liver, cut it in small portions, make a batter of 2 tablespoonfuls of self-raising flour, a pinch of salt and cold water. Have ready a pan of boiling fat, dip each piece of liver in the batter, and fry till a nice golden brown. Serve hot with vegetables.

From Miss W. Palmer, Norfolk.

LIVER POTATO ROLL

1½ lbs. liver.
1 oz. flour.
1 onion.

¼ pint milk.
4 ozs. mashed potato.
Salt and pepper.

SLICE liver and fry with onion and chop when fried. Make gravy with flour and milk, and to the gravy add liver, onion and potato and seasoning. Mix thoroughly and shape into roll. Put in baking tin with dripping and bake 45 minutes.

From Miss Bond, Somersetshire.

ROAST LIVER

YOU will be surprised to discover how good roast liver is. Have 1 lb. cut off in a solid piece. Ask the butcher to gash it in the centre, almost through to the other side, so as to make a sort of pocket. Stuff this with a dressing made by chopping a thin rasher of bacon and 1 onion, and mixing them with breadcrumbs, 1 egg well beaten, and enough hot water to moisten the crumbs. Tie a string round the liver to hold it together, lard it with thin rashers of bacon, and bake until tender. Make a brown gravy with the fat in the baking-dish. Serve with currant jelly.

From Mrs. A. E. Godfrey, Surrey.

STUFFED LOIN OF LAMB

GET your butcher to bone a loin of lamb before sending it. Then mix together 3 ozs. breadcrumbs, 1½ ozs. shredded suet, ½ teaspoonful of mixed herbs, a little grated lemon rind, 1 small teaspoonful of chopped parsley and seasoning. Mix together into a crumbly paste with beaten egg. Put this into the loin where the bone was removed, roll the meat round and tie firmly with tape in several places. Roast for 1 hour 20 minutes.

To serve, cut in neat slices and arrange in the centre of a hot dish. Put little heaps of vegetables round: green peas, potatoes and asparagus look very attractive.

From Mrs. Bartlett, Somersetshire.

MARKET DAY SAVOURY

THIS can be left cooking on the stove while you go to market. Take 6 small pork chops, 2 pigs' kidneys, 1 lb. onions, 1½ lb. potatoes, 1 small apple, 1 teaspoonful dried sage,

1 tablespoonful tomato sauce. Peel and slice potatoes and onions, put in a stew-jar in layers with the chops and sliced kidneys. Sprinkle sliced onion, apple and seasoning among them. Cover with a layer of potatoes. Pour over a teacupful of water, put on a tight-fitting lid and cook slowly for 2 or 3 hours. The longer you cook this dish the more savoury it will be.

From Mrs. M. Arundel, Leicestershire.

MEAT LOAF

1½ lbs. neck of beef.
¼ lb. fresh pork from shoulder.
½ cupful breadcrumbs, soaked in milk or water.
1 tablespoonful minced parsley.
1¼ teaspoonfuls salt.

¼ teaspoonful paprika.
½ cupful tomatoes.
⅓ teaspoonful celery salt.
Dash of black pepper.
1 tablespoonful grated onion.

RUN the meat through the mincer, and let it remain on a plate for 1 hour or longer. Then add the soaked breadcrumbs, tomato, onion, parsley and celery salt and seasoning. Mix thoroughly, shape into a loaf, or press into a greased baking-tin (deep). Brush with beaten egg, sprinkle with crumbs, and bake 1½ hours in a moderate oven. Baste with melted butter or bacon dripping and hot water. Serve with tomato sauce.

From Dorothy Alder, Shropshire.

MEAT PUFFS

2 ozs. breadcrumbs.
1 lb. mashed potatoes.
2 ozs. flour.
2 eggs.

1 oz. butter.
Minced cold meat.
Pepper and salt.

THIS is to use up left-overs of meat, bread and potatoes. First mash the potatoes, then add butter, breadcrumbs, flour and seasoning, and last of all 1 egg well beaten. Make this into a paste, dredge with flour and roll out. Cut into squares about ¼ in. thick and fill these with minced meat. Fold over corner-ways, egg and bread crumb the rolls, shake off all the loose crumbs and fry a rich brown. Serve with a good gravy.

From Mrs. G. Carnell, Nottinghamshire.

MEAT ROCK CAKES

½ lb. finely chopped meat.
2 ozs. flour.
Salt and pepper.
A little gravy to mix.

1 grated onion.
1 oz. suet (this may be omitted if
the meat is fat).

MIX flour, suet, salt, pepper, and chopped meat. Add the grated onion. Moisten with gravy to the consistency of rock-cake mixture. Place on greased baking-tin in rough heaps. Bake in a fairly brisk oven for about ½ hour, or till the cakes are brown and crisp.

Serve with thick brown gravy and vegetables as a dinner dish, or with scrambled egg as a supper dish.

From Mrs. C. P. Rowan, Yorkshire.

MEAT ROLY-POLY

¾ lb. self-raising flour.
6 ozs. chopped suet.
½ lb. any cold roast meat, minced.
2 large onions, minced.

½ teaspoonful salt.
¼ teaspoonful pepper.
½ pint good gravy.

MAKE suet crust with flour, suet and water. Roll out ½ in. thick. Mix together the chopped onion and minced meat, season well and spread over the pastry. Wet the edges and roll up. Press the ends before covering with a scalded and floured pudding cloth. Place in pan of boiling water. Boil for 2 hours.

From Mrs. Edith Williams, Monmouthshire.

MOCK GOOSE

1 bullock's heart.
2 bay leaves.
4 cloves.
2 meat cubes.
4 large onions, grated.
1 tablespoonful cornflour.

8 or 10 large sage leaves, chopped
fine.
¼ lb. chopped suet or bacon.
½ lb. breadcrumbs.
1 egg.
Pepper and salt.
Dripping.

WELL wash the heart and place in a saucepan with enough water to cover. Add the pepper and salt, bay leaves, cloves and meat cubes. Simmer gently for 4 or 5 hours on the side of the stove. (It must only simmer to ensure tenderness.) Set aside until next day. Take off the fat from the stock. Mix together, with the egg to bind, the onions, sage leaves, chopped suet or bacon and breadcrumbs. Make into forcemeat balls, leaving a little to stuff the heart. Put the heart with the forcemeat balls round it in a baking-tin, cover with dripping and bake in a sharp oven for $\frac{1}{2}$ hour. Strain the stock in which the heart was boiled: use about 1 pint to thicken with the corn-flour. This makes a good brown gravy to serve with the heart.

The remainder of the stock makes an excellent soup if all kinds of vegetables are cut up and added. Thicken with corn-flour. The remainder of the heart can be minced for next day's dinner, and served with brown gravy and baked potatoes.

From Mrs. Arthur Hurst, Buckinghamshire.

MUTTON AND PICKLE DISH

Cold mutton.   Salt and pepper.
Gravy.   Breadcrumbs.
3 pickled walnuts.   3 large pickled onions.

CUT some cold mutton in slices, sprinkle with salt and pepper. Dip the slices first in gravy, then in breadcrumbs, and put into a greased pie-dish. Chop finely the pickled walnuts and pickled onions. Spread a layer of pickles over the meat, add a spoonful of liquor from the pickles, then another layer of mutton and pickles. Set the dish in the oven to get thoroughly hot, put some snippets of toasted bread on top and serve.

From Miss A. E. Parry, Flintshire.

MUTTON SPICE PIES

Short crust pastry.   Sugar.
Cold mutton.   Nutmeg.
An equal amount, by weight, of A few chopped prunes.
    windfall apples.

MAKE your short crust pastry of mutton fat if possible keeping a little back for the top of the pies. Cut the cold mutton into small pieces, pack the pie dish with this, alternating with the chopped apples, and plenty of seasoning. Sprinkle with a little sugar as you fill the pie dish, add a few chopped prunes, and a grating of nutmeg. Finally cover the last layer with a little finely grated mutton suet. Put on the pastry crust, and bake in a good oven until a pale golden brown.

Do not add water as the apples will cook to a spicy sauce over the meat. If the pies are to be eaten cold, then a slit should be left in the top of each pie, and when hot, red currant jelly is run into the pies. When cold, this will set stiffly again and form a delicious layer of sweetness on the surface of the meat layer.

From Kathleen Thomas.

OATMEAL SCRAPPLE

3 lb. lean pork.
1 large bone.
1 lb. oatmeal.
5 teaspoonsfuls salt.

1½ teaspoonsfuls ground black pepper.
5 teaspoonsfuls onion juice.

PUT pork and bone into a large saucepan and cover with water, cook until meat is tender. Remove meat and bone, put meat through mincer. Return minced meat to liquid, bring to the boil and stir in the oatmeal, seasonings and onion juice. Cook slowly for 1 hour. Pour into bread tins and set aside to cool. When required, cut into thin slices and fry in hot fat until crisp and brown—a very good breakfast dish with fried eggs.

From Mrs. H. Fooks, Lancashire.

PORK CHEESE

IN Scotland we are very fond of cold meats and brawns for Sunday supper, and this is a nice dish which is always a favourite.

Chop coarsely 1 lb. of lean pork and 1 lb. of inside fat. Strew over and thoroughly mix in 3 teaspoonfuls of salt, half as much pepper, 1 teaspoonful of finely-chopped parsley, thyme and sage (mixed), and 1 tablespoonful of chopped chives, or spring onions.

Press the meat closely and evenly into a shallow tin, such as we use for a Yorkshire pudding, and bake in a gentle oven for 1 hour. When done, pour over ½ pint of aspic jelly that has been made with some well-seasoned bone stock. Allow to set, then serve the pork cheese cold, in slices, with a green salad. Minced mushrooms are very nice added to the pork, when they are available.

From Mrs. R. Johnstone, Scotland.

PORK PIE

3½ lbs. flour, heated quite hot.
1 lb. lard.

1 pint water.
½ teaspoonful salt.

For the filling:

3 lbs. pork (2 parts lean and 1 part fat) cut very small and well mixed.

1 oz. salt.
1 teaspoonful of anchovy essence or sauce.

94

THIS is a recipe that has been in my family for over a century, and at Christmas time is very much sought after, having a most subtle flavour.

Boil lard, water and salt together. Pour over the heated flour and mix with a wooden spoon. When cool enough to handle, knead well for 15 minutes. If you have no mould, a 2lb. jar will do to shape the pastry. When set, take off the mould and fill, packing the meat well to form a good shape when baking.

Fasten a band of greaseproof paper around the pastry, fix on a pastry lid and decorate with fancy shape in bold designs, leaves, etc. Make a centre hole and bake for $2\frac{1}{2}$ hours in a hot oven first, then moderate the heat to finish. Make your jelly by stewing the gristle and pig's foot. Pour a little into the pie when baked. This will make a good family-size pie or two smaller ones.

From Mrs. M. Hemsley, Nottinghamshire.

PORK PUDDING

1 lb. flour.
$\frac{3}{4}$ lb. raisins.

$\frac{1}{2}$ lb. salt pork (fat).
A little salt.
1 egg.

CHOP up the pork, but not too finely, and mix with the flour and a little salt; then add the raisins, previously stoned, and mix all to a stiff batter with milk and egg. Put into a well-greased baking tin, and bake until well cooked.

From Mrs. E. M., Kent.

POTATO, HAM AND CHEESE PASTY

$\frac{1}{4}$ lb. fat ham.
$\frac{1}{4}$ lb. mashed potatoes.
1 large onion.

2 ozs. cheese.
4 sage leaves.
Pepper and salt.

MAKE an ordinary pastry crust of $\frac{1}{2}$ lb. self-raising flour and $\frac{1}{4}$ lb. lard, water and salt, and roll out flat on the board. Cut the ham into small squares, grate the cheese and cut the onion into strips. Cut the sage leaves finely, have the potatoes mashed ready and mix with the other ingredients. Add the pepper and salt to taste. Put on to the pastry, wet the edges all round and press together. Put on a greased baking-tin, and bake for 1 hour in a moderate oven. This is very nice hot or cold.

From Mrs. E. Macey, Kent.

PRESSED BEEF

3 lbs. of brisket or flat ribs of beef.   1 meat cube.
½ cow's heel.

PUT these into a saucepan with seasoning and enough cold water to nearly cover the beef. Let the water come to the boil and draw the saucepan on to the side of the fire and let the water simmer for 2½ hours. Now lift out beef, remove bones carefully, and put it into a pudding-dish. Sprinkle a little salt over to taste and pour over some of the liquid. Then put a plate on the top and weight down. Leave until next day, then turn out. The beef will be covered with brown jelly.

From Mrs. M. Rogers, Wrexham.

QUORN BACON ROLL

THIS is a dish for a cold day, very popular in the Quorn country.

Make a suet paste with equal quantities of flour and shredded suet, a pinch of salt and enough water to moisten. Roll out, about ¼ in. thick. Lay rashers of lean bacon—collar is best—on the paste, and sprinkle with sage and chopped onion. Roll up, wrap in a pudding-cloth and boil for about 2 hours. (Allow about ½ lb. bacon for 3 people.) Serve on a hot dish, sprinkled with chopped parsley and surrounded with potatoes, carrots and turnips.

From Miss P. Crawford, Leicestershire.

SANDWICH FILLING

1 lb. sausage meat.   1 rasher fat bacon.
1 small onion.   Sage to taste and pepper and salt.
1 teacupful of mashed potato.   2 tablespoonfuls milk.
1 egg.

CHOP finely the bacon and onion and mix well with rest of ingredients, put into a greased basin and steam 2 hours.

From Mrs. Rogers, Wrexham.

SANDWICH SPREAD

1 teacupful water.	2 or more cooked potatoes.
1 meat cube.	Pepper and salt to taste.
1 tablespoonful oatmeal.	2 ozs. margarine.

PUT all in a small saucepan and simmer for 5 minutes. Add 2 ozs. margarine, stir well. A little cooked meat can be added to this mixture. Cool before using. Grated onion can be used in the mixture if liked.

From Mrs. A. W. Dickman, Northumberland.

SAUSAGE GALANTINE

¼ lb. grated carrots.	¼ lb. cooked peas.
½ lb. sausage meat.	2 tablespoonfuls each chopped
1 tablespoonful chopped parsley.	beetroot and chopped onion.
2 tablespoonfuls oatmeal.	½ teaspoonful sage.
Salt and pepper.	2 eggs.

GREASE a mould or small cake-tin and put a very small quantity of each of the different vegetables at the bottom, to form a decorated top when the galantine is turned out. Mix the sausage, oatmeal and the remaining vegetables and seasoning in a bowl, add the beaten eggs and mix well together. Place carefully in the decorated mould, cover with greased paper and steam for 1½ hours. When cold, turn out and serve with green salad.

From Mrs. Rogers, Wrexham.

SAVOURY MUTTON PIE

2 lbs. fillet mutton.	1 lb. sausages.
4 tomatoes.	1 teaspoonful barley.
1 large onion.	Salt and pepper.

For the crust:

1 lb. flour.	1 teaspoonful baking powder.
⅓ lb. lard.	

LAY mutton flat in saucepan and cover with water. Add barley, onion (chopped), salt and pepper to taste. Simmer till tender, then lift it bodily into a pie-dish with some gravy. Next fry the sausages gently and drain on to greaseproof paper for 2 minutes, and lay round the mutton. Place a tomato in each corner.

For pie crust, put flour into a warm bowl, add salt and 1 teaspoonful of baking powder and mix well. Rub half the lard into flour and make up the pastry with water. Roll out flat. Divide remaining lard into 3 portions. Take 1 portion and with the end of a knife distribute in small portions at equal distances over pastry. Fold over 4 times and roll out again. Repeat this twice more and then place pastry on pie and bake in a hot oven for 40 minutes.

From Miss M. Scott, Yorkshire.

SCALLOPED MEAT WITH MACARONI

2 cupfuls tomato soup or gravy.
1 cupful cooked macaroni.
2 cupfuls cooked meat (chopped).
1 cupful browned breadcrumbs.
Salt and pepper to taste.
Butter.

ARRANGE the cooked macaroni, meat and gravy in alternate layers in a casserole. Sprinkle each layer with salt and pepper, cover the top with browned breadcrumbs. Dot with butter and bake in moderate oven until mixture is heated through.

From Miss L. Pound, Kent.

SCOTCH SCRAPPLE

1 cup oatmeal.
1¼ cups water.
½ teaspoonful salt.
½ cup pork sausage meat.

ADD the oatmeal to the boiling, salted water. Cook for 20 minutes or until thick, stirring constantly to prevent sticking.

Stir in the crumbled sausage meat and mix thoroughly. Season to taste, pour into a narrow dish and leave overnight. Cut into slices, dip the slices in flour and fry in a little fat until brown both sides. Nice served with fried tomatoes.

From Miss Webster, Lancashire.

SCOTCH MUTTON PIE

1 lb. self-raising flour.
6 ozs. lard, or a mixture of fat.
1 lb. lean mutton.
A little powdered mace or nutmeg.
½ teaspoonful salt.
¼ pint water.
Seasonings.
A little stock or gravy.

TAKE about one-third of the pastry, and put aside. Divide the rest into six pieces and shape each into a small case—a tumbler may be used to help with shaping. Fill the cases with the meat, cut into very small pieces, add seasonings and flavourings and moisten with stock or gravy.

Divide the smaller piece of pastry into six and shape each piece, pressing the edges firmly together. Trim with a pair of scissors, and pinch all round the edge. Make a hole in the centre of each pie, brush the top with a little milk or egg, and bake 1 hour in a moderate oven. When cooked, add some hot gravy through the hole made in the top of pastry, and serve hot.

From Mrs. Bridges, Surrey.

SAVOURY SHEEP'S HEAD

1 sheep's head.	1 medium-sized onion.
½ lb. rice.	¼ teaspoonful mixed herbs.
¼ lb. breadcrumbs.	Pepper and salt.

SOAK the head overnight in plenty of salt and water. Wash off well and boil very slowly for about 1½ to 2 hours with the onion. Add rice ½ hour before it is ready. When nearly cold, carefully cut the meat off the bones and mince or cut up very fine.

Now mix the herbs, salt and pepper with the breadcrumbs. Well grease the pie-dish and put alternate layers of breadcrumbs, meat and rice; top your dish with breadcrumbs. You may also add a skinned tomato, cut up, to decorate and give colour to your dish. Pour over a little gravy and brown in the oven for ½ hour.

This dish can be prepared overnight and heated up in the morning, and is both nourishing and cheap.

From Mrs. Stone, Devonshire.

BRAISED SHEEP'S TONGUES

3 sheep's tongues.	A few slices of bacon.
2 small turnips.	1 onion.
1 carrot.	A bouquet of herbs.

LAY the sheep's tongues in salt and water for 12 hours and then put them in cold water. Bring rapidly to the boil. Drain the tongues dry, fry a few slices of bacon in a stew-pan and in this put a sliced carrot, an onion and the turnips, with a bouquet of herbs. On this place the tongues, and lay another slice of bacon over them. Pour in a pint of stock and simmer gently for 3 hours. Skin the tongues, slice them lengthwise, and put the pieces in the stew-pan with the strained gravy till they are hot.

From Miss A. E. Parry, Flintshire.

SHEPHERD'S PIE WITH VEGETABLES

Boiled potatoes.	Cooked carrots.
Turnips.	Peas and parsnips.
Cold meat.	Onion.
Seasoning.	Water (about ½ teacupful).

MINCE meat and put into a roasting-tin. Add sliced onion, pepper, salt and water. Add a layer of each of the sliced carrots, turnips and parsnips. Add a layer of peas. Then cover with mashed potatoes. Mark with fork and cook in a brisk oven until potatoes are nicely browned.

From Mrs. Birkett, Cumberland.

SPICED MUTTON

BONE the joint, rub it well with black pepper, a little powdered thyme, a pinch of mace and fine oatmeal; do not use salt. Cover thickly with mutton dripping and wrap the whole in cabbage leaves. Roast very slowly, allowing 20 minutes for each pound of meat. Baste well at least twice during the cooking and when basting add a cupful of cider to the fat in the pan. This can be eaten either hot or cold.

From Kathleen Thomas.

SPRING LAMB

PUT 2 cupfuls of fine breadcrumbs into a basin, add 2 table-spoonfuls shredded suet, 2 teaspoonfuls chopped mint, seasoning of salt and pepper. Mix with a beaten egg and a little milk.

Have the bone taken out of a shoulder of lamb. Well skewer the shoulder after the stuffing has been put in. Dredge the outer skin with flour, put 2 or 3 knobs of dripping on top, and roast in a hot oven for 1½ hours.

From Miss F. Smithson, Lincolnshire.

ROLLED STEAK AND PUFFS

SELECTS 2 lbs. juicy steak, cut in one piece about ¾ in. thick. Make a seasoning as follows: Rub 1 teaspoonful dripping into 1 cupful fine breadcrumbs; add a little mixed

herbs, pepper and salt, and a small onion finely minced.
Spread this mixture over the steak, roll up and fasten with a
skewer. Dust over the roll a little flour and a pinch of sugar
(the sugar imparts a delicious flavour and makes a nice brown
gravy), place in a greased baking-dish, and put dripping on
top. Roast about 1½ hours. Baste frequently.

About 20 minutes before it is cooked, pour into the dish,
1 dessertspoonful at a time, a Yorkshire pudding batter. For
batter, beat 1 egg thoroughly, add ½ pint milk, sift in ¼ lb. flour
and pinch of salt. Leave a space between the spoonfuls. When
cooked, place roast on dish with Yorkshire puffs, and serve
with brown gravy and vegetables.

From Mrs. H. Mewton, Cornwall.

STUFFED SUMMER CABBAGE

1 cabbage.	¼ lb. whole rice.
1 lb. minced pork (lean).	1 onion.
1 ozs. butter.	1 egg.

SEPARATE leaves of cabbage, keeping larger leaves whole
for stuffing. Mince remainder of cabbage finely and boil in
salted water for 8 minutes, allowing to steam for 8 minutes
longer with lid on pan. Strain cabbage thoroughly. Grease
pan and put layer of minced cabbage on bottom, then fill each
large leaf with stuffing and lay on top, covering all with
remainder of cabbage and small nuts of butter.

Prepare stuffing thus: Mix minced meat with rice previously boiled, and egg (not beaten), onion finely minced with
salt and pepper to taste. Stew slowly for 1½ hours.

From Mrs. Cromar, Aberdeenshire.

SWEDES WITH BACON

TAKE thin slices of smoked bacon and put a layer in the
bottom of a saucepan, then a layer of swede turnip, and
so on, in alternate layers till you have as much as required.
Then add 2 tablespoonfuls of cold water and place at side of
stove and simmer gently till cooked. The swedes stew in their
own liquid and absorb the flavour of the bacon, and in con-
sequence are altogether more delicious than when cooked in
the usual way.

From Miss K. Murphy, Cork.

SIMMERED STEAK

TAKE 2 lbs. steak and pound well with the back of a large wooden spoon. Sprinkle with about ½ cup of flour, beat this well in. Put the steak in a frying-pan and brown on both sides. When nicely browned, cover with boiling water, add 4 or 5 sliced onions, pepper and salt, and simmer for 2 hours, adding a little more water if necessary.

From Miss W. Palmer, Norfolk.

TIPPERARY IRISH STEW PIE

½ lb. lean shin of beef.	Gravy browning.
3 carrots.	6 large potatoes.
3 turnips.	A few pieces of celery.
1 onion.	1 dessertspoonful seasoning.
1 pint of water.	

Suet-crust paste composed of:

¼ lb. flour.	¼ teaspoonful baking powder.
2 ozs. suet.	½ gill water.
¼ teaspoonful salt.	

CUT up the meat into pieces 1 in. square. Put the meat into a casserole (one with a lid), and slice into this the onion, carrots, turnips, celery and seasoning. Add the water and simmer for an hour. Add the sliced potatoes and boil a further ¼ of an hour. Make the paste and roll it out, so that it will just fit into the casserole, and place on top of the stew. Put the casserole lid on: boil gently for ½ an hour.

From Mrs. G. Dean, Cheshire.

TOAD SPECIAL

FIRST make a batter with 2 eggs, 5 ozs. flour, a pinch of salt, tablespoonful water and sufficient milk to make to a thick creamy consistency. Allow this to stand 1 hour or longer. In well-greased flat fireproof dish lay tiny rolls of thinly-cut veal, stuffed with breadcrumbs, parsley, milk and seasoning and a quarter slice of a rasher of bacon. Pour the batter over the neatly-arranged rolls, and cook for ½ to ¾ hour in a moderate to hot oven. Ornament the top, when nearly cooked, with cooked mushrooms or uncooked slices of tomato. This is a good way of using up remains of a joint.

From Mrs. Kitchener, Buckinghamshire.

TRANSVAAL ROAST

THIS is a far more interesting way of cooking breast of mutton than stewing it, and is, moreover, delicious when cold, and very economical. Buy the meat ready boned (the butcher does it much better than oneself). See that you have the bones, though, for gravy. For 2 cups of breadcrumbs, take ¾ teaspoonful of salt, a good dash of pepper, a finely-chopped onion, 1 level tablespoonful (not more) each of dried (or fresh) parsley and thyme. Mix well with 2 eggs. Open the meat, spread it evenly with the stuffing, roll and tie tightly. If you can bake it in a pie-dish, just to fit, so much the better. Baste well and cook slowly for at least 2 hours. Serve with apple jelly and the usual gravy and vegetables.

From Mrs. W. Levers, South Africa.

TRIPE WITH TOMATOES

THIS is a good spring dish, and one which all tripe eaters may like to try. You will need 2 lbs. of tripe, a bunch of herbs, 1 lb. of tomatoes, 2 onions, 2 ozs. of dripping, pepper, salt and 1 large tablespoonful of flour.

First, cut up the tripe and blanch it. Fry the herbs and sliced onions in the fat, and when browned a little, stir in the flour. Pass the tomatoes through a sieve, put into the stew-pan with the onions, etc., and stir till very hot. Add the tripe to the sauce; season all, and simmer slowly for 1½ hours. Chop some parsley very finely and scatter over all. Have fried pieces of bread for a further garnish.

From Mrs. A. D. Jones, Cheshire.

TURKEY PORK

A leg of pork.   Dripping.
Flour.   Forcemeat balls.

COOKED in the following way a leg of pork will taste like turkey. Take off the skin and bone the leg; make a plain crust with the flour and dripping, roll out very thin, and fold the pork in it. Bake it in a moderate oven; allowing 25 minutes to each pound of pork. Break off the crust; and you will find your pork beautifully white and tender. Serve with brown gravy, forcemeat balls and bread sauce. Cut the crust into neat pieces and serve on a separate dish.

From Mrs. C. Ball, Bedfordshire.

VEAL AND HAM PIE

1 lb. filleted veal.	½ teaspoonful herbs.
¼ lb. ham.	A little grated lemon rind.
2 hard-boiled eggs.	Salt and pepper.
1 teaspoonful chopped parsley.	Stock.

For the pastry:

10 ozs. flour.	Water to mix.
6 ozs. butter and lard mixed.	Egg to glaze.

COOK the veal in enough cold water to cover, with an onion stuck with 2 cloves. When cold, cut into thin slices, put a pinch of seasoning (parsley, herbs, lemon peel, salt and pepper) on each slice and roll up. Pack the rolls in a pie-dish, not too tightly, with the ham and hard-boiled eggs cut in slices. Reduce the stock, adding a leaf of gelatine if necessary, and pour it into the pie-dish.

Cover with pastry, decorate with leaves and a rose, brush over with egg, bake for 1½ to 1¾ hours, remove the rose and pour in the remainder of the stock through the hole. Rough puff or flaky pastry can be used for this dish.

From Mrs. F. Mayne, Bedfordshire.

WILTSHIRE PORKIES

MIX ¼ lb. flour with ½ teaspoonful salt in a basin, add the yolk of 1 egg, 1 tablespoonful salad oil and enough water to make a batter which will coat the back of a spoon. Beat well and let it stand for ½ hour. Form 1 lb. sausage meat into small, neat rolls, flouring the hands and board to prevent sticking. Whisk the white of the egg stiffly, stir into the batter, then coat each roll with batter and fry in deep, boiling fat until brown. Pile on a hot dish and serve with apple rings fried in the batter. Garnish with fried parsley.

From Mrs. C. Gibbons, Cheshire.

PUDDINGS

SPICED APPLE CAKE

1 lb. apples.
3 ozs. sugar.
Rind of ½ lemon.

A little water.
Teacupful of cake or biscuit crumbs.

For the pastry:

3 ozs. flour.
3 ozs. cornflour.
2 ozs. butter.
2 ozs. castor sugar.

½ teaspoonful spice.
Yolk of an egg.
A pinch of salt.

PUT the apples in a saucepan with sugar, lemon and a little water. Stew until the apples are reduced to a pulp. Turn out to cool. To make the pastry: sieve all the dry ingredients and rub in the butter until fine as breadcrumbs. Bind together with the egg yolk beaten with a little water. Do not make the pastry too soft. Knead this until free from cracks, and roll out thinly.

Grease a tart ring, line it with pastry, sprinkle half the crumbs at the bottom, fill up with the apple mixture, and cover with the rest of the crumbs. Roll out the remainder of the pastry and cover, wetting the edges in the usual way. Bake in a moderate oven for about 1 hour. Sprinkle with sugar. It is delicious with custard, cold.

From Mrs. R. Noble, Cambridgeshire.

APPLE CRACKNEL

1 lb. cooking apples.
½ to ¾ lb. self-raising flour.
Just a little sugar to the flour.

Sugar to taste.
2 to 4 ozs. margarine (not lard).

BOIL the apples until soft, and mash up. Sweeten to taste. Put flour and margarine into basin. Rub well together until quite crumbly. Do not wet.

Pour apple into a greased pie-dish evenly, then sprinkle the flour mixture well over to cover apple. There must not be any liquid in the apple, so when you cook them use only just enough water to keep from burning. Put in a moderate oven and bake till a nice brown.

From Mrs. A. Lawford, Sussex.

APPLE CREAM

PEEL, core and grate apples according to quantity required. Mix quickly with sweetened condensed milk. Heaped into a glass dish this makes a delicious sweet, which children especially love.

From Miss E. Rutherford, Northumberland.

APPLE CREAM SPONGE

2 lbs. apples.
Sponge cake or any stale pieces of plain cake.

2 eggs.
1 pint milk.

PEEL and cut apples in slices and cook with a little water until they resemble apple sauce. Leave until cool. Sweeten a little and pour half over the sponge pieces, then make a little custard with yolks of eggs, whisk the whites and other half of apples until it's like a lovely fruity cream.

Put a custard on top of sponge cake and apples, and then the cream on top. It makes a nice treat for the children, and only takes 15 minutes to make.

From Mrs. F. Janney, Lincolnshire.

APPLE CRISPS

4 good-sized cooking apples.
¼ cupful margarine.

1 cupful brown sugar.
1 cupful flour.

GREASE a baking-dish, and ¾ fill with sliced apple. Work the margarine, sugar, and flour together until the mixture is like granulated sugar. Spread it over the apples. Bake in a hot oven for 10 minutes, then reduce the heat, and bake until the apples are soft and the crumbs nicely browned. Serve with cream or thin egg custard.

From Mrs. G. Rose, Huntingdonshire.

APPLE DELIGHT

6 ozs. self-raising flour.	2 ozs. sugar.
3 ozs. lard.	1 egg white.
1 lb. cooking apples.	A pinch of salt.

MAKE a short pastry by rubbing the fat and a pinch of salt into the flour. Roll out pastry and line a sandwich-tin; bake until golden brown. Peel, core and slice the apples, cook with sugar and a little water until very soft. Beat up with a fork and fill the pastry. Whisk the egg white until stiff and spread evenly on apple. Return to the oven for a few minutes to brown and when cold decorate with a little blackcurrant jam. Serve cold with custard.

From Miss A. Everall, Warwickshire.

APPLE MARMALADE CHARLOTTE

Left-over bread and butter or thin slices of plain bread, about ½ lb.

½ to 2 ozs. marmalade.	1 egg.
½ pint milk.	Sugar to taste.
½ lb. apples.	

PUT layer of bread into a greased pie-dish and cover with a layer of sliced apple and a little marmalade. Cover with bread. Fill the dish in this way and then beat up the egg in the milk and pour over. Bake in moderate oven for 30 to 35 minutes.

From Anne Coltman, Leicestershire.

APPLE MERINGUE
(*With a difference*)

6 cooking apples.	1 tablespoonful of castor sugar.
2 egg whites.	½ cupful sugar.
½ cupful water.	Pinch of ground cloves.
A little raspberry jam.	

PEEL the apples, remove cores and slice thinly. Place in a pan with water and sugar and cloves. Stew very gently until tender. Take from the pan and place in a small pie-dish. Allow to cool. Whisk the egg whites briskly with the castor sugar until very stiff. Spread a little raspberry jam over the top of the apples. Pile the whisked egg white in heaps on top. Return to the oven for a minute or two to set and brown very slightly. Serve cold.

From Miss Christian Milne, Aberdeenshire.

APPLE MINCE PIE

PEEL and chop 3 or 4 large cooking apples, add any fruit such as sultanas, currants, dates, etc., that you have, 2 tablespoonfuls syrup, pinch of mixed spice, and mix all together.

Line a plate with pastry, place mixture on it and cover with more pastry. Cook in a good oven. This makes a good substitute for mince pie.

From Mrs. H. Baldwin, Essex.

APPLE AND SYRUP TART WITH OATMEAL PASTRY

Pastry:

4 ozs. flour.	4 ozs. fine oatmeal.
2 ozs. fat.	Pinch of salt.
Water to mix.	

Filling:

1 lb. apples.	2 ozs. sugar.
¼ cloves.	2 tablespoonfuls brown bread-
3 tablespoonfuls golden syrup.	crumbs.
2 oz. sultanas.	

TO make the pastry, mix flour, oatmeal and salt together; rub in fat. Form to a stiff paste with a little water. Roll out. Line a rather deep, round tin with pastry.

Peel, core and slice the apples. Stew till tender in very little water, with cloves. Strain off any liquid. Stir in sugar. Put mixture in pastry case, and sprinkle breadcrumbs over. Cover with warm golden syrup and add sultanas. Bake in a moderate oven 30 minutes. The tart, when it is cold, will be solid and carries well in a tin.

From Miss E. Hughes, Buckinghamshire.

APPLE TANSY

3 large apples (soft).	3 eggs.
Sugar to taste.	A little mixed spice.
1 pint milk.	1 cupful fine breadcrumbs.

PEEL and slice the apples, cook gently in a little butter until soft, and pour into a greased fireproof dish. Beat the eggs, add them to the milk, sweeten to taste, and add a pinch of mixed spice and a pinch of nutmeg. Pour this mixture over the breadcrumbs and beat lightly, then pour all the mixture over the apples and bake very slowly till set.

From Kathleen Thomas.

STUFFED APPLES WITH BLACKBERRIES

PEEL and core apples. Press blackberries to a pulp, and mix with sugar or golden syrup. Press this pulp down well in the opening of apples, and if there is any left, throw among the apples when you put them in a casserole or pie-dish. Put just a little water round them. Cover with a plate, and cook in a moderate oven till soft.

From Mrs. Livingstone, Warwickshire.

STUFFED APPLES

TAKE some large cooking apples and core them. Prick over with a fork to prevent them bursting. Next prepare the filling as follows: 2 ozs. stoned dates (chopped), 1 oz. walnuts, 1 oz. brown sugar, grated rind of 1 lemon, juice of 1 lemon. Mix all the ingredients together. Put some of the filling into the core. Put the apples in a pie-dish, with some water. Cook in a moderate oven until the apples are soft.

From Miss L. Rice, Glamorganshire.

APRICOT CASTLE

¼ lb. dried apricots.	3 ozs. margarine.
8 ozs. flour.	3 ozs. sugar.
½ pint milk and a little water beaten together.	1 egg.
	2 teaspoonfuls baking powder.

SOAK the apricots for 24 hours. Stew with a little sugar until quite soft. Add baking powder to flour. Cream fat and sugar. Add egg mixture and flour alternately to creamed fat, beating well all the time. The mixture must be very smooth, so if too stiff add more water and beat well. Pour into greased flan case and bake ½ hour in a moderate oven. Turn out in plate. Pour warmed stewed apricots into centre.

From Mrs. Birkett, Cumberland.

BEESTINGS

(Beestings is the milk a cow gives after she has freshly calved)

WE do not use the very first as it is so deep in colour. I always test it by putting a little on a saucer in the oven. If it sets too "thick", I put a pint of milk to 3 pints of beestings (or in proportion, according to the way it sets), sprinkle a little pudding-spice on top, and add a little sugar, Let it simmer in the oven, but not boil, just as if you were making an egg custard.

I make tarts with it just as one would make egg custard tarts.

From Mrs. H. M. Watkins, Wrexham.

FRUIT BEESTINGS

TAKE the third milking of the cow and set in a pan. After 6 to 12 hours, skim off about 2 pints of the rich head of the milk. Take a good size pie-dish, grease well. Mix 1 oz. cornflour, with a little of the milk in a basin until smooth. Put the remainder of the milk into pie-dish. Add 1 oz. sugar (brown is best), 2 ozs. sultanas or currants. Then stir in the cornflour and bake in a moderate oven until golden brown and set.

When served, the fruit will be in a layer on bottom.

From Mrs. E. J. Cottey, Devonshire.

BEESTINGS CHEESE

FILL a pudding-dish with milk from second milking; stir in 2 tablespoonfuls syrup and mix well. Spread on top the cream from the first milking, put into a moderate oven, and bake until firm to touch and golden brown. This cheese cuts into smooth, creamy slices and is short and free in texture.

From Mrs. McLennan, Argyllshire.

BEESTINGS CURD

2 pints new milk.
1 breakfastcupful water.

1 breakfastcupful beestings (the first milkings after a cow calves).

HEATED quickly on a bright fire, makes about 1½ lbs. delicious curd.

One teacupful beestings is equal to 2 eggs in Yorkshire puddings. And do they rise!

From Mrs. Duckles, Yorkshire.

BEESTINGS CUSTARD

TAKE 1 pint beestings milk; 2 tablespoonfuls sugar; pinch of salt. Add salt and sugar to milk in pie-dish. Stir well. Cook in moderate oven until set. The result is a delicious custard-like pudding; but much depends on correct oven heat.

From Mrs. Birkett, Cumberland.

BEESTINGS PUDDINGS

TO make 1 dozen small puddings, allow 3 tablespoonfuls batter to each tin (teacake size). Tins should be warm, bottoms just covered with melted fat. I use: 2 breakfastcupfuls flour; 1 breakfastcupful beestings; 2 tablespoonfuls water; 1 level teaspoonful salt; ½ pint milk.

Mix flour and salt; pour in beestings and water. Beat out lumps, thin down with milk (separated, or milk and water) to creamy mixture. Bake in hot oven 20 to 30 minutes. As with Yorkshire puddings, do not open the oven door till they should be ready; it only wastes heat and may make the puddings go flop.

In case you should be tempted to use more beestings, *don't;* you will get better results with less if it's the first time you have tried them.

From Mrs. Duckles, Yorkshire.

BEESTINGS TARTS

ADD 2 parts beestings to 1 part water and stir over a fire or stove till it thickens. Don't let it boil. To this add 3 eggs, ½ lb. sugar, a little nutmeg, currants (sultanas will do), a little marmalade instead of peel, add if possible a small quantity of rum.

Line tins or saucers with paste and put a good filling of the mixture, and you will find this delicious.

From Mrs. W. Johnson, Yorkshire.

BEESTINGS "NEW CHEESE"

I WONDER how many country women make that old-fashioned farmhouse dainty "new cheese"?

For this you fill a pudding-dish with milk from the second milking of a newly-calved cow. Heat 2 tablespoonfuls of syrup and add, stirring until thoroughly blended. Remove cream carefully from first milking, and use to "top" cheese. Bake in a moderate oven until golden brown and firm to touch. (An oven suitable for a baked custard is just right.) New cheese made thus cuts in smooth, creamy slices, and is short and free in texture. Served with cream, it is a delicious change from the usual milk pudding.

N.B.—A too intense oven ruins the texture of new cheese, making it tough and leathery instead of tender.

From Miss Christian Milne, Aberdeenshire.

BLACKBERRY AND APPLE CREAM

1 lb. of blackberries.	2 tablespoonfuls water.
2 large cooking apples.	Sugar to sweeten.
¾ oz. gelatine.	Little lemon essence.
½ pint custard.	Few drops cochineal.

PEEL and slice the apples, put with the blackberries, add sugar and stew gently till soft. Put through a sieve, dissolve the gelatine in water; and stir into the warm purée; add lemon essence and cochineal. When lukewarm, whisk in the custard, and turn into a wetted mould. Leave to set.

From Miss Mabel Roddis, Buckinghamshire.

BLACKBERRY ROLL

SIEVE half a pound of flour with ½ teaspoonful salt and 3 level teaspoonfuls baking powder. Cut in 2 ozs. margarine or other suitable fat and when well mixed, add milk up to a teacupful and a half; until you have a soft but not sticky dough.

Knead just enough to shape it into a smooth ball and then pat this out to ½ in. thickness. Sprinkle a pint of ripe, uncooked blackberries on this and sprinkle them with sugar (brown if possible) and a little cinnamon.

Roll up the paste like a roly-poly, place seam downwards on a greased baking sheet and bake in a hot oven for about ½ hour. Brush the roll over with a little melted margarine before baking.

From Mrs. F. A. Haynes, Warwickshire.

BLACKBERRY SNOW

TAKE 1 pint of blackberry juice (prepared as for jelly) and add 2 tablespoonfuls of syrup and one of sugar. Heat gently, stirring in ½ oz. of gelatine. Allow the mixture to become partially set, then beat in the white of an egg. Served in a glass dish with custard or creamy milk, this makes a delicious sweet.

From Mrs. E. Watson, Yorkshire.

BLACKBERRY SOLID

Blackberries.	Water.
½ pint milk.	2 to 3 tablespoonfuls sugar.
1 oz. gelatine.	

PLACE blackberries in a saucepan, just cover with water and simmer until all juice is extracted; then strain. Soak gelatine in 3 dessertspoonfuls water. To $\frac{1}{2}$ pint blackberry juice add $\frac{1}{2}$ pint milk. Put in a saucepan with the sugar and bring to blood heat. Add the gelatine and stir well until it dissolves and the mixture curdles, but do not boil. Then pour into a mould and put aside to set.

When the blackberry solid is turned into a dish it should be a deep purple, clear jelly at the bottom and a pale mauve, curdled mixture at the top.

From Mrs. Pitts, Hampshire.

BLACKBERRY SPONGE

4 ozs. flour.	2 tablespoonfuls sugar.
Teacupful blackberry jam.	3 ozs. shredded suet.
Pinch salt.	Little milk.

MIX the flour together with the suet, add the sugar, the salt, and the milk. Stir well. Now add the blackberry jam and stir again.

Pour the mixture into a buttered pudding-basin, cover with a greaseproof paper and steam for 2 hours. Serve with a sweetened white sauce.

From Mrs. E. Isaac, Carmarthenshire.

BLACKCURRANT LEAF CREAM

BLACKCURRANT leaves are most delicately scented in the spring and then is the time to use them for flavouring sweets and all kinds of creams and puddings.

This is my own special recipe: Boil 1 lb. white sugar with $\frac{1}{2}$ pint water and a cupful of *young* blackcurrant leaves. Boil, without stirring, for 15 minutes; then strain and pour the hot syrup *very gently* on to 2 beaten egg whites. Beat all the time, until the mixture begins to thicken; then stir in the juice of a lemon and a gill of whipped cream.

Served in individual glasses, it is the most delicious sweet.

From Mrs. R. Johnstone, Kirkcudbright, Scotland.

BLANCMANGE VARIATIONS

FOLLOW the usual routine for making the ordinary corn-flour pudding with 1 pint of milk and a little extra sugar to $2\frac{1}{2}$ tablespoonfuls cornflour.

(1) With a little cold milk, mix into a smooth paste 2 table-spoonfuls of ground almonds and 1 heaped tablespoonful of chocolate powder. Add this paste gradually to the cornflour pudding while still very hot, and mix thoroughly. The result makes an appetising and nourishing sweet, which is equally palatable, either cold or hot. If cold it looks most attractive in individual dishes garnished with whipped cream, whole blanched almonds, glacé cherries or angelica.

(2) Desiccated coconut may be substituted for ground almonds, in which case it is better to cook the coconut in the pudding to bring out the flavour.

(3) Coffee flavouring may be preferred to either of the chocolate-nut combinations. In this case, care must be taken that the milk pudding is definitely well below boiling-point before adding coffee essence, or the milk may curdle.

From Mrs. Mary Cowles, Suffolk.

"BREAD BETTY"

SOMETIMES I have toast left over as well as bread and butter, and this is how I use it up:

Butter the toast and cut it into dice, enough to fill 4 cupfuls. Mix it with ½ cupful of grated or chopped walnuts and 2 cupfuls of raisins previously soaked in orange juice. Arrange this mixture in a well-buttered pie-dish and sprinkle a little brown sugar among the layers.

Have ready a few slices of buttered bread, which should be put on top as a lid, buttered side on top. Pour over all ½ pint of milk, in which you have beaten an egg and a teaspoonful of honey, and sprinkle a little nutmeg on top. Bake as you would an ordinary egg custard in not too hot an oven.

Mrs. Constance Berry, Warwickshire.

BREAD AND MIXED FRUIT PUDDING

STALE bread, of course, need never be wasted; there are endless ways in which it can be used up. One of the best ways is in a bread pudding, and here is a recipe I can recommend.

Cut some bread into neat dice, put them in a greased pie-dish, and pour sufficient milk over just to cover. Leave till soft, then add more cold milk, to which has been added 1 or 2 eggs according to the size of the pudding; some sultanas, currants, raisins or stoned dates and sugar to taste. Stir the mixture very carefully with a fork, being careful not to break the dice: put a few pieces of butter here and there and bake in a moderate oven until a golden brown.

Mrs. H. Handy, Leicestershire.

BUTTERED APPLE CRISPS

Some large apples (firm).   Butter.
2 or 3 thick slices of white bread.   Sugar.

PEEL and cut up the apples, cut the crusts off the bread, and cut it into cubes. Fry the apples in the butter in a frying pan, and as soon as they are cooked lift them out and put into a dish, and sprinkle them with sugar. Fry the bread cubes in the remaining butter, lift out to drain, then mix with the apples and serve with custard and cream.

From Kathleen Thomas.

CHOCOLATE AND DATE BAKED PUDDING

Brown bread. $\frac{1}{4}$ lb. dates.
Treacle. $\frac{3}{4}$ pint of cocoa.

GREASE a pie-dish and line with two or more slices of brown bread spread with treacle. Put a layer of dates and then pour half the cocoa over. Add more brown bread and treacle slices, and pour over remaining cocoa. Put in a moderate oven and bake for 20 minutes.

Make cocoa extra thick with 3 heaped teaspoonfuls of cocoa and sugar.

Mix with water to a smooth paste and then stir on $\frac{3}{4}$ pint of boiling milk.

This is a special favourite with the children, and the cost is only a few pence. For special occasions, when pudding is half baked, put a few walnuts on top.

From Mrs. R. Pritchard, Herefordshire.

CHOCOLATE APPLE PUDDING

1 pint apple puree.   2 ozs. sugar.
2 ozs. brown breadcrumbs.   Cream.
4 ozs. chocolate.   Juice of $\frac{1}{2}$ a lemon.

SWEETEN the apple purée to taste, add lemon juice, crumb the breadcrumbs finely, whip the cream, and grate the chocolate. In a buttered dish put first a layer of breadcrumbs, then a layer of apple purée, then grated chocolate. Build up the pudding like this until all the ingredients are used, finishing with chocolate. Top with whipped cream and allow to set in a cold place for 2–3 hours.

From Kathleen Thomas.

CHOCOLATE APPLE STIRABOUT

¼ lb. flour.	1½ ozs. sugar.
3 or 4 cooking apples.	1 tablespoonful of cocoa.
Pinch of salt and milk to mix.	2 ozs. margarine.

MIX flour, cocoa and salt, rub in margarine. Add sugar and apples, pared, cored and cut into small pieces. Mix with milk to the consistency of a thick batter. Pour into a greased baking-dish and bake in a hot oven for 20 to 30 minutes. Serve with golden syrup.

From Miss E. Rutherford, Northumberland.

CHOCOLATE PLUM DESSERT

SOAK overnight 4 tablespoonfuls oatmeal in ¾ pint of milk. Cook until oatmeal is soft, then add 1 tablespoonful of sugar and 1 dessertspoonful of cocoa, and cook slowly for 15 minutes more. Add a few drops of vanilla essence.

Stone ½ lb. plums and stew until tender. Put alternate layers of fruit and oatmeal into a wetted mould until all is used up. Leave to set.

From Miss E. Rutherford, Northumberland.

CHOCOLATE TART

FOR this you will need 8 ozs. short pastry and a filling made from the following ingredients: 3 ozs. breadcrumbs; 1 tablespoonful sugar; 1 egg; 2 teaspoonfuls cocoa; ⅓ cupful milk; vanilla essence.

Make the pastry and line a plate with it, slightly raise and decorate the edge. Filling: Make the breadcrumbs, heat the milk, and dissolve the sugar in it. Pour over the crumbs and cocoa, then add the beaten egg, and stir over the heat for a few minutes. Add flavouring; cool and spread on pastry. Decorate with strips of pastry. Bake 25-35 minutes.

From Miss A. Kerr Caskey, Co. Derry.

CHERRY PIE WITH MERINGUE

About ½ lb. cherries (stewed with a little sugar).
2 ozs. each margarine, flour and sugar.

2 eggs.
1 tablespoonful milk.
½ teaspoonful baking powder.
Short-crust pastry.

LINE a pie-dish with the short-crust. Pour in the cherries, be careful to keep them whole. Cream butter and sugar together. Add flour and baking-powder alternately, with the beaten egg yolks, mixed with milk. Mix well. Flavour with vanilla, pour over the cherries and bake for half an hour.

Next make a meringue from the two whisked egg whites and 2 ozs. sugar. Pile on top of the pie and return to the oven for the meringue to set and become delicately browned. Serve with cream.

From Mrs. W. Herbert, Bedfordshire.

ECONOMY BREAD PUDDING

1 lb. soaked bread.
6 ozs. self-raising flour.
6 ozs. moist sugar.
2 tablespoonfuls marmalade.

4 ozs. margarine.
½ teacupful milk.
1 dessertspoonful vinegar.

FOR this you can use your stale crusts or pieces of dry bread, and the quantity given here is ample for 4 or 5 persons. The bread must, of course, be well soaked in water, and also well squeezed out of the water. Beat the margarine and sugar together, then add the bread and flour. When it is well mixed, add the milk; to which the vinegar has been added. Beat well and put in a basin that has been well greased and lined with the marmalade. Cover with greaseproof paper and a cloth, plunge into boiling water, and boil steadily for 2 hours.

If preferred, jam may be used in place of marmalade; or 6 ozs. of fruit added to the mixture makes a delightful change. Again, chopped dates could be added in place of either; so it is really a recipe from which you can make three different puddings.

From Mrs. I. Goldsmith, Sussex.

EGG CUSTARD

For each person allow

1 egg.
1 breakfastcupful milk.

1 tablespoonful sugar.
1 pinch of salt.

BEAT all together until frothy. Pour into greased fireproof dish and cook in a moderate oven until set and slightly browned. Serve cold.

From Mrs. Birkett, Cumberland.

EMERGENCY FRUIT PUDDING

1 lb. seedless raisins.	¾ lb. flour.
1 lb. currants.	¾ lb. breadcrumbs.
1 lb. stoned dates.	1 lb. each of grated apples and
½ lb. chopped mixed peel.	carrots.
1 lb. sugar.	3 eggs.
1 lb. suet.	The juice of a lemon.
½ oz. mixed spice.	A little milk.

MIX together dry ingredients, beat up the eggs with a little milk, add the juice of a lemon and blend thoroughly with the other ingredients. Prepare some stone jam-jars; fill with the mixture, cover with greased paper and boil for 4 hours. When cool store on a shelf where they will keep for weeks ready for use.

When required stand the jar in a saucepan of boiling water to re-heat; and in the same pan stand another jar of milk which can be sweetened and thickened with eggs to make a sauce for the pudding.

From Miss Joyce Francis, Huntingdonshire.

FIG PUDDING

5 ozs. flour.	1 egg.
2½ ozs. grated suet.	¼ teaspoonful grated nutmeg.
¼ lb. chopped figs.	½ teaspoonful cinnamon.
¾ gill syrup.	½ teaspoonful ginger.
¾ gill sour milk.	½ teaspoonful bicarbonate of soda.

MIX the dry ingredients, suet and figs together, add the warmed syrup, beaten egg and milk. Pour into a greased basin and steam for 2 hours. Serve with sugar and cream.

From Miss M. C. Utley, Somerset.

FIG AND RAISIN PASTIES

1 lb. cooking figs.	1 lemon.
1 lb. stoned raisins.	1 teaspoonful ground cinnamon.
1 lb. Demerara sugar.	1 tablespoonful cornflour.

WASH and soak the figs until plump. Cut them in small pieces, put in saucepan with raisins, and sugar and lemon, cover with water, and stew until very tender. Mix the cornflour and cinnamon with a little water, add to the mixture, and cook for another $\frac{1}{4}$ of an hour. Then pot for use. It should be of the consistency of jam. Roll out short pastry the size of a dinner plate, spread half with some of the fig and raisin mixture, moisten edges, turn over the plain half, pinch edges and cut a row of holes down the pastry with fork or pastry scissors. Bake in a steady oven.

From Mrs. E. G. Mactier, Wigtownshire.

FRESH CURRANT LAYER PUDDING

PLACE in a greased pudding-basin a layer of stewed red or blackcurrants, then a layer of suet pastry; repeat until basin is almost filled. Cover with greaseproof paper, and steam for 2 hours. When cooked cut into footsteps and serve with custard.

From Mrs. Rogers, Wrexham.

FRUIT FRUSHIE

THIS is an excellent way of using up windfalls quickly. Take 1 lb. apples, cut up small, cook with some brown sugar, a teaspoonful of lemon juice and a little water. When almost done add $\frac{1}{4}$ lb. each of currants and sultanas. Stir for 2 minutes and then stand aside. Make a sweet paste with $\frac{1}{2}$ lb. flour, $\frac{1}{4}$ lb. butter, 2 ozs. sugar and milk. Line a tart plate with half the paste. Put in the fruit, then cover with the other half. Brush with milk and bake in a hot oven 20 to 30 minutes. This is a delicious dessert dish or sliced for tea.

From Mrs. T. Weddell, Nottinghamshire.

FRUIT POPOVERS

MIX together 1 cupful flour with 1 cupful milk, 1 unbeaten egg and a pinch of salt. Stir thoroughly, using a wooden spoon. Butter some cups and place them in the oven; and when hissing hot, pour in the batter, filling each cup half full. Drop into each a piece of banana. Bake in a hot oven until puffed and golden brown, then cover with paper and finish baking. (Other fruit can replace banana.)

From Miss M. Palmer, Norfolk.

FRUMENTY AND FLUFFIN

FRUMENTY, which is an old yeoman farmer's dish, and Fluffin were made at Christmas time. The old custom was to sup a wee bowl on Christmas Eve, and offer it to the stranger within the door. It is a great favourite in the districts of Stockton-on-Tees and Coxhoe.

To make Fluffin, simmer enough barley and milk until it is as smooth as velvet. Add enough grated nutmeg and sugar to taste, and a few drops of brandy.

Frumenty takes a lot of cooking. Simmer enough kibbled wheat for 12 hours; then add a nut of butter, mixed spice, currants (if liked), sugar, cream and rum. It is as near a liquid spice loaf as one can imagine, delightful and fragrant. One farmer I heard described it as "Gruel with its best clothes on."

From Mrs. E. Symes, Northumberland.

GINGER APPLE

1 lb. cooking apples.	3 ozs. margarine.
1 oz. sugar.	2 tablespoonfuls golden syrup.
6 ozs. self-raising flour.	1 teaspoonful ground ginger.
2 eggs.	Milk to mix.

PUT stewed apple into pie-dish. Cream margarine, sugar and syrup together, beat in eggs, add flour, ginger and milk. Beat well until creamy and of a "dropping" consistency. Pour mixture over the apple and bake in a moderate oven until golden brown.

From Mrs. G. Prosser, Salop.

GOLDEN PUDDING (1)

SPREAD a layer of halved prunes in a deep pie-dish or Pyrex dish, then a layer of breadcrusts spread with margarine, either cut into fingers or roughly broken. Then sprinkle on cut-up prunes. Fill dish nearly full of these layers, finishing with margarine on top. Fill up dish with fresh milk and 2 tablespoonfuls of sugar. Cover over tightly and leave to soak 2 or 3 hours if possible, adding a little more milk as the crusts soak it up. Leave cover on, and bake in a medium oven, removing cover just to crisp the top a little.

To add richness, beat up one or two eggs and a little milk with a whisk of sugar, and when pudding is about half-baked, pour in, lifting edges with fork to let the custard layer itself in.

Crusts are much better than breadcrumbs for this.

Good hot, but better cold.

From Mrs. M. Marsh, Staffordshire.

GOLDEN PUDDING (2)

SMEAR a dish with treacle; then put in it layers of bread spread with margarine. Partly cook some sweetened rhubarb; fill centre and place more bread and margarine on top. Put in hot oven for 15 minutes. Then turn out on to dish. This is very nice with or without custard.

From Mrs. G. Wood, Gloucestershire.

GOOSEBERRY BREAD PUDDING

1 pint young gooseberries.　　　　1½ gills milk.
1 thick slice of white bread.　　　2 eggs.

CUT the crust off the bread, on to which pour the boiling milk. Cover this with a plate and let it stand for ½ hour, then crush the bread and beat in the eggs. Add 1 pint of young gooseberries which have previously been topped, tailed and washed. Mix well together, put into a well-greased basin and cover with greased paper. Steam for 1 hour. Do not add sugar before cooking.

From Mrs. W. Evans, Salop.

GOOSEBERRY CREAM

½ lb. gooseberries.　　　　　1 dessertspoonful powdered gela-
½ pint thick sweetened custard.　　　　tine.
　　　　　　　　　　　　　　　Sugar to sweeten.

TOP and tail gooseberries and simmer in enough water to cover till soft. Rub through a sieve and sweeten to taste. Dissolve gelatine in 2 or 3 tablespoonfuls of hot water and add to the gooseberry purée—making the whole a little less than ½ pint. Stir this into the sweetened custard, then pour into individual glasses. Chill and serve with a little mock cream.

From Mrs. Rogers, Northumberland.

GOOSEBERRY CREAM (2)

1 quart green gooseberries.　　　4 yolks of eggs.
2 ozs. butter.　　　　　　　　Cold water.
6 ozs. castor sugar.

WASH and "top and tail" the gooseberries and put them in a stew pan with the butter and sufficient water to cover them. Simmer gently till gooseberries are tender, and rub them through a hair sieve. Add the castor sugar and yolks of eggs well beaten, and stir the mixture over the fire for a few minutes to cook the yolks of eggs. It must NOT boil, or it will curdle. When cold, serve in a glass dish or in small glasses. Other fruits treated in the same way are very delicious.

From Mrs. J. S. Fountain, Pembrokeshire.

GOOSEBERRY CUSTARD CAKE

½ pint stewed, sweetened gooseberries.	The grated rind of 1 orange.
	½ cupful orange juice.
2 eggs.	1 tablespoonful lemon juice.
1 cupful castor sugar.	½ pint thick custard sauce.
1¼ cupfuls self-raising flour.	⅛ cupful of margarine or vegetable cooking fat.

BEAT the fat to a cream in a basin. Stir in the sugar and beaten egg yolks. Beat thoroughly and then add the grated orange rind and the strained lemon juice. Sift the flour and a pinch of salt together, then add alternately with the strained orange juice. Fold in the stiffly frothed egg whites and bake in two deep round sandwich-tins for about 20 minutes, until firm and golden.

Remove from the oven, allow to stand for a few minutes, then turn on to a hot dish lined with a lace paper doyley, sprinkled with castor sugar. Put the two halves together with thick custard sauce, place the drained gooseberries on top and add more custard sauce.

From Miss E. Williams, Monmouthshire.

GOOSEBERRY FLUMMERY

6 ozs. rice.	2 pints milk.
2 ozs. sugar.	2 cupfuls gooseberries.

WASH the rice and place in a pan with milk. Allow to cook slowly till soft and thick. Add sugar and stir well, then allow to cool. Grease a mould and cover the inside with a layer of rice about an inch thick, leaving the inside of the mould empty until the rice sets. Fill up with gooseberries stewed until soft, and sweetened to taste. Stand until the mould firms and becomes cold, then turn out, being careful not to break it. If preferred, the flummery can be steamed after the fruit is added and served with custard sauce.

From Miss Christian Milne, Aberdeenshire.

GOOSEBERRY PUDDING

1 quart green gooseberries.	1 oz. butter.
¼ lb. sugar.	¼ lb. breadcrumbs.
2 eggs.	

STEW the fruit gently till it will pulp, then beat it up. Take 1 pint of this pulp, add the other ingredients, mix all together except the eggs which should not be added till the mixture is quite cool, and then stirred in thoroughly. Put the mixture into a buttered dish and bake for ½ hour. Strew a little sifted sugar over the pudding before serving.

From Mrs. E. A. Thomas, Glamorganshire.

GOOSEBERRY ROLL

MIX together 8 ozs. flour, 1 teaspoonful baking powder, and 2 ozs. shredded suet or grated margarine or dripping. Add just enough water to make a stiff dough. Roll out into an oblong shape. Spread thinly with syrup, then with a layer of gooseberries. Roll up, roly-poly fashion, securing the ends firmly. Put on large baking-dish or tin and bake in moderate oven, 1 hour, or steam for 2 hours.

From Mrs. A. A. Mactier, Wigtownshire.

GOOSEBERRY TART

TAKE 1 lb. of gooseberries and cook gently in a saucepan, until soft, with 2 tablespoonfuls of water and ¼ lb. sugar. Mash to a pulp, adding a little lemon essence, and, when cool, add the beaten yolk of egg.

Meanwhile, line a sandwich-tin with pastry made from 6 ozs. flour; 3 ozs. lard or margarine; mix with a little water and roll to about ¼ in. thick. Pour in gooseberry pulp, and put another round of thinner pastry on top. Make two sharp cuts in the form of a cross in the centre of tart.

Place in a hot oven and bake for 20 minutes until it is a light brown. Finally, whisk the white of egg to a stiff froth and spread over the top of the tart and sprinkle with sugar. Put it back in the oven again for 3 minutes. Serve hot or cold.

From Mrs. P. W. Newbury, Devonshire.

GOOSEBERRY TRIFLE

1 lb. gooseberries.   Sugar to taste.
A very little water.   ½ pint custard.
Vanilla essence.   Slices of sponge cake.

STEW the gooseberries until tender, and rub through a sieve. Sweeten to taste.

Lay thin slices of sponge cake in a glass dish. Soak these

with a little flavoured and sweetened milk. Spread over the gooseberry purée, and, when quite cold, pour over the custard flavoured with vanilla essence.

Whipped cream piled on the top of the custard makes a hot-weather sweet even more tempting.

From Miss Christian Milne, Aberdeenshire.

GRAPES IN A PIE

Pastry:

2 cupfuls flour.	½ teaspoonful salt.
1 teaspoonful cream of tartar.	4 tablespoonfuls butter.
½ teaspoonful bicarbonate of soda.	Milk or water to mix.

Filling:

½ lb. grapes.	2 tablespoonfuls flour.
1 cupful sugar.	1 tablespoonful butter.
1 tablespoonful lemon juice.	

MAKE the pastry, using half to line an 8 in. pie-dish. Wash the grapes, and then, using a sharp knife, cut them in half, when the seeds are easily removed. Leave the skins on. Mix the flour and sugar together and sprinkle about half of it over the grapes. Pour over the lemon juice and mix well. Sprinkle the remaining flour and sugar over the bottom of the pastry case (to prevent sogginess). Place the grapes in the case, put dabs of butter here and there on the top and cover with more pastry. Bake for ½ hour to 40 minutes in a moderate oven. Serve hot or cold with fairly thin custard. This makes a delicious sweet.

From Mrs. M. Moulam, Derbyshire.

GREEN CURRANT PIE

THESE are the red currants before they ripen. Pick and wash clean, then place in a deep enamel plate, fire-proof glass or pie-dish, with just enough water to cover. Add sugar to sweeten, and place in oven while you make pastry.

Take the plate or dish out of the oven, grease round the edge. Put a funnel in the middle if a pie-dish is used, or prick the pastry top if a plate. Cover the fruit with pastry, brush over with a little cold milk, and cook in a quick oven.

From Mrs. Lakin, Warwickshire.

124

HONEY NUT TARTLETS

6 ozs. flour.
½ cupful sour cream.
Salt.
2 ozs. butter (slightly salted or fresh).

1 yolk of egg.
Honey.
Walnuts.
Castor sugar (or Demerara).

SIFT the flour with a pinch of salt, rub in the butter, and blend with the beaten egg yolk and cream. Leave in a cool place for a time, then roll out and line small tartlet-tins with the paste. Mix together 1 teaspoonful of honey with 1 teaspoonful of Demerara sugar and 1 teaspoonful of minced walnuts, for each tartlet, fill and bake in a moderate oven till brown and crisp.

From Mrs. V. Cantwell, Hampshire.

HATTED KIT
(*A very old Highland dish*)

WARM slightly over the fire 2 pints of buttermilk. Pour it into a dish and carry it to the side of a cow. Milk into it about 1 pint of milk, having previously put into the dish sufficient rennet for the whole.

After allowing it to stand for a while, lift the curd, place it on a sieve, and press the whey through until the curd is quite stiff. Season with sugar and nutmeg before serving. Whip some thick cream, season it also with a little grated nutmeg and sugar, and mix gently with the curd. This dish can quite well be made without milking the cow into it, although direct milking puts a better "hat" on the Kit.

From Miss H. Stuart, Wigtownshire, Scotland.

JAM SLICES

Stale bread in slices.
Jam.

Dripping.
Water.

CUT the bread into slices about 3 inches long by 2 inches wide, without crusts (these can be used otherwise). Damp one side of each slice with water, but not enough to make it sodden. Heat some dripping in a pan until very hot, then drop the bread pieces into this, dry side up.

Fry the damp side a golden brown, then turn over the bread and fry the dry side. Spread this second side with warmed jam and serve hot.

Cooking time 10 minutes.

From Mrs. Rogers, Wrexham.

JANE'S CHOCOLATE SPONGE

7 ozs. self-raising flour.
1 small teaspoonful salt.
3 ozs. drinking chocolate.
5 ozs. butter.
2 eggs.

1 large tablespoonful of coffee essence.
A few drops of vanilla essence.
3 ozs. sugar.

SLIGHTLY warm butter, add sugar, beat until creamy. Beat yolks of eggs well, and add to butter and sugar. Mix chocolate powder, salt and flour together, stir into the mixture. Add coffee essence in a tablespoonful of warm milk. Beat the whites of eggs to a stiff froth, add vanilla essence and fold into the mixture gently. Add 1 teaspoonful of boiling water just before putting the mixture into well-papered tin. Bake in fairly sharp oven for 1 to 1½ hours.

Care must be taken not to have the milk too warm.

From Mrs. D. L. Brown, Essex.

JELLY CREAM

For the jelly:

I oz. gelatine.
½ pint cold water.
Pinch of citric acid.

½ pint hot water (cordial or fruit juice).
3 dessertspoonfuls sugar.
Flavouring as desired.

For the cream:

¼ tin evaporated milk.

2 tablespoonfuls sugar (optional).

TO make the jelly, dissolve gelatine in hot water; add sugar and acid, stir in cold water; add flavouring and colouring as desired. Leave to cool while making the cream.

Whip the milk until light and very stiff. Fold into the sugar and whisk again. Now add to the jelly; stir well, then place in mould to set.

From Miss I. L. Dixon, Lincolnshire.

LEMON CHIFFON PIE

2 oz. butter.
2 tablespoonsfuls golden syrup.
2 oz. cornflakes.
4 oz. sugar.
2 eggs.

Grated rind of 1 lemon.
Juice of 2 lemons.
½ oz. gelatine.
Chocolate shavings.

MELT the fat and syrup and add the cornflakes, press into a pie plate and leave to become quite firm. Combine the sugar and egg yolks with the grated lemon rind and juice, and beat over a pan of hot water until the mixture thickens.

Add the gelatine, dissolved in a small quantity of water. When the mixture is cool, fold in the egg whites, and pour into the prepared case to set. Just before serving, decorate with chocolate shavings.

From Kathleen Thomas.

LEMON CURD DUMPLINGS

THESE dumplings are better made in small individual moulds to prevent any water getting in to spoil lemon curd centres.

Well grease some small moulds and line with thinly-rolled suet paste made with 4 ozs. shredded suet, 8 ozs. flour, salt, and mixed with cold water. Make a curd-filling by well beating 2 eggs and adding 1 teacupful castor sugar, juice and grated rind of 1 large, or 2 small lemons, and 2 ozs. fresh melted butter. Whip all together and nearly fill each dumpling. Cover tops with a lid of paste. Squeeze the edges together well. Tie over with greased paper and steam for 1¼ hours. Turn out carefully and sift with a little fine sugar and serve hot.

From Mrs. R. Cruse, Worcestershire.

LEMON CURD SPONGE PUDDING

4 ozs. margarine or butter.	1 oz. currants.
4 ozs. sugar.	Lemon curd.
4 ozs. flour.	A pinch of salt.
2 eggs.	A little milk.
½ teaspoonful baking powder.	

BEAT butter and sugar to a cream, add well-beaten eggs, sift in flour by degrees, stirring all the time; add about 2 tablespoonfuls of milk and beat well. Put about two-thirds of the mixture in a well greased pie-dish, then a layer of lemon curd, sprinkle currants over the lemon curd, then the remainder of the mixture. Bake in a moderate oven for about 40 minutes. For 5 or 6 people.

From Mrs. M. I. Bell, Lincolnshire.

LEMON MERINGUE PIE
(*Made the day before use*)

Short pastry:

2 small lemons.	2 eggs (yolks separate).
½ pint of milk.	1 heaped dessertspoonful of corn-
2 tablespoonfuls of sugar.	flour.

LINE greased pie-dish with pastry. Blend cornflour with a little milk. Boil rest and pour on cornflour, stirring well. Add sugar, grated rind of lemon and juice and beaten egg yolks. Pour into pie-dish. Cook in a fairly hot oven until set. Whisk egg whites with a little sugar. Pile on pie. Brown in cool oven.

From Mrs. Birkett, Cumberland.

LEMON PIE

LINE a deep plate with your favourite pastry. Make a custard by taking ¾ pint milk and 1½ tablespoonfuls cornflour, mixed to a paste with a little of the milk. Grate the rind and juice of 2 lemons into the custard when cooled down a little, add sugar to taste. Then stir in the yolks of 2 eggs, place mixture on pastry, and bake in a nice oven. When ready, whip up the whites very stiffly, fold in 2 tablespoonfuls of castor sugar, and brown in a cool oven.

From A. E. Lamb, Derbyshire.

LITTLE BILLINGHAM PUDDING

6 ozs. self-raising flour.	6 ozs. chopped stoned dates.
A pinch of salt.	4 ozs. shredded suet.
2 ozs. white breadcrumbs.	2 ozs. seedless raisins.
Milk (less than ½ pint).	2 tablespoonfuls liquid honey.

MIX together all the dry ingredients. Then add sufficient milk to make into a stiff dough, and finally stir in the honey. Put the mixture into a well-greased basin, allowing room to rise. Cover with 2 thicknesses of greaseproof paper and steam for 2½ to 3 hours. Turn out and serve hot with whipped cream, sweet sauce or hard sauce as desired.

From Mrs. M. B. N. Allender, I.O.W.

LUNCHEON CAKE

1½ lbs. flour.	1 teaspoonful bicarbonate of soda.
1 lb. sultanas.	A pinch of salt.
¾ lb. butter.	1 pint buttermilk, or as much as
6 ozs. brown sugar.	is needed to mix to a nice
1 oz. nutmeg, grated	consistency.

RUB the butter into the flour and mix thoroughly all the dry ingredients. Stir in the buttermilk last, with the bicarbonate of soda dissolved in it (sour milk can be used). Bake in a slow oven for 2 hours.

From Mrs. Rose Davies, Worcestershire.

MARROW AND APPLE PIE

1 lb. prepared marrow.
½ lb. sliced apples.
Short-crust pastry.

2 ozs. seedless raisins.
1 lemon.
Sugar.

PREPARE the marrow, and cut into small pieces. Fill a pie-dish with layers of marrow, sliced apples and raisins, sprinkling each layer with a little sugar and grated lemon rind. Pile the mixture rather high in the centre of the dish, and add just a little water. Cover with pastry, and bake in a good oven for 1 hour or a little longer according to the apples.

Pears also can be used in this way.

From Mrs. R. Weston, Lincolnshire.

MIXED FRUIT PIE

WHILE fresh fruit is scarce, the following mixture will be found most economical, and very suitable for pies, or with custard, blancmange, etc.

Take ½ lb. dried apple rings, ¼ lb. dried apricots, cover with water and leave overnight. Next day add about ½ lb. rhubarb, cut fine, and ¼ lb. brown sugar. Cook gently, adding more water if fruit gets too thick, until the apple rings and apricots look clear. Leave to get cold before covering with pie-crust.

From Mrs. F. E. Crisp, Norfolk.

MINCEMEAT AND ALMOND DELIGHT

5 ozs. self-raising flour.
2 ozs. butter.
1 oz. lard.

½ teaspoonful lemon juice.
The yolk of 1 egg.

For the filling:

4 tablespoonfuls mincemeat.
2 bananas.
2 eggs.
2 ozs. castor sugar.

2 ozs. butter.
2 ozs. ground almonds.
Almonds for decoration.
Almond essence.

SIEVE the flour into a basin, add a pinch of salt, then lightly rub in the lard and butter. Beat the egg yolk, add the lemon juice and 1 tablespoonful of cold water: add gradually to the flour. Mix to a stiff paste, adding more water if required.

For the filling: Cream the butter and sugar together, stir in the beaten eggs, ground almonds, almond essence: mix well.

Line a pie-dish with the pastry; almost fill it with alternate layers of mincemeat and the sliced bananas, then spread the almond mixture on the top. Decorate with the almonds (blanched and halved), bake in a quick oven for ½ hour.

From Mrs. Vincent, Devonshire.

MIXED FRUIT STIRABOUT

THIS is an old farmhouse recipe and can be used with all kinds of fresh fruit, rhubarb, gooseberries, currants, raspberries, etc., alone or mixed. Mix 4 ozs. flour with 2 ozs. butter and a pinch of salt, add 2 ozs. sugar and 2 breakfast-cupfuls of picked fruit (if rhubarb, cut into neat cubes). Mix with milk to the consistency of a thick batter and bake in a hot oven for about 30 minutes. Serve with sugar and thick cream.

From Miss Peggy Crawford, Leicestershire.

OCTOBER COBBLER

1 quart blackberries.	1 tablespoonful lemon juice.
2½ tablespoonfuls milk.	1 teaspoonful salt.
2 cupfuls s.r. flour.	2 tablespoonfuls butter.
5 tablespoonfuls lard.	½ cupful water.
1½ tablespoonfuls castor sugar.	

PLACE the berries, sweetened to taste, in a buttered pie-dish and sprinkle with the lemon juice, and dab with pieces of butter. Rub the lard lightly into the flour, sifted with the baking powder and salt. Stir in the sugar and milk and roll out the paste to the size of the pie-dish. Place on top of the fruit, neatening the edges, which must not come over the brim, and prick with a fork. Bake in a hot oven for ½ hour and serve with custard sauce or cream. This is enough for 6 people, and is delicious.

From Mrs. Godfrey, Somerset.

OATMEAL PUDDING

½ lb. plain flour.	1 teaspoonful baking powder.
½ lb. fine oatmeal.	¼ lb. sugar.
1½ teaspoonfuls ground ginger.	3 tablespoonfuls golden syrup.
1 egg.	½ lb. shredded suet.
Little milk for mixing.	

MIX dry ingredients together, add beaten egg to the warmed golden syrup, and stir into the dry ingredients. Mix to about the consistency of a cake, adding as much milk as required. Put into a greased pie-dish, and bake in a moderate oven for about 1½ hours. Turn out on to a hot dish, and serve with hot golden syrup.

From Mrs. L. Stean, Cheshire,

OLDBURY TARTS (GLOUCESTERSHIRE)

2 lbs. flour.	½ lb. butter.
½ lb. lard.	1 small teacupful boiling water.
Gooseberries.	Demerara sugar.

PUT the flour into the pastry bowl, and make a well in the middle of it: into the well put the butter and lard, cutting it into rough chunks. Have ready the boiling water and pour the teacupful quickly over the butter and lard. Stir with a knife till the fat has dissolved and then stir in the flour till the whole is a not too stiff paste. Flour the pastry board, and take out two pieces for each tart, a larger and a smaller. Roll out the larger piece to about the size of a saucer, turn up the edges all round, about 1 in. high, cover the bottom with gooseberries, and over this put 1 large dessertspoonful of Demerara sugar. Take a smaller bit of paste, and roll out to about the size of a tea-cup, and put over the sugar, pressing the edges of the pastry well together to prevent the syrup escaping when cooking. Pinch the edges all round to form a fluted edge. Cook in a quick oven.

Many people think the edges stand up more perfectly, when cooked, if the tarts are made a day before cooking.

From Mrs. T. Gazard, Gloucestershire.

OUR FAVOURITE PUDDING

GREASE a plain mould and strew thickly with black, red or white currants. Blend 2 ozs. cornflour with 1 pint of milk, and cook for a few minutes. When cool, stir in 1 or 2 beaten eggs, 3 ozs. sponge cake crumbs, 1 oz. finely chopped suet, a dash of cinnamon, a few drops of lemon and almond essence, and 3 ozs. sugar.

Fill the prepared mould, and steam for 1½ hours. Serve with cream or custard.

From Mrs. Rogers, Wrexham.

PEAR AND GINGER PUDDING

BUTTER a pudding-basin and coat with breadcrumbs. Mix 4 ozs. breadcrumbs with 2 ozs. grated suet. Prepare 1 lb. pears and grate them with the rind of a lemon, adding sugar to taste, and 1 oz. chopped preserved ginger. Put a third of the bread mixture into the basin; then half of the pears; another third of the bread; then the remainder of the pears; and cover with the rest of the bread mixture. Cover with greased paper and steam for 2 hours. Serve with sweet white sauce. This has a delicious flavour.

From Mrs. W. Symes, Northumberland.

PEASE-MEAL BROX

PUT 2 tablespoonfuls pease-meal in a bowl, add a pinch of salt and a dessertspoonful of syrup. Make smooth with the back of a spoon. Now pour on sufficient boiling water to make a soft, smooth mixture, stirring vigorously to be sure knots do not form.

Serve immediately with a generous pour of cream on top.

From Miss Christian Milne, Aberdeenshire.

PINEAPPLE UPSIDE-DOWN PUDDING

BUTTER a round pan about 8 in. in diameter and 3 in. deep. In it melt 1 cup brown sugar and 2 tablespoonfuls butter. On the sugar, after melting, lay as many slices of pineapple as the pan will hold. Pour over the fruit a batter of $\frac{3}{4}$ cupful milk, $\frac{1}{2}$ cupful butter, $\frac{3}{4}$ cupful granulated sugar, 2 well-beaten eggs, 2 teaspoonfuls baking powder, $\frac{1}{2}$ teaspoonful salt, $\frac{1}{2}$ teaspoonful flavouring, 2 cupfuls flour. Beat the butter and sugar to a cream, add the eggs with a little of the flour. Sieve the dry ingredients and fold in. Bake in a moderate oven from 45 to 60 minutes. Turn at once on to a hot dish. Serve with whipped cream or custard.

From Mrs. Anderson, Ayrshire.

PLUM CARAMEL PUDDING

Dry bread. Margarine.
Ripe plums. Sugar.

SPREAD the sides and bottom of a pie-dish with margarine. Sprinkle over with sugar. Line it all neatly with slices of bread about $\frac{1}{4}$ in. thick.

Place a layer of plums, cut in halves and stones removed, over the bread and sprinkle with sugar. Cover with another layer of bread and a second layer of plums and sugar. Finish the top with nice, even slices of bread and dab over with margarine.

Cover with a piece of greasy paper and bake in a good oven for an hour. Turn out on a hot dish and serve with milk.

From Mrs. Thomson, Nottinghamshire.

POTATO APPLE CAKE

1½ lbs. cooked potatoes.	5 ozs. flour.
1 teaspoonful salt.	1½ ozs. melted margarine.
3 medium-sized apples.	

USE the potatoes while they are still hot. Mash them carefully with a little margarine. Place on a board and sprinkle with salt. Add the melted fat, and knead in enough flour to make a soft, pliable dough. Care should be taken not to add too much flour. Roll out and divide into two cakes. On one piece put a layer of three medium-sized sliced apples, place the other piece on top, and pinch the edges together. Bake in a moderate oven. When cooked, split the cake open, then turn the top over and put small pieces of margarine on, together with some sugar. Then put the top back and return to the oven until the margarine and sugar are melted.

From Mrs. H. Handy, Leicestershire.

POTATO CHEESE CAKES (SWEET)

¼ lb. mashed potatoes.	1 egg.
¼ lb. butter.	A little jam.
¼ lb. sugar.	Puff pastry.
2 ozs. currants.	

BEAT the butter and sugar to a cream, add to the potatoes and currants; then add the egg, well beaten. Line tins with puff pastry, put in a little jam and add 1 teaspoonful of the above mixture. Bake in a quick oven until light brown.

From Mrs. J. R. Robinson, Cumberland.

RAISIN CHOCOLATE PUDDING

½ pint milk.	3 dessertspoonfuls sugar.
¼ lb. raisins.	4 tablespoonfuls custard powder.
2 dessertspoonfuls cocoa.	

MIX custard powder and cocoa to a smooth paste with a little of the milk. Boil the rest of the milk with sugar. Pour over the mixture, stirring well. Add raisins last. Serve cold.

From Mrs. Birkett, Cumberland.

RAISIN AND RHUBARB PASTY

MAKE sufficient short-crust pastry to line and cover a plate or sandwich tin. Grease and line with pastry. Cover with a handful of coarse oatmeal, and pour a tablespoonful of treacle over this.

Wash and cut up six or seven sticks of tender rhubarb, and place these on the treacle and oatmeal. Sprinkle a handful of seedless raisins over the top, and cover the whole with short-crust pastry, wetting the edges and pressing them firmly together. Prick the top and decorate with any pieces left over. Bake in a hot oven 20 to 30 minutes. Serve hot or cold.

From Mrs. L. Gardiner, Worcestershire.

RASPBERRY CUSTARD

1 lb. raspberries.	3 ozs. sugar.
2 eggs.	1 pint milk.
A little margarine.	

GREASE a pie-dish with the margarine and put in the raspberries. Sprinkle with 2 ozs. sugar.

Beat the eggs with the remainder of the sugar and add the milk. Whisk well, pour it over the fruit and bake in a moderate oven until done and slightly browned.

From Mrs. E. Holland, Cheshire.

RASPBERRY RINGS

4 ozs. margarine.	2 eggs.
4 ozs. sugar.	1 bottle raspberries.
4 ozs. flour.	Some sweetened condensed milk.

MAKE a sponge with the margarine, sugar, eggs and flour in the usual way, baking in a flat swiss roll tin. When cool cut the sponge in rounds with a pastry cutter and scoop a little out of each with a smaller pastry cutter.

Place each sponge cake cup on an individual dish (the odd pieces of sponge come in for trifle), pile the bottled raspberries into each hollow, place a dab of condensed milk on the top of each and decorate with a few of the raspberries.

From Mrs. F. J. Sparey, Herefordshire.

RHUBARB AND BANANA PIE

1 lb. rhubarb.	1 egg white.
3 ozs. sugar.	2 ozs. almonds.
The grated rind of $\frac{1}{2}$ a lemon.	2 tablespoonfuls castor sugar.
4 bananas.	

WASH the rhubarb and cut into small lengths, put into a pie-dish and sprinkle with lemon rind and the sugar. Peel the bananas, crush and beat to pulp with the castor sugar; when soft beat in the white of the egg. Continue beating until quite stiff. Spread on the top of rhubarb to form a crust, sprinkle the top with blanched almonds, and bake in a moderate oven for $\frac{1}{2}$ hour. Serve hot with custard or cream.

From Mrs. J. W. Foster, Yorkshire.

RHUBARB CHARLOTTE

2 cupfuls breadcrumbs.	$\frac{1}{4}$ teaspoonful lemon juice.
1 tablespoonful (heaped) brown sugar.	$\frac{1}{4}$ teaspoonful grated nutmeg or mixed spice.
1 tablespoonful suet (grated).	

STEW 1 lb. rhubarb with very little water and 1 tablespoonful brown sugar. Mash when cooked. Grease a pie-dish and fill with alternate layers of fruit and the above mixture. The last layer should be crumbs.

Bake in a moderate oven for 30 minutes—covering it at first, but allowing the crumbs to brown after 20 minutes.

From Mrs. W. P. Baker, Cambridgeshire.

RHUBARB AND DATE BAKE

LINE a shallow tin with short-crust pastry; spread with a generous layer of rhubarb cut into small pieces, and stoned dates cut in halves. Add the grated rind of a lemon and a sprinkling of powdered cinnamon. Sugar should not be necessary, as the dates give the required sweetness. Cover with thinly rolled out pastry. Press down well and lightly score the top, criss-cross fashion. Bake for about $\frac{1}{2}$ hour until the pastry is well browned.

From Mrs. J. Green, Wrexham.

RHUBARB GINGERBREAD

6 sticks rhubarb.	2 ozs. fat.
2 ozs. sugar.	3 ozs. treacle.
8 ozs. self-raising flour.	Level teaspoonful cinnamon.
Heaped teaspoonful ground ginger.	1 egg. Gill milk.

PUT milk, treacle, fat, spice and ginger in saucepan, and melt over low heat. Sift in flour gradually, and finally add beaten egg. Pour half into greased dish; place chopped rhubarb and sugar on top, pour over remainder of mixture. Bake in moderate oven 1 hour. This can be served as it comes out of the oven, or it is delicious with hot milk poured over it.

From Mrs. L. Shallcross, Essex.

RHUBARB MOULD

STEW some rhubarb with a very little water and sugar to sweeten. When tender allow to cool.

Line a pudding-basin with slices of stale sponge cake or bread. Pour in the rhubarb, making a top of the cake or bread. Cover with a plate. Permit to set overnight. Then turn out carefully and serve with cream.

From Miss Christian Milne, Aberdeenshire.

RHUBARB PUDDING

¼ lb. flour.	2 teaspoonfuls cocoa.
2 ozs. dates.	2 ozs. margarine.
Tablespoonful syrup.	A few sticks rhubarb.
Pinch of salt and milk to mix.	

MIX flour, salt and cocoa, rub in margarine, add melted syrup, stoned and chopped dates, and rhubarb cut into pieces. Mix with milk to the consistency of a thick batter. Pour into greased baking-tin and bake in hot oven for 20 to 30 minutes. Serve hot.

From Miss E. Rutherford, Northumberland.

RHUBARB IN SPICED BATTER

SIEVE into a bowl 6 ozs. flour, and pinch of salt. Stir in 2 eggs and enough milk to make a batter, beat well and stand while preparing the rhubarb.

Wipe and cut rhubarb into small pieces. Arrange in a well-greased pie-dish. Sprinkle with sugar. Beat into the batter

½ teaspoonful each of ground ginger, mixed spice and cocoa. Pour over rhubarb and bake in a hot oven until crisp. Serve hot or cold.

From Miss E. Rutherford, Northumberland.

RHUBARB SPONGE

1 large cupful cooked rhubarb (cold).	1 egg.
	2 ozs. sugar.
2 ozs. butter.	½ teaspoonful baking powder.
1 large cupful flour.	¼ teaspoonful salt.

GREASE a pie-dish well, pour in the stewed rhubarb. Beat the butter and sugar until creamy, add the egg, salt and baking powder, then sift in the flour gradually, stirring all together until the mixture is well blended. If it is rather thick, a little milk should be added. Spread the mixture evenly over the rhubarb, and cook in a hot oven for 20 minutes. Serve hot or cold with custard.

From Miss M. Broad, Cheshire.

COVERED RHUBARB TART AND RHUBARB JELLY
(*From one boiling*)

BOIL rhubarb in water with sugar to taste. When tender, pour into a strainer (keeping the juice). Line a baking-plate with pastry, put in the rhubarb pulp, cover with a lid of pastry, brush over with milk, and bake until brown. To the hot juice add gelatine (½ oz. to 1 pint of juice). Stir till dissolved. Add some drops of red colouring to improve the appearance of the jelly (but this is not essential). Pour into a wetted mould and leave to set.

From Mrs G. M. Fisher, Northamptonshire.

ROSE HIP CREAM

SPLIT open the rose hips with a knife, and remove all the seeds and small hairs. The larger the rose hips the easier this is to do. They must be ripe and red for Rose Hip Cream.

Take ½ pint of these split hips, rinse them and place them in from 1¾ to 2 pints water and bring them slowly to the boil. Allow them to boil until they are soft, occasionally stirring the mixture rather briskly. Pass the mixture through a fine sieve, and boil up the juice obtained together with about ¼ lb. of sugar and (if liked) a small piece of cinnamon. When it has boiled, remove any scum floating on the surface.

Next take 3 or 4 tablespoonfuls of cornflour, mix up with a little cold water to a thin cream, and pour this into the hot rose hip syrup mixture. Boil up again for a short time and pour out into jelly moulds or a basin. Serve with custard or with milk in small fruit plates.

Rose hips, after splitting and removing the seeds, can be dried in a cool oven or in the sun, and stored away in glass jars for use during the winter.

From Mrs. A. E. Jansson, Yorkshire.

ROSEMARY SUGAR

CLEAN and dry well several sprigs of rosemary. Place them in a canister or screw-topped jar and cover with 1 lb. of sugar. Shake well and leave for 24 hours. Shake well again and stand for several days. Remove rosemary sprigs—and the sugar is ready for use with milk puddings, egg custards, and so on. The faint flavour of rosemary is good with any milk sweet.

From Miss E. Rutherford, Northumberland.

SPICE BUN

1 oz. butter.	1 teaspoonful baking powder.
4 ozs. flour.	1 egg.
2 ozs. sugar.	1 tablespoonful golden syrup.
2 ozs. currants.	1 oz. sultanas.
Short pastry.	

LINE a sandwich-tin with short pastry, leaving enough pastry for cross bars. Rub butter into flour; add all dry ingredients and syrup; add the egg (well beaten) and baking powder.

Turn into lined tin, put the cross bars over the top, bake ½ hour in moderate oven.

From Mrs. Steward, Essex.

SNOW BALLS

PARE as many apples as you will require; take out the cores with a small scoop; do not break the apples. Fill the space with stoned raisins. Have some rice that has been well steeped in milk, place enough rice on a cloth to hold an apple, then draw up corners and tie round with tape or string as you would a dumpling.

Set in a shallow pan with enough cold water to cover them; bring to the boil and simmer for 1 hour. Remove them carefully without breaking, and serve with cream or melted butter.

From Mrs. Goad, Yorkshire.

SOUR CREAM TART

GET the exact third and fourth milkings of a freshly-calved cow, sieve it into a bowl and leave overnight for the cream to rise to top. When you have sufficient cream (cream only) prepare your best pastry. Line a dish with the pastry and sprinkle it well with sugar, and a dash of sultanas. When the oven is moderately hot, pour the cream over the pastry and place it gently into the oven. No cover is required, but be sure the pastry comes up the sides fully an inch all round: and do avoid any holes or pricks in this bottom pastry—should the milk get in between pastry and tin it is spoilt, for it rises in bubbles and has an ugly appearance. We call it sour cream tart—if done carefully it is delicious.

From Mrs. Davies, Carmarthenshire.

SPICED PLUM TART

Pastry:

8 ozs. flour.	A pinch of mixed spice.
4 ozs. butter.	2 teaspoonfuls castor sugar.
¼ teaspoonful cinnamon.	Water.

Filling:

1 lb. plums.	4 ozs. castor sugar.
4 small apples.	2 tablespoonfuls water.

MIX all dry ingredients together to a stiff paste with cold water. Line a shallow tin with some of the paste.

Put in fruit filling. Cover with the rest of the pastry and bake ¾ hour. Remove from tin and serve hot or cold.

From Mrs. E. J. Waters, Pembrokeshire.

SPICED RHUBARB TART

LINE a deep enamel plate with pastry. Cook rhubarb to a pulp, adding as little water as possible. Sweeten to taste, and add ¼ teaspoonful ground ginger and ¼ teaspoonful cinnamon. Allow to cool and spread on pastry. Over this sprinkle the following mixture: ½ oz. margarine rubbed into 2 tablespoonfuls flour, with ½ oz. sugar added.

Bake for 20 minutes, when the mixture on top will become crisp.

From Mrs. Erwen Thomas, Glamorganshire.

STRAWBERRY ANGEL FOOD PIE

For the flan:

6 ozs. flour.	Pinch salt.
3 ozs. shortening.	Very little cold water to mix.

R UB fat into flour and mix to a stiff dough with water. Roll out and line a 7-inch flan tin. Bake blind in a hot oven, Mark 6, 425 deg. F., for about 20 minutes, until pale golden brown.

For the filling:

3 egg whites.	1 breakfast cup mashed strawberries.
4 ozs. castor sugar.	
1 teaspoonful vanilla essence.	Whipped cream and whole fruit to decorate.

B EAT egg whites stiffly, gradually add sugar and vanilla. Stand basin over a pan of hot water and beat again until mixture holds its shape well. (This takes about 5 or 6 minutes but makes sure the meringue will not become leathery when cold.) Spread this (or pipe) into the flan case and return to moderate oven, Mark 3, 350 deg. F., until a pale golden brown. Cool, then coat top with strawberry pulp. Decorate with cream and whole fruit.

From Mrs. Jean C. Fife, Kent.

THREE-DECKER RHUBARB TART

L INE a pie-dish with short pastry, made from ½ lb. flour, ¼ lb. lard and 2 ozs. of butter, salted to taste and mixed with water. Put in layer of sliced young rhubarb, sprinkle liberally with sugar and cover with a piece of pastry. Repeat this until there are three layers of rhubarb. Covering the top with pastry, cut 3 slits in the centre. Bake in a moderate oven for 1 hour. The secret in making this tart lies in using plenty of sugar, so that there is an abundance of sweet syrup when the pie is opened. No water must be added.

Any fruit can be used.

From Mrs. Vincent, Devonshire.

TARTS SIONED
(*Welsh Cheesecakes*)

Pastry:

6 ozs. flour.	Salt.
3 ozs. lard.	Cold water.

Raspberry jam.

LINE patty-tins with short crust made with above ingredients. Put into each a small quantity of raspberry jam, and on the top of the jam a teaspoonful of the mixture (see below). Bake *immediately* in a fairly quick oven till nicely browned. Cool on a sieve. Before serving sift over with castor sugar.

Mixture:

1 egg and its weight in butter, sugar and flour.	A pinch of baking powder. The grated rind of $\frac{1}{2}$ a lemon.

Beat the butter and sugar to a cream, add flour and egg alternately (beating well between each addition), then the lemon rind and, lastly, the baking powder.

From Mary Stokes, Caernarvonshire.

TREACLE SPONGE

6 ozs. flour.	4 ozs. suet.
A good teaspoonful baking powder (or, if a very dark sponge is preferred, use bicarbonate of soda, mixed smooth in a spoonful of milk).	Grated rind of 1 lemon. 1 egg. 1 gill milk. 6 ozs. golden syrup.

MIX the flour and suet together, add lemon rind, beaten egg, bicarbonate of soda (if used), milk and syrup. Put in a greased basin with 2 pieces of greaseproof paper tied very securely over the top. Place basin in a saucepan with boiling water to come half-way up, and steam for 3 hours. Serve with hot custard.

(The best way to measure syrup is to scatter plenty of flour on the scales, and pour syrup on the flour. It will be found to come away all together.)

From Miss M. I. Owen ,Nottinghamshire.

VELVET CREAM

¾ ozs. gelatine.	Rind of 1 lemon.
2 ozs. castor sugar.	½ pint double cream.
1 glass sherry or 3 tablespoonfuls jam.	1 gill lukewarm water.

MELT the gelatine in water and add sugar and rind chopped fine. Whisk cream stiff and add with the wine, etc. Turn into mould and allow to set.

From Mrs. Anderson, Aberdeenshire.

WEST COUNTRY JUNKET

MASH 2 very ripe bananas well, whip them with a fork until frothy and light, then spread the banana pulp at the bottom of an earthenware dish. Make a junket, flavouring it by adding a few drops of vanilla essence to the warm milk before adding the rennet. Pour the junket mixture over the banana purée, and grate a little nutmeg over the top. Leave to set, and serve, if possible, with Devonshire cream.

From Kathleen Thomas.

WINTER TARTS

LINE some tartlet-tins with good short crust; place a little mincemeat in each, then cover with a mixture made by beating together 2 ozs. each butter and sugar, 1 egg, 1 tablespoonful of cake crumbs (rice or Madeira), and a little baking powder; or crumbs of fruit cake may be used and mincemeat left out. Bake in a moderate oven for 15 to 20 minutes.

From Mrs. S. E. Hodgson, Yorkshire.

YORKSHIRE APPLE PUDDING

½ lb. self-raising flour.	A good pinch of salt.
2 eggs.	2 large baking apples.
1 pint milk.	Dripping.

SIFT flour and salt into a basin, break in the eggs and add half the milk. Stir with a wooden spoon to a smooth paste and beat well. Then add the rest of the milk a little at a time.

See that the mixture is free from lumps. Peel 2 large baking apples and grate them into a mixture, stirring well. Melt about 2 ozs. dripping in a Yorkshire pudding-tin until very hot; then pour in the batter at once and bake in a hot oven for about 40 minutes. Serve dredged well with sugar.

From Miss Sumnel, Cheshire.

CHRISTMAS FARE

APRICOT MINCEMEAT

1 lb. apricots.
1 lb. dates.
1 lb. currants.
1 lb. shredded suet.
1 lb. apples.
1 lb. raisins.

1 lb. brown sugar.
2 ozs. chopped almonds.
1 oz. nutmeg.
The rind and juice of 1 large lemon.

SOAK the apricots in a very little cold water overnight. Drain and chop them. Stone the dates and raisins. Peel, core and chop the apples.

Add all the other ingredients with grated nutmeg and lemon rind, then add the juice of the lemon.

From Mrs. Scarlett, Suffolk.

CHRISTMAS CAKE WITH CHERRIES

1 lb. flour.
¼ teaspoonful nutmeg.
¼ teaspoonful cinnamon.
A little salt.
½ lb. butter.
¾ lb. soft sugar (brown).
½ lb. currants.

½ lb. sultanas.
¼ lb. shredded candied peel and almonds.
4 eggs.
Teaspoonful bicarbonate of soda.
¼ lb. glacé cherries.
½ pint stout or milk.

PASS the flour through a sieve; add the nutmeg and cinnamon together with the salt. Rub in the butter; add sugar, currants, sultanas, shredded candied peel and almonds. Lightly beat the eggs, and add the bicarbonate of soda dissolved in a little milk or water, and mix with the dry ingredients. Add the cherries.

Mix with the stout or milk. (The stout gives colour and flavour to the cake.) Put the cake in a well-greased tin; line the bottom. Bake in a moderate oven.

From Mrs. Hartley, Yorkshire.

CHRISTMAS CAKE WITHOUT EGGS

½ lb. plain flour.	¼ lb. mixed peel.
½ lb. ground rice.	¾ lb. butter or good margarine.
⅛ lb. granulated sugar.	1 teaspoonful bicarbonate of soda.
⅓ lb. currants.	12 drops essence of almonds.
⅛ lb. sultanas.	½ pint boiling milk.

MIX the flour, rice, sugar, fruit and peel all together. Cream the butter and stir well. Put the soda into a tablespoonful of cold milk, add the essence to the boiling milk, then gradually blend the milk into the mixture while boiling hot. Beat well all together, put into a fairly large tin, and bake in a good oven for 4 hours.

The cake will keep for months and improve.

From Mrs. L. E. Brook, Sussex.

CHRISTMAS PUDDING USING CARROTS AND OLD ALE

7 ozs. flour.	7 ozs. breadcrumbs.
14 ozs. beef suet.	½ lb. mixed peel.
14 ozs. currants.	10 ozs. sultanas.
½ lb. Demerara sugar.	1 oz. ground almonds.
½ lemon.	⅛ teaspoonful grated nutmeg.
3 eggs.	¼ lb. carrots.
1 gill old ale.	¼ teaspoonful ground cinnamon.
½ lb. stoned raisins.	⅛ teaspoonful mixed spice.
⅛ oz. baking powder.	Silver pudding favours.

PREPARE suet, currants, peel, raisins and sultanas as for mincemeat. Sift flour with salt, spices, and baking powder into a large mixing-bowl. Rub crumbs through a wire sieve. Scrape, wash and dry carrots, then grate them. Turn into basin containing fruit and suet. Stir crumbs and sugar into flour mixture. Add suet and fruit and mix well. Stir in washed, dried and grated lemon rind. Cover basin with a clean cloth and stand overnight in a cool but dry place.

Next day stir in the ale and strained lemon juice with your hand, and keep mixing until well incorporated. Beat eggs well together in a basin, and stir in with your hand. If eggs are small you may need 2 more, or add a little more ale. Beat well, then bury the pudding favours in the mixture.

Fill buttered basins or moulds with the mixture, but only to within 1 in. of the top, to allow for swelling. Cover with buttered paper, tie securely, then tie up with pudding-cloths.

Steam for 7 hours. Store in a dry but airy cupboard till required, then put to steam for another 2 hours. The quantities given will make 2 large puddings.

From Miss Maisie Williams, Montgomeryshire.

CHRISTMAS SPICED BEEF
For about 15 lbs. of beef (boneless meat is best)

1 oz. bay salt.
8 ozs. Demerara sugar.
¼ oz. Jamaica pepper.
1 oz. saltpetre.

½ oz. cloves.
2 ozs. black pepper.
Salt.

RUB the beef well with sugar, bay salt, salt and saltpetre. Then cover with the peppers, and stick the cloves in the meat. Let it stand for about 3 weeks, turning and basting every day. Before cooking take out the cloves and roast in the usual way.

From Mrs. H. Jarvis, Buckinghamshire.

RUSSET MINCEMEAT

8 ozs. each of shredded suet, dried apricots, cooking apples, large prunes, sultanas.
4 ozs. each of glace cherries, mixed peel and soft brown sugar.
2 ozs. sweet almonds.

1 tablespoonful syrup.
1 teaspoonful ground cinnamon.
½ teaspoonful ground cloves.
1 lemon.
1 orange.
1 pint ginger wine.

PEEL, core and chop apples, chop nuts, prunes and apricots. Add suet, mix with the cherries, nuts and spices. Grate the lemon and orange, squeeze out the juice. Add rind and juice to other ingredients. Stir all well together and then add the wine. Allow to stand 24 hours before bottling.

From Mrs. Turner Herts.

KING GEORGE I's CHRISTMAS PUDDING
(*This is not to be listed as an economy recipe; nor do Sandringham kitchens prepare it nowadays. But we include it to represent the rich old Christmas tradition.*)

KING GEORGE I, sometimes called the "Pudding King," ate this pudding at six o'clock on December 25, 1714—his first Christmas in England. Practically the same ingredients were mixed in huge earthenware bowls at Sandringham for his descendants:

146

1½ lbs. finely-shredded suet.
1 lb. eggs, weighed in their shells.
1 lb. each dried plums, stoned and halved; mixed peel, cut in long strips; small raisins; sultanas; currants; sifted flour; sugar and brown crumbs.

1 teaspoonful (heaped) of mixed spice.
½ nutmeg, grated.
2 teaspoonfuls salt.
½ pint new milk.
Juice of 1 lemon.
A very large wineglassful brandy.

Mix the dry ingredients, moisten with eggs, beaten to a froth, and the milk, lemon juice and brandy mixed. Stand for at least 12 hours in a cool place, then turn into buttered moulds. Boil for 8 hours at first, then for 2 hours before serving. This quantity makes 3 puddings of about 3 lbs. each.

From Mrs. M. Johnson, Nottinghamshire.

MINCE PIES

12 ozs. flour.
9 ozs. butter.

¼ pint cold milk.
Mincemeat.

RUB lightly into the flour one-third of the butter, add milk, mix into a smooth paste, and roll out into a long narrow strip. Divide remainder of butter into 3 equal portions. Put one portion on paste in small pieces, dredge lightly with flour, fold evenly in three, turn it round so that the folded edges lie right and left when rolling. Press edges lightly with rolling-pin to prevent air escaping, and roll out as before. Repeat process with other portions of butter. Then roll out to about a ¼ in. in thickness, and cut covers for pies. Roll pieces out thinner, cut out rounds, and line patty-tins.

Put in some mincemeat, cover with pastry, brush lightly with milk, and dredge with castor sugar. Bake in a hot oven for about 20 minutes.

From Miss A. Griffiths, Montgomeryshire.

MINCEMEAT
(*With Raspberry Jam*)

1 lb. raisins (stoned).
1 lb. sultanas.
1 lb. currants.
1 lb. castor sugar.
1 lb. suet.
Grated rind of 2 lemons.

2 lbs. cooking apples (after peeling).
¾ lb. mixed peel.
¾ lb. raspberry jam.
Juice of 3 lemons.
1 nutmeg (grated).

MINCE finely the fruit, apples, peel and suet. Stir in sugar, lemon rind and juice, nutmeg and jam. Add a few whole currants and a little brandy or whisky. Mix well, and put into pots and cover closely.

From Miss Margaret Sheffield, Birmingham.

WHITE CHRISTMAS CAKE

8 ozs. butter.
8 ozs. castor sugar.
4 large eggs.
12 ozs. plain flour.
Pinch of salt.
1 level teaspoonful baking powder.
6 ozs. stem ginger (drained and
chopped).

6 oz. glacé pineapple (chopped).
4 ozs. candied peel (chopped).
4 ozs. walnuts (chopped).
Grated rind of 1 lemon.
Juice of ½ lemon.

CREAM the butter and sugar until light and fluffy. Beat in the eggs gradually. Sieve together the flour, salt and baking powder and fold into the creamed mixture. Add the fruit, nuts, lemon rind and juice. Mix gently. Put mixture into an 8-inch round lined cake tin and bake in a very moderate oven, 325 deg. F., mark 3, for 2½–3 hours, covering with greaseproof paper if necessary for the last hour.

From Kathleen Thomas,

YULE BREAD

PUT 1 lb. flour into a basin with a pinch of salt. Dissolve
½ oz. yeast in a cupful of warm water and stir into the
flour. Let it stand for 1 hour in a warm place then add ½ lb.
butter (creamed), ½ lb. sugar, ½ grated nutmeg, ¾ lb. currants,
¼ lb. candied peel and 2 beaten eggs. Mix all together well
and pour into tins; bake in a moderate oven about 2 hours.
It is very nice buttered.

From Mrs. L. Butler, Yorkshire.

SAUCES, PICKLES, CHUTNEYS

APPLE CHUTNEY

4 lbs. apples (windfalls are suitable).	½ lb. sultanas or dates.
	Salt.
2 lbs. onions.	Cayenne pepper.
¼ lb. sugar.	Vinegar (spiced).

CORE and chop the apples, add the onions, sugar and sultanas or dates (chopped finely). Sprinkle with a tablespoonful of salt and a pinch of cayenne pepper (if available). Cover with a pint of spiced vinegar, and simmer gently for 2 hours, stirring frequently. Put into jars and cover tightly.

From Mrs. M. Marsh, Staffordshire.

APPLE PICKLE

TAKE 6 lbs. of good cooking apples (Bramley Seedlings), peel, cut up into ¾-in. cubes, spread on dish and strew with a little salt; stand for 24 hours then drain. Put into a saucepan 3 pints of vinegar, 12 shallots cut up, ¾ lb. of lump sugar, 1 oz. of turmeric, ½ oz. ground ginger, ½ oz. mustard, 1 doz. cloves and peppercorns, the last two tied in muslin. Boil for 10 minutes, remove muslin bag, then add the strained apple chunks and cook for 15 minutes or until tender, without smashing.

From Mrs. W. J. Ford, Gloucestershire.

APPLE AND TOMATO CHUTNEY

1 lb. apples, cut small.
1 lb. onions (chopped).
1 lb. ripe tomatoes, skinned and
 sliced.
½ pint vinegar.

½ lb. very dark brown sugar.
½ oz. mixed pickling spice, tied in
 muslin (taken out after); 1
 teaspoonful salt.
¼ lb. sultanas; ¼ lb. mustard seeds
 if liked.

MIX all ingredients well and simmer for about 4 hours.

From Mrs. M. E. Lenton, Huntingdonshire.

BEET RELISH

1 quart cooked beetroot (which
 has been chopped fine).
1 quart chopped uncooked cabbage.
1 cupful freshly-grated horseradish.

½ lb. sugar.
Pinch of cayenne.
1 saltspoonful white pepper.
1 tablespoonful mustard.
1 teaspoonful of salt.
1 pint vinegar.

MIX the ingredients well together and cook for ½ hour. Put into jars and cover closely. This is very good served with fish.

From Mrs. H. Handy, Leicestershire.

BENGAL CHUTNEY

1 lb. Demerara sugar.
½ tablespoonful salt.
2 ozs. mustard seed.
2 ozs. ground ginger.
½ oz. cayenne pepper.

½ lb. stoned raisins.
3 pints vinegar.
¼ lb. garlic.
¼ lb. onions.
15 large sour apples.

BAKE apples down to a pulp, and boil onions until tender in a little water. Bring the garlic to the boil, skim; then, with the raisins, put all the ingredients into a preserving-pan and boil for ¼ hour. Put into jars and seal down. This chutney will keep for 2 or 3 years and improves with keeping.

From Miss M. C. Wood, Oxfordshire.

BLACKBERRY PICKLE

1 quart blackberries.
1 pint white vinegar.
2 lbs. sugar.

1½ ozs. allspice.
½ oz. ground ginger.

STEEP the blackberries and ginger for 12 hours. Then bring the vinegar to the boil. Add the berries and the sugar and boil for ½ hour. When cold add spice. Mix well, put into jars and cover.

From Mrs. A. Johns, Flintshire.

151

CRANBERRY CHUTNEY

PICK over 2 quarts of cranberries, put them into a pan with 3½ lbs. white sugar; 1 lb. stoned coarsely chopped raisins, the thinly pared and finely chopped rinds of two oranges, ½ lb. chopped onions. Add ½ pint of good vinegar and the strained juice of the oranges; ½ oz. mustard seed and a level teaspoonful each of ground ginger and powdered cloves and cinnamon and a little salt and pepper. Boil until thick and bottle.

From Mrs. Rogers, Northumberland.

DAMSON PICKLE

4 lbs. damsons.
3 lbs. Demerara sugar.
½ pint vinegar.

¼ oz. cinnamon.
¼ oz. cloves.

BOIL sugar, cinnamon and cloves in vinegar for 10 minutes; take out spices (which should be in muslin bag), and add fruit. Boil for 10 minutes, being careful not to break fruit when stirring. Put all into a large jar and tie down when cold. Prepared in this way, they will keep for years, and improve with keeping. Splendid with cold meat. Plums may be prepared the same way.

From Mrs. E. F. Crick, Suffolk.

DATE AND BANANA CHUTNEY

TWELVE bananas cut in slices, 2 lbs. onions cut small, 1 lb. dates chopped. Pour over about 1 pint vinegar and cook until tender. Beat to a pulp, add 2 teaspoonfuls of curry powder, ½ lb. crystallized ginger cut small, 1 tablespoonful salt and 1 lb. treacle. Cook again until a rich brown colour. This is a delicious chutney and can be made at any time.

From Mrs. H. Bampkin, Northamptonshire.

DATE PICKLE

2 lbs. dates (stoned).
1¼ pints vinegar.

2 ozs. pickling spice.
Pinch of salt.

BOIL the vinegar and spice together and pour over the dates while hot. Place in jars and tie down. This pickle is ready for use in 3 months.

From Mrs. A. Lount, Rutlandshire

DELICIOUS SWEET CHUTNEY

1 lb. dates, stoned and chopped.
3 lbs. apples peeled, cored and chopped.
1 quart vinegar.

1 lb. onions.
2 ozs. ground ginger.
Pinch of cayenne pepper.
A few cloves.

BOIL together for 1 hour and bottle when cold.

From Mrs. L. E. Long, Hampshire.

ELDERBERRY PICKLE

1 lb. elderberries.
2 tablespoonfuls sugar or 1 tablespoonful syrup.
1 small onion.

$\frac{1}{2}$ teaspoonful ground ginger.
$\frac{1}{2}$ teaspoonful ground mixed spice.
$\frac{1}{2}$ pint vinegar.
Pinch salt.

WASH berries, taking away the stalks and mash them well. Put all ingredients into an enamelled pan, bring to boil. Cook slowly till thick, stirring so that the mixture does not burn. Bottle while hot in hot jars and tie down.

From Mrs. Rogers, Northumberland.

FIG PICKLE

1 lb. dried figs (cooking).

Pickling mixture:

$\frac{1}{2}$ pint vinegar.
1 lb. Demerara sugar.
1 dessertspoonful ground cloves.

1 dessertspoonful ground cinnamon.
1 teaspoonful ground mace.
1 teaspoonful allspice.

WASH 1 lb. of figs in cold water. Leave them to soak overnight in a basin just covered with cold water. The next day drain them in a colander. For the pickling mixture, boil the sugar and vinegar till it is thick, then add cloves, cinnamon, ground mace and allspice. Simmer for a minute or two, then add the figs and cook very gently for 1 hour. Put into jars and cover. It is delicious with pork, cold meat or cold bacon.

From Mrs. A. Williams, Monmouthshire.

GOLDEN CHUTNEY

1 pint of apple pulp.   3 good sized shallots.

SIMMER in a $\frac{1}{4}$ pint of vinegar till thick. Remove from stove and add 1 teaspoonful each of ginger, mustard, curry powder, turmeric, mace, salt and 2 teaspoonfuls of powdered

153

garlic, or 2 cloves of same, finely chopped; and 2 tablespoonfuls sugar. Mix well, turn into a bowl and bottle when quite
cold. This is liked by those who cannot take anything really
hot, being quite mild.

From Mrs. M. Johnstone, Northumberland.

GOOSEBERRY KETCHUP

PUT 2 quarts of gooseberries, 2 cups vinegar, 3 lbs. brown
sugar, and a dessertspoonful each of cinnamon, cloves
and allspice in a lined pan.

Cook slowly for 2 hours, being careful that it does not burn.
Put into wide-mouthed bottles and seal down tightly. This is
a delightful adjunct to cold meat.

From Miss Christian Milne, Aberdeenshire.

GOOSEBERRY PICKLE

3 lbs. gooseberries.
1¼ lbs. sugar.

¼ oz. ground cloves.
½ pint vinegar.

PUT the ingredients in an enamel pan and boil; stirring
carefully till the mixture is the consistency of jam. Put into
jam-pots and cover when cold.

From Mrs. G. Theobold, N. Wales.

GOVERNOR'S SAUCE

12 lbs. green tomatoes.
12 large onions.
1 cup salt.
1 lb. brown sugar.
4 teaspoonfuls red pepper (if
   liked).

1½ teaspoonfuls ground white
   pepper.
1½ teaspoonfuls mustard.
Vinegar to cover the whole.
In a small muslin bag put two teaspoonfuls each of cloves,
   whole pepper and ginger.

WASH and cut tomatoes, peel onions and cut in slices,
sprinkle over them the salt. Mix all together and let
stand all night. In the morning drain off the water and put
fruit in preserving-pan (not copper), add vinegar, etc., and
boil until soft. Remove muslin bag and put sauce in jars for
use.

From Mrs. G. E. Jones, Hampshire.

GREEN GOOSEBERRY JELLY

TOP and tail some green gooseberries and wash them. Dry in the sun, and place in the preserving-pan with a ¼ pint of cold water to every pound of fruit. Boil gently to a soft pulp, strain through a jelly bag, and measure the juice.

Allow 1 lb. sugar to every pint of juice, and make this hot in the oven while the juice is boiling for 10 minutes.

Boil both together for 20 minutes and pour into hot jars. The jelly should be perfectly clear and bright.

From Miss D. Morphet, Lancashire.

GREEN TOMATO CHUTNEY

3 lbs. green tomatoes.	2 tablespoonfuls mustard.
4 large apples.	1½ teaspoonfuls ground ginger.
2 small cucumbers.	1 level teaspoonful cayenne.
3 large onions.	1½ tablespoonfuls salt.
6 ozs. sultanas.	4¼ gills vinegar.
¾ lb. Demerara sugar.	

REMOVE stalks from tomatoes. Slice and peel onions and apples, slice cucumbers and put all the ingredients into a large pan. Bring to boil. Allow to simmer for 2 to 3 hours, or until quite soft, stirring frequently. Put into jars and seal down.

From Mrs. H. Nelson, Pembrokeshire.

HAW SAUCE

1½ lbs. haws.	3 gills vinegar.
4 ozs. sugar.	½ teaspoonful white pepper.
1 oz. salt.	

GATHER the haws and wash them well. Put into an enamel pan with the vinegar and cook over a gentle heat for 30 minutes; then press through a sieve; return to the pan with sugar, salt and pepper, and boil for 10 minutes. Pour into pots and seal. This sauce keeps splendidly.

From Miss E. Rutherford, Northumberland.

HOME-MADE HOT SAUCE

1 pint vinegar.	2 tablespoonfuls treacle.
2 tablespoonfuls flour.	1 tablespoonful mustard.
3 tablespoonfuls sugar.	1 oz. pickling spice.
1 teaspoonful salt.	

MIX all together and boil for 20 minutes, then put through a strainer. When cold, bottle and cork. This is very tasty.

From Miss Dilys Morgan, Flintshire.

INDIAN CHUTNEY

TAKE 3 lbs. apples, peeled and quartered, 2 large onions, finely chopped; boil to a pulp, in 1 quart of malt vinegar. Add 2 lbs. Barbados sugar; 1 lb. raisins, stoned and chopped; ½ lb. crystallized ginger, cut up very fine; ½ teaspoonful red pepper, 1 dessertspoonful dry mustard, 1 teaspoonful salt. Mix well together. Boil again for ½ hour, stirring often; then put into jars, and cover down. A little of this, added to meat stews or hashes before dishing up, is delicious. It also makes welcome Christmas presents if put in small fancy jars.

From Miss Wescott, Devonshire.

MANGOLD CHUTNEY

4 lbs. mangolds.	3 pints spiced vinegar.
1 lb. shallots.	Small tablespoonful turmeric.
¾ lb. sugar.	

TAKE the mangolds, cut up and put through the mincer, using the largest knife. Sprinkle well with salt. Leave until next day. Then strain and add shallots, minced fine, sugar and vinegar. Boil altogether for about 1 hour. Just before taking off, put in the turmeric. This quantity makes 8 lbs. of chutney.

From Miss Hawkins, Berkshire.

MARROW CHUTNEY

4 lbs. marrow.	9 chillies.
½ lb. pickling onions.	1½ ozs. ground ginger.
6 cloves.	1½ ozs. mustard.
1½ lbs. loaf sugar.	2 pints vinegar.
½ oz. turmeric.	Salt.

CUT the marrow into small squares (about ½ in.), lay on a dish and shake some salt over it, leaving overnight. Now drain. Boil the other ingredients for 10 minutes, then add the marrow and boil for ½ hour, or until tender, and put into jars.

From Mrs. T. Metcalfe, Yorkshire.

MAYONNAISE

MIX together 1 dessertspoonful flour, 1 tablespoonful castor sugar, 1 teaspoonful dry mustard, 1 teaspoonful salt, and a dash of pepper. Break in 2 eggs, beat thoroughly with a spoon, then stir in gradually a breakfastcupful of milk and a teacupful of vinegar, adding them alternately. When all is blended, stir over a gentle heat until it thickens, then beat in 2 ozs. fresh butter.

From Mrs. D. M. Munn, Buckinghamshire.

MINT CHUTNEY (uncooked)

3 tablespoonfuls mint.	½ teacupful muscatel raisins.
½ teacupful raisins.	1 tablespoonful brown sugar.
2 tablespoonfuls tomato-ketchup.	Pinch salt, lemon juice.

WASH the mint, dry the leaves and chop very finely. Have the raisins seeded and chopped and mix with the mint. Add moist brown sugar, the ketchup and salt and a squeeze of lemon juice. Work all together until the chutney is thick and juicy. Bottle and store in a dry place. This chutney is delicious with cold lamb.

From Miss Christian Milne, Aberdeenshire.

MINT SAUCE

TAKE 1 teacupful of finely-chopped mint, ½ pint of vinegar and 6 ozs. of sugar. Boil vinegar and sugar together. Withdraw from heat. Add chopped mint. Bottle when cold in glass-stoppered bottles. When required for use, add more vinegar, as the sauce should be quite thick when made. This sauce will keep for a year.

From Miss E. Rutherford, Northumberland.

MUSHROOM KETCHUP SAUCE

USE the large black mushrooms. Break them up into small pieces and put in an earthenware pan. Cover with salt, stand in a cool place, and leave for three days, stirring frequently with a wooden spoon.

Strain; put liquor into a saucepan, and simmer for 20 to

30 minutes. Add pepper, mixed spice and onion, if a flavoured sauce is preferred. When cold, put into bottles.

If a thick sauce is wanted, mix in a little flour, and simmer until the right thickness is obtained.

From Mrs. G. E. Jones, Hampshire.

MUSTARD PICKLE

¼ lb. dry mustard.	1 quart small onions.
1 cupful fresh butter.	1 quart sliced onions.
1 cupful sugar.	1 quart green tomatoes.
2 ozs. flour.	1 quart kidney beans.
1 oz. turmeric.	1 quart sliced cucumber.
1 quart vinegar.	1 cupful nasturtium seeds.
1 head cauliflower.	1 teaspoonful celery seed.

PUT all the vegetables into salt water overnight: in the morning strain them and boil in weak salt water until tender (a little underdone rather than overdone). Have the sauce, made with the mustard, butter, sugar, flour, turmeric and vinegar, ready in a double boiler.

Mix the flour, sugar and turmeric with the vinegar, and when the vinegar is very hot add the butter, stirring all the time. Add the mustard last after taking the mixture from the fire. Put the pickles into a large basin and cover with the hot sauce. Mix well and tie down with a cloth. After 3 days make a second lot of sauce, like the first, adding a little more sugar and 1½ ozs. turmeric. Mix thoroughly.

From Mrs. E. Hyatt, Staffordshire.

NASTURTIUM SAUCE

1 quart pressed nasturtium flowers.	1 teaspoonful salt.
1 quart vinegar.	½ level teaspoonful cayenne pepper
8 shallots, well bruised.	A little Indian soy.
6 cloves.	

SIMMER all except the flowers together for 10 minutes, then pour over the flowers. Cover closely for 2 months. Strain, and pour into bottles, adding a little Indian soy before corking securely.

From Mrs. F. S. Ashford, Wiltshire.

ORANGE CHUTNEY

4 oranges; 2 apples.	½ oz. chopped chillies.
4 lb. brown sugar.	1 pint malt vinegar.
½ oz. raisins.	1 oz. salt; a little pepper.
4 ozs. preserved ginger.	1 onion.

PEEL the oranges, remove pips and pith and cut into small pieces. Peel, core and chop apples finely. Chop the onion. Put these into a pan with the other ingredients and boil slowly until the fruit is tender (about 1 hour). Bottle and cover hot.

From Mrs. S. Allen, Leicestershire.

ORANGE PICKLE

6 oranges.
3 cupfuls white sugar.
2 cupfuls white vinegar.

1 teaspoonful each of cloves, cinnamon, lemon peel and mace all tied up in a muslin bag.

PEEL the oranges, cut into thick slices, remove pith and pips, then steam in a double saucepan, till clear and tender. Boil the sugar, vinegar and spices for $\frac{1}{2}$ hour. Take out the muslin bag. Add the fruit and simmer very gently for 1 hour. Bottle in the usual way. This is delicious with cheese.

From Mrs. C. Gibbons, Cheshire.

PEAR CATSUP

STEW 1 quart of pears, mash, and rub through a sieve. Add 1 cupful sugar, $\frac{1}{2}$ cupful vinegar, 1 teaspoonful salt, $\frac{1}{2}$ teaspoonful each of pepper, ground cinnamon and ground cloves.

Boil gently until thick, then put into bottles and seal tightly.

From Miss E. Rutherford, Northumberland.

PICCALILLI

2 cauliflowers.
2 medium-sized cucumbers.
16 French beans (young).
1 lb. onions.
1 medium-sized marrow.
1 quart vinegar.

1 oz. whole spice.
$\frac{1}{4}$ lb. Demerara sugar.
$\frac{1}{2}$ oz. ground ginger.
1 oz. mustard.
$\frac{1}{2}$ oz. turmeric.
1 tablespoonful flour.

CUT the vegetables into small pieces, lay on a dish, and sprinkle with salt. Leave for 12 hours. Drain off water, boil nearly all the vinegar with the spice, then strain. Mix the other ingredients, with the remaining cold vinegar, into a smooth paste; then mix with boiled vinegar. Pour into saucepan, add vegetables, and boil for 15 minutes.

From Miss I. Underwood, Hertfordshire.

PLUM CHUTNEY

6 lbs. plums.
½ lb. onions.
2 lbs. sour apples.
Salt.
Allspice.

1½ lbs. dates.
½ lb. sugar.
Vinegar.
Ginger.

REMOVE stones from plums, cut all ingredients into small pieces. Put in a pan and cover with a pint of vinegar. Add 1 oz. salt, a heaped teaspoonful of ground ginger and allspice, also a small teaspoonful of ground clove, mustard, and nutmeg mixed smoothly together. Stir well into other ingredients. Simmer gently for 2 hours, or even a little longer. Put into ars and cover tightly.

From Mrs. M. Marsh, Staffordshire.

PICKLED EGGS

16 hard-boiled eggs.
1 quart vinegar.
½ oz. black peppercorns.

½ oz. allspice.
¼ oz. ginger (whole).

REMOVE eggshells and place eggs in wide-necked jars. Boil the peppercorns, spice and ginger in the vinegar for 10 minutes; pour it, while boiling hot, over the eggs. When cold cover closely and store in a cool dry place.

These are ready for use in about a fortnight and are delicious when eaten with cold meat or cheese.

From Mrs. J. C. Beakley, Cambridgeshire.

PICKLED GREEN CABBAGE

CUT up finely 1 large cabbage and 4 large onions, sprinkle with salt and allow to stand for 24 hours. Drain well through a colander or sieve, and then boil slowly in 1 quart of vinegar for 20 minutes.

Mix together 1 cupful of plain flour, 2 cupfuls of sugar, 2 teaspoonfuls of curry powder, and 2 tablespoonfuls of mustard in 1 pint of vinegar. Pour over the cabbage and boil all together for another 5 minutes. Bottle while hot, leave till cold, then cover and tie down in the usual way.

From Mrs. V. Cantwell, Hampshire.

PICKLED MUSHROOMS

USE best vinegar and small button mushrooms. Prepare them by rubbing with a damp flannel dipped in salt. Put the mushrooms, sprinkled with a little salt and cayenne pepper, in a saucepan by the side of the fire. As the moisture runs out of them be careful they do not burn; and when the moisture has been reabsorbed, cover them with vinegar. Leave them to simmer, but do not boil. Put them into jars and tie down when cold.

From Mrs. W. Roberts, Warwickshire.

PICKLED ONIONS

2 quarts onions.	½ packet pickling spice
⅓ cupful sugar.	Cloves and peppercorns.
⅓ cupful salt.	1 quart pure malt vinegar.

PEEL the onions and place in a basin; sprinkle with salt. Stand overnight. Rinse well and dry. Boil the sugar, spices and vinegar for 5 minutes. Throw in the onions and boil up. Pack in bottles or jars and pour vinegar to overflowing. When cold cover closely.

From Miss C. M. Jones. Cardiganshire.

PICKLED PEARS

7 lbs. (stewing or hard) pears.	½ pint white vinegar.
3½ lbs. lump sugar.	½ oz. root ginger (bruised).
1 large lemon.	A few cloves.

BOIL ingredients together for 2 minutes, add pears (peeled and halved—if placed in cold water as soon as peeled they will keep white). Boil until tender. It is advisable to keep a cover on the stewing-pan to keep in all steam until sufficient liquid covers the pears.

Turn into dry bottles and tie down securely.

From Mrs. Arthur Lea, Cornwall.

PICKLED PLUMS

USE firm, not quite ripe, plums if possible. Take 6 lbs. of plums, stick a clove in one end and a piece of cinnamon in the other end. Put them in the jar in which they are to be cooked. Add 3 lbs. of Demerara sugar and 1 pint of best vinegar. Put the cover on the jar and stand in the oven until it reaches boiling-point.

Take out the jar and leave until next day. Draw off liquid, boil it gently for ½ hour, pour it over the plums. Tie down when cold. This pickle keeps well.

From Mrs. A. M. Duckett, Somerset.

RHUBARB CHUTNEY

1 lb. chopped rhubarb.
2 chopped onions (or several spring onions).
2 teaspoonfuls curry powder.
10 tablespoonfuls vinegar.

1 teaspoonful salt.
¼ teaspoonful pepper (cayenne if possible).
2 tablespoonfuls brown sugar.

PUT all ingredients into a pan. Cook slowly till they soften. Then boil rapidly till thoroughly cooked. This will keep well.

From Mrs. W. P. Baker, Cambridgeshire.

RHUBARB MINT JELLY

WIPE and cut up some rhubarb. Add a little water and cook until it is reduced to a pulp. To each pint of juice, allow 1 lb. of sugar and return to pan.

Take a bunch of fresh mint, tie together and add to contents of pan. Boil till jelly thickens, removing mint when jelly is flavoured to taste.

Pour into small pots and tie down. This is delicious with lamb instead of mint sauce.

From Miss E. Rutherford, Northumberland.

RHUBARB SAUCE

3 lbs. rhubarb.
¾ pint vinegar.
1 lb. sugar.
½ lb. onions.
1 oz. salt.

Pinch cayenne pepper.
3 teaspoonfuls turmeric.
2 teaspoonfuls mustard.
6 cloves

PEEL and cut rhubarb as for stewing; peel onions and cut up, put into pan with a little of the vinegar, salt, cloves, and pepper; boil gently about 1 hour. Pass mixture through a sieve, return to pan, add remains of vinegar and sugar, bring to boil and add turmeric and mustard, mixed with a little vinegar to a smooth paste. Boil gently about ¾ to 1 hour, till thick; cool a little and bottle and cork tightly.

From Mrs. L. J. Feltham, Gloucestershire.

RIPE TOMATO CHUTNEY

8 lbs. ripe tomatoes.
1 lb. onions.
3 ozs. salt.
½ oz. cloves.

Cayenne pepper and ground ginger
to taste, about ¾ teaspoonful
of each.

BOIL for 2 hours, then beat through a sieve until nothing remains but the seeds, skin, etc. Return to pan, add 1 pint vinegar and 6 ozs. sugar, boil for ½ hour or until thick. This is appetizing with fish, hot or cold, or with other meat dishes.

From Miss E. Henton, Lancashire.

ROAST APPLE CHUTNEY

ROAST 6 large cooking apples, mash them to a pulp and colour them red with beetroot juice. Add two finely-chopped shallots, 1 tablespoonful of chili vinegar, 1 saltspoonful of cayenne and of salt and simmer very gently till the chutney is the consistency of thick cream. Bottle and seal.

From Mrs. Rogers, Northumberland.

SALAD CREAM

1 tablespoonful mustard.
1 tablespoonful sugar.
1 teaspoonful flour.
½ teaspoonful salt.

2 eggs.
¾ breakfastcupful vinegar.
Cream.

MIX mustard, sugar, flour and salt together; add the eggs, then vinegar. Stand in boiling water and stir until mixture thickens. Allow it to get quite cold, then add cream (and a little milk, if necessary) till mixture is the required thickness. This salad cream will keep 12 months.

From Mrs. G. R. Smith, Lancashire.

SALAD DRESSING (with oil)

2 pints milk.
4 dessertspoonfuls mustard.
2 tablespoonfuls flour.
2 dessertspoonfuls salt.
4 tablespoonfuls sugar.

1 teaspoonful pepper.
1 pint vinegar.
2 eggs.
2 tablespoonfuls salad oil.

MIX together flour, sugar, salt, pepper, mustard and oil. Well beat the eggs, add milk, and stir gradually into the other ingredients. Lastly add vinegar, drop by drop. Pour into the saucepan, and stir over fire until simmering. Simmer for 5 minutes. Use double saucepan to prevent burning.

From Mrs. S. Yates, Buckinghamshire.

SALAD DRESSING (without oil)

2 small dessertspoonfuls flour.
1½ ozs. margarine
Breakfastcupful milk.
2 teaspoonfuls mustard.

2 teaspoonfuls sugar.
½ teaspoonful salt.
½ teacupful vinegar.

MELT margarine in saucepan. Mix flour and other dry ingredients with it. Add milk and cook until mixture thickens. Add vinegar last. Beat well.

From Mrs. Birkett, Cumberland.

A SAUCE FOR COLD MEAT

SLICE 6 smooth-skinned lemons, rub 3 ozs. salt into them, after removing the pips. Mix together 2 ozs. each of allspice, mustard seed, white pepper and horseradish, and 1 oz. each of mace, cayenne and cloves. Put the lemon slices in layers in a jar. Sprinkle the mixed spices between, and pour over them 2 quarts vinegar at boiling-point. Set aside for 24 hours; squeeze, strain and bottle.

From Miss H. West, Devonshire.

SIMPLE PLUM SAUCE

STEW 1 lb. stoned plums gently in ½ pint of white wine vinegar. Add just enough sugar to remove excessive sourness.

When quite cooked stir in a dessertspoonful of freshly chopped mint. Serve very hot. Delicious with any cooked meat.

From Miss E. Rutherford, Northumberland.

SPICED CARROTS

BOIL together ½ pint vinegar, ½ pint water, a few cloves, a little cinnamon, and salt to taste. Prepare about 12 medium-sized boiled carrots. Place in jars, allow the spiced vinegar to become cold, then pour over the carrots and tie down. Ready for use in a fortnight.

From Mrs. C. Gibbons, Cheshire.

SPICED VINEGAR

¼ oz. blade mace.
¼ oz. allspice.
¼ oz. cloves.
¼ oz. stick cinnamon.

6 peppercorns.
1 qt. vinegar,
and if you like a very hot pickle.
¼ oz. root ginger.

164

TIE spices in a muslin bag, put in a covered pan with the vinegar, and heat slowly to boiling point. Leave to stand about 2 hours, then remove the bag of spices, and allow to cool before bottling.

TOMATO CURD

1 lb. English tomatoes.	1 lemon.
6 ozs. sugar.	2 eggs.
3 ozs. butter or margarine.	

WIPE the tomatoes and put them into a stew pan with a little water and stew until tender. Pass through a sieve and return the purée to the pan with the sugar, butter, grated lemon rind and the lemon juice; when the sugar has dissolved add the well-beaten eggs and cook until thick, but do not allow to boil.

Pour into warmed pots and tie down.

Will keep 2-3 months.

From Mrs. J. Whitelock, Surrey.

TURNIP CHUTNEY

2 lbs. turnips.	½ oz. turmeric powder.
1 lb. apples.	1 teaspoonful mustard.
1 lb. onions.	½ teaspoonful pepper.
½ lb. sultanas.	2 ozs. salt.
½ lb. moist sugar.	1 quart brown vinegar.

CUT up the turnips and boil until soft. Drain out the water, beat to a pulp. Prepare the apples and onions, chopping them finely. Mix the turmeric powder and the mustard together, with a little vinegar. Put all the ingredients into the pan and boil for 1 hour. Stir. Put into jars and cover when cold.

From Mrs. Robinson, Staffordshire.

UNCOOKED GOOSEBERRY CHUTNEY

1 lb. of gooseberries.	½ lb. sugar.
1 lb. of onions (or ¼ lb. shallots).	¼ lb. mustard seed if liked *or*
½ lb. of raisins (or sultanas).	1 tablespoonful dry mustard.
Add dry ginger to taste and cold vinegar to cover.	1 tablespoonful salt.

TOP and tail gooseberries; peel onions; cut into quarters and put through mincer; add the dry ingredients and mix very well. Add vinegar (not boiled) but cold. Cover just to the top of the ingredients in stone jar. Cover tightly. This will keep many weeks. If it seems to be getting rather dry, add a little more vinegar—but keep well covered.

From Mrs. R. Jackson, Durham.

VICTORIA PLUM CHUTNEY

2 lbs. chopped Victoria plums.
½ lb. chopped onions.
¼ lb. sugar (Demerara if possible).
¼ oz. peppercorns.

1 lb. chopped cooking apples.
½ lb. chopped raisins.
¼ oz. root ginger.

TIE ginger and peppercorns in a muslin bag, and put everything together into a pan over medium heat, and cook until of a jam consistency.

The jars must be well tied down, and the covers brushed over with paraffin wax. This chutney must be kept for at least three months before use.

From Mrs. Walkinton, Sussex.

BREAD

APPLE BREAD

A VERY light pleasant bread is made by a mixture of apples and flour in proportion of 1 lb. of apples to 2 lbs. of flour. The usual quantity of yeast is required as in making ordinary bread, and is mixed with flour and warm pulp of apples—after they have been cooked. The dough is allowed to rise for 3 to 4 hours.

Then put into long tins and bake in a moderate oven for about 1 to 1¼ hours.

Very little water is needed, none generally, if the apples are very fresh.

From Mrs. H. Shirt, Derbyshire.

APRICOT BREAD

14 ozs. flour.
6 ozs. sugar.
3 ozs. raisins or nuts.
1½ teaspoonsfuls baking powder.
½ teaspoonful bicarbonate soda.
⅓ teaspoonful salt.
6 oz. dried apricots, cut small and soaked in warm water.

1 egg, well beaten.
1 oz. melted butter.
Rind and juice of 1 orange, made up to two-thirds cup of liquid with more juice or orange squash.

167

SIEVE all dry ingredients, add apricots and mix well. Make a well in the centre of the mixture, add egg, butter and juice. Put into a 2-lb. bread tin which has been well greased. Bake 50–60 minutes at 350 deg. F. When cold, wrap and keep for 24 hours.

From Mrs. D. Jackson, York.

HOME-MADE BREAD

TWO things have contributed to the rise in interest in home-baked bread: the poor quality of much of the steam-baked, sliced, wrapped bread on the market, and the introduction of several brands of "strong" bread-making flour. Also the increased distribution of dried yeast which can now be bought at many chemists and some good grocers.

This method we give below is the simplest one there is; you will need:—

3 lbs. bread-making flour.	1¾ pints of hand-hot water, or
2 tablespoonsfuls salt.	milk and water.
1 tablespoonful dried yeast.	Fat for greasing tins.

PUT the sieved flour into a big bowl, stand in a warm place, add to it the salt.

Take 4 tablespoonfuls from the warm water or milk and water, put into a small bowl or measuring jug. Sprinkle on to the top of the water the dried yeast. Leave in a warm place until the top shows a froth rising on it, stir gently and beat a little with a fork, then add this to the rest of the warm liquid.

Make a well in the centre of your flour, pour in the yeast mixture and stir really well with a wooden spoon or your hand. When the mixture is really smooth and feels spongy and elastic, put the bowl back on to the top of the stove or in an equally warm place, cover with a piece of oiled polythene and leave until the mixture has doubled in size—this will probably take 1½–2 hours.

Flour a board liberally, turn the dough on to it and knead, really hard for 5–6 minutes, seeing that you get right to the inside of the dough.

Grease two 2-lb. bread tins, warm them, divide the dough into two equal pieces, put one piece in each tin, make one or two deep cuts with a knife right down into the centre of each loaf (this releases any small air pockets there may be in the dough), then put to prove again in a warm place until the dough has risen well above the top of the tins.

Bake in a hot oven for 45 minutes, 400 deg. F. for the first 15 minutes, then reducing to 350 deg. F. for the rest of baking time.

Test for "done-ness" by taking the bread out of the tins and tapping sharply with your knuckles on the bottom and sides, they will sound hollow if the loaves are done. If not done the bread can be put back in the oven out of the tins and finished that way, this makes for a nice crisp crust.

Overnight rising.

If you find this method irritating because you have to wait while the dough rises try letting it prove overnight. Start the bread last thing at night and when you have done the first process, and the yeast and flour are well mixed, put the bowl, covered with greased polythene in a COOL place, the floor of the larder for instance, until the morning. Then it will be ready to go on with the making just as in the previous recipe.

Recipes from Kathleen Thomas.

HOT APPLE MUFFINS

3 large cooking apples.	1 egg.
8 ozs. flour.	2 ozs. moist sugar.
3 ozs. lard.	A little castor sugar.
1 teaspoonful baking powder.	A little butter.

MIX baking powder and flour together, rub in the lard and add the moist sugar. Peel, core and mince the apples. Beat the egg well and, with the minced apples, add to the flour, etc. Work all well together and add a little milk if too dry, but on no account should it be too wet, as apples moisten it in baking. Put into a greased flat tin and bake in a moderate oven. When done, cut in rounds, split open and butter, dusting with castor sugar before serving. Time for cooking: about $\frac{1}{2}$ hour.

From Miss H. Tibbs, Somertetshire.

AUSTRALIAN BROWNIE LOAF

3 breakfastcupfuls flour.	2 teaspoonfuls cream of tartar.
1 breakfastcupful brown sugar.	1 cupful mixed fruit and peel.
1 teaspoonful mixed spice.	Pinch of salt.
1 teaspoonful bicarbonate of soda.	Cupful of milk, or milk and hot water.

MIX all dry ingredients, then add fruit and mix with the milk until the consistency of dough. Bake in a square bread-tin, well greased, in a hot oven for about ¾ to 1 hour. Cut in thin slices and butter.

From Mrs. R. R. Watson, Sussex.

BARA BRITH

1 lb. self-raising flour.
½ lb. brown sugar.
¼ lb. lard or butter.
½ lb. currants or sultanas.
1 small egg.
1 lemon.

1 teaspoonful caraway seeds, if liked.
Salt and spice to taste.
1 teaspoonful bicarbonate of soda.
1 large tablespoonful of treacle.
½ pint buttermilk.

MIX fat well into flour, add sugar, beaten egg, grated rind of lemon, fruit, salt, spice and (last of all) juice of lemon and treacle.

Mix all well together with the bicarbonate of soda in the buttermilk. Put into a bread-tin and bake 1¾ to 2 hours.

From Miss A. M. Davies, Montgomeryshire.

BROWN BREAD (STEAMED)

1 large cupful bran.
1 cupful wholemeal flour.
2 cupfuls plain flour.
1½ cupfuls thick sour milk.
1 tablespoonful black treacle.

1 tablespoonful sugar.
½ teaspoonful salt.
1 teaspoonful bicarbonate of soda.
½ cupful sultanas or raisins.

MIX the dry ingredients; heat the sour milk and add the treacle, mixing well. Stir in the dry ingredients, and lastly the sultanas. Pour into greased tins two-thirds full and steam for 3 hours. Straight marmalade jars are excellent for making, as they turn out nice shapes which can be cut into dainty rounds to be spread with butter for afternoon tea. Rye flour, oatmeal, Indian corn meal, or any coarse flour can be substituted for the bran.

From Mrs. M. Stokes, Caernarvonshire.

COTTAGE LOAF

1 lb. flour.
½ teaspoonful salt.
½ pint hot milk.

2 ozs. margarine.
2 teaspoonfuls baking powder.

MIX flour, salt and baking powder in a basin. Melt the margarine in the hot milk and stir into the flour.

Turn quickly on to a floured board, knead lightly for a second only and then turn into a greased loaf tin. Bake in a brisk oven for ¾ hour.

From Miss E. Walker, Lanarkshire.

DATE BREAD

1 lb. dates. | 1 lb. flour.
1½ cupfuls boiling water. | ½ lb. sugar.
1½ teaspoonfuls bicarbonate soda. | 2 eggs.
2 ozs. butter.

STONE and cut up the dates, pour over them the boiling water with the bicarbonate of soda dissolved in it. Leave till cold. Rub the butter into the flour, add the sugar. Beat up the eggs and add to flour with the dates and water. Knead into two loaves and place in well greased tins. Bake in a moderate oven for 1½ hours.

From Mrs. Livingston, Warwickshire.

FRUIT BREAD

1½ lbs. flour. | 1 teaspoonful salt.
2 ozs. margarine. | ½ oz. good, fresh yeast.
2½ gills tepid milk. | 1 tablespoonful castor or ordinary
Currants, raisins, sultanas or dates. | sugar.
1 or 2 eggs. | A little finely-chopped peel is nice.

SIEVE flour and salt. Rub in fat. Mix in clean fruit, quantity according to taste, about 8 to 12 ozs. to the above quantity is quite good. Thoroughly mix all dry ingredients except 1 teaspoonful of the sugar which must be kept to cream the yeast. Add tepid milk and beaten egg to creamed yeast. Make a well in centre of flour, pour in yeast and milk, leave in warm place covered with cloth for ¾ hour to set the sponge. Afterwards mix to a soft dough. Turn out on to floured board, and knead well. Put into greased tins and set to rise 1½ to 2 hours. Bake in hot oven; time according to size of loaves.

From Mrs. McLennan, Argyllshire.

HEALTH BREAD

1½ lbs. self-raising flour. | 1 breakfastcupful large raisins,
1 teacupful granulated sugar. | stoned.
1 breakfastcupful syrup. | 1 breakfastcupful milk.
1 egg. | A pinch of salt.

MIX flour, sugar and a pinch of salt together and add raisins. Well beat egg and add together with milk. Thoroughly mix all ingredients (sufficient for 2 loaves) and bake in well-greased bread-tins in a moderate oven for 1½ hours. After a couple of days the loaf can be buttered and cut into slices, wafer thin, or as required for the menfolk. If kept in a tin cake-bin, these loaves will retain their flavour and moisture for at least a month.

I have made them myself for home use regularly for over 20 years, and they have always been thoroughly enjoyed.

From Mr. John E. Lines, Middlesex.

IRISH OATEN BREAD

2 breakfastcupfuls of rolled oats.
2½ breakfastcupfuls flour.
1 teaspoonful salt.

2 breakfastcupfuls sour milk or buttermilk.
1 teaspoonful bicarbonate of soda.

STEEP the rolled oats in the buttermilk overnight. Sift the flour, salt and soda together. Stir in the rolled oats. Keep the dough stiff and knead lightly until smooth. Cut in four or make into scones 2—2½ inches thick. Bake in a moderate oven for 25 minutes.

From Miss M. Dowse, Co. Wicklow.

IRISH TREACLE LOAF

2 ozs. butter.
½ gill water.
1 heaped tablespoonful black treacle.
2 ozs. moist sugar.
2 ozs. each currants and raisins.

1 egg.
½ lb. flour.
½ teaspoonful mixed spice.
½ teaspoonful ground ginger.
1 small teaspoonful bicarbonate of soda.

PUT the butter and water in a pan and leave on a low heat until the butter is melted. Meanwhile, beat together the treacle, sugar and egg. Sift into this the flour mixed with the mixed spice, ginger and bicarbonate of soda. Add the fruit, then the butter and water. Mix up well, turn into a greased loaf tin and bake in a moderate oven until firm to touch—about 1¼—1½ hours.

From Mrs. Gillespie, Co. Roscommon.

MALT LOAF

½ lb. flour.
¼ lb. sugar.
3 ozs. lard.
2 ozs. sultanas.
1 teaspoonful baking powder.

¼ teaspoonful bicarbonate of soda.
1 dessertspoonful treacle.
1 egg.
Milk to mix.

MIX all the dry ingredients, rub in the lard, then add the treacle, milk and egg, well beaten. Make a fairly stiff mixture. Bake for about 1 hour in a slow oven.

From Mrs. E. Donaldson, Lancashire.

" MIXED BREAD "

About 2 lbs. flour.	1 teaspoonful cream of tartar.
About ¼ lb. (1 breakfastcupful)	A pinch of salt.
best Indian meal.	Buttermilk.
1 teaspoonful baking soda.	

MIX all dry ingredients together, and sift through the fingers to make the dough light. Make into a firm dough with buttermilk (preferably a few days old). Turn on to a floured board, knead and roll out. Cut into farls, and bake on a moderately hot griddle, turning the farls when done on one side and finishing on the other.

This makes a pleasant variety from all-flour and wheaten bread, and is often regarded as quite a novelty. We call it " mixed bread."

Farls are usually about ½ in. thick, and this amount of flour and meal would make 5 or 6 farls, taking about 17 minutes to cook—10 minutes on the first side and 7 minutes after being turned.

From Miss M. Stevenson, Co. Down, N.I.

PLANK BREAD

2 lbs. flour.	1 teaspoonful salt.
1 oz. yeast.	1 teaspoonful sugar.
1 oz. lard.	1 breakfastcupful milk and water.

WARM the flour and put into a large bowl, which should have been warmed. Rub the lard into the flour. Put the yeast into a jug with the sugar, and mix with the milk and water, which must be just tepid.

Make a well in the centre of the flour and pour in the liquid. Make into a soft dough, cover with a warm cloth and leave it to rise for 1 hour in a warm place, out of the draught. Mould into a large flat cake, kneading and pressing with the hands towards the sides. When shaped it should not be more than 1 in. or 1¼ ins. thick. Leave to rise for 15 minutes.

Place carefully on the plank, which should not be too hot. Bake for 20 minutes on one side, then turn and bake for another 20 minutes on the other side.

The plank, or baking-iron of Wales, is placed over the top of a clear fire, and it is important that it should never be made too hot, otherwise the dough will scorch instead of baking slowly and thoroughly.

From Mrs. Owens, Anglesey.

SPICE BREAD

MIX the following ingredients together, adding the two whipped eggs last:

3 teacupfuls self-raising flour.
4 ozs. margarine or butter.
4 ozs. sugar.
2 eggs whipped.

1 dessertspoonful mixed spice.
2 ozs. each sultanas and currants.
Little milk to mix.

Mix until a smooth paste. Put into a well-greased tin and bake for one hour in a moderate oven.

From Mrs. D. M. Smith, E. Yorkshire.

SYRUP AND NUT LOAF

8 ozs. self-raising flour.
¼ pint milk.
3 ozs. dates (chopped).
1½ ozs. chopped nuts (optional).

2 heaped tablespoonfuls syrup or honey.
1 level teaspoonful bicarbonate of soda.

WARM milk and syrup together in a pan over a low heat. Stir in the sieved flour and bicarbonate of soda, mixing well.

Sprinkle in 1 oz. chopped nuts and the chopped dates, distributing well. The consistency should be like a stiffish batter. Put into a greased and floured bread or cake tin and sprinkle remaining nuts on top.

Bake in a very moderate oven for about one hour.

From Mrs. Rogers, Northumberland,

TREACLE BREAD

2 breakfastcupfuls brown flour.
2 breakfastcupfuls white flour.
½ breakfastcupful sugar.
1 breakfastcupful treacle.
1 breakfastcupful raisins.

Few chopped nuts.
1 egg.
½ pint warm milk.
½ teaspoonful bicarbonate of soda.

MIX together the flour, sugar, raisins and chopped nuts, then pour the treacle in and mix together well. Add the egg well beaten, then work the warm milk in gradually, leaving a drop to dissolve the bicarbonate of soda. Stir well and put into greased tins. Bake in a moderate oven for 1½ hours. This amount makes 2 nice-sized loaves and is spread with butter to serve.

From Mrs. Bosworth, Derbyshire.

VIENNA LOAVES

1 lb. flour.
Approximately ½ pint milk.
1½ ozs. margarine.
1 teaspoonful castor sugar or ordinary granulated sugar.

1 teaspoonful salt.
1 egg well beaten.
½ oz. yeast.

174

SIEVE flour and salt into a basin. Melt the margarine, add the milk and make tepid. Cream yeast and sugar until liquid. Pour tepid milk over prepared egg, add to the yeast and pour into flour and make a soft, smooth dough. Beat well. Cover with a cloth and put to rise in a warm place for about 1 hour when it should be well risen. Form into loaves, place on greased baking-sheet for about 15 minutes. Bake in a quick oven for 20 to 30 minutes.

From Mrs. McLennan, Argyllshire.

WHITE BREAD

2 lbs. flour.
1 oz. yeast.
1 pint warm milk.

1 oz. sugar.
1 oz. butter or lard.
1 dessertspoonful salt.

CREAM the yeast with a little of the sugar, and add the pint of milk. Mix all dry ingredients. Make a well in the centre, and add half of the fluid. Mix well. Stand in a warm place for $\frac{1}{4}$ of an hour. When risen add the remainder of the liquid. Knead well. Divide into 2 baking-tins. Set aside to rise in a warm atmosphere. Bake for 1 hour.

From Mrs. K. W. Mollard, Cornwall.

WHOLEMEAL BREAD

3 lbs. wholemeal flour.
2 lbs. white flour.
Pinch of salt.
2½ pints tepid milk.

2 ozs. lard.
1½ ozs. yeast.
2 mashed potatoes

RUB the lard into the flour, add the potatoes and salt; mix together; make a well in the flour. Cream the yeast and the sugar and the warm milk, pour into the well, cover with flour, set to rise. Then mix into a dough. Put in tins, keep in a warm place to rise, and bake in a good oven.

From Mrs. K. W. Mollard, Cornwall.

WHOLEMEAL DATE TEA-SCONES

1 lb. wheaten-meal.
1 level teaspoonful bread-soda.
1 level teaspoonful cream of tartar.
1 level teaspoonful salt.
3 ozs. butter (or margarine).

6 teaspoonfuls fine sugar.
½ lb. dates, stoned and cut into pieces the size of sultanas.
Buttermilk.

175

MIX well together the wheaten-meal, bread-soda, cream of tartar and salt. Rub in the shortening, mix in the sugar, add dates and mix. Then add sufficient buttermilk to knead to a firm dough (slightly softer than for bread); cut in triangles and bake in a good oven for about 20 minutes. These are delicious hot with butter for tea.

From Miss E. M. Walker, Eire.

WILTSHIRE LARDY CAKE

1 lb. of white bread dough.	Granulated sugar.
Lard.	Mixed spice if liked.

ROLL the dough on a floured pastry-board. On it put dabs of lard about the size of a walnut and about $1\frac{1}{2}$ ins. apart. Sprinkle with granulated sugar. Fold into three from the ends, and then into three from the sides. Turn to the right and roll out again. Repeat this process twice, each time putting on dabs of lard. After three foldings and lardings, roll out to size of baking-tin, score across and across with a knife, and bake in a moderate oven. If liked, mixed spice may be mixed with the sugar, and currants or sultanas may be added as well. This cake is sometimes called " Shaley Cake " by the older people, and is usually served hot for tea on Saturdays or Sundays.

From Miss Doris Hiskins, Wiltshire.

YEAST SPICED LOAF

4 ozs. butter.	Pinch salt.
$1\frac{1}{2}$ ozs. lard.	1 oz. yeast.
10 ozs. flour.	9 ozs. soft brown sugar.
$1\frac{1}{2}$ ozs. candied peel.	One-third pint of milk (warm).
$\frac{1}{4}$ teaspoonful nutmeg.	1 egg.
$\frac{1}{4}$ teaspoonful cinnamon.	10 ozs. currants.
$\frac{1}{4}$ teaspoonful ginger.	

RUB fat into flour, add spices, dried fruit and salt, but not sugar. Cream yeast with a little sugar and mix with the warm milk and egg. Knead liquid into the flour and leave in a warm place to rise for about an hour. Then knead in the sugar, and place the dough into a 2-lb. loaf tin, it will be two-thirds full. Leave to rise till the tin is full (about 20 minutes), bake in a moderate oven for about 2 hours.

From Mrs K. Mason, Ilkley.

CAKES,
BUNS
and BISCUITS

AFTERNOON TEA CAKES

4 ozs. margarine.
8 ozs. flour.
1 teaspoonful baking powder.
A few drops of lemon or vanilla essence.

1 tin sweetened condensed milk.
2 eggs.
Pinch of salt.

MELT the margarine and mix with condensed milk, then add the eggs and beat well. Sift flour, baking powder and salt together; add to the margarine mixture and then add the essence.

Grease patty-tins, half fill with mixture and bake in a hot oven for 10 to 15 minutes.

From Mrs. Heydon, Co. Kildare.

APPLE GINGERBREAD WITH CINNAMON ICING

½ lb. cooking apples.
3 ozs. Demerara sugar.
¼ lb. golden syrup.
3 ozs. butter.

6 ozs. self-raising flour.
1 teaspoonful ground ginger.
¼ teaspoonful ground cloves.
1 egg.

177

PEEL and slice apples, and put in a pan with 1 dessertspoonful sugar, and just sufficient water to keep them from
burning. Stew gently until tender. Mash up and leave to get
cold. Put the golden syrup in a pan with the butter, and the
remainder of the sugar; dissolve slowly, then leave to cool.

Sift the flour into a basin with the ground ginger and
ground cloves. Whisk up the egg, add the dissolved syrup and
fat, etc., and whisk together; then add to the flour. Mix well,
stir in the apple pulp and beat all together. Turn into a well-
greased oblong tin. Bake in a moderate oven, about ½ hour.
When cooked, let stand for a little before turning out of tin.
The icing is optional.

CINNAMON ICING

6 ozs. icing sugar.	1 level teaspoonful ground
2 to 3 dessertspoonfuls water.	cinnamon.

RUB sugar through a sieve and mix with the ground cinnamon. Then stir in sufficient moderately hot water to make
a thick coating consistency. Spread on top of gingerbread and
leave to set.

From Miss Mary MacDonald, Inverness-shire.

APRICOT SHORTBREAD

6 ozs. flour.	3 ozs. sugar.
1½ teaspoonfuls baking powder.	1 egg.
1 tablespoonful milk.	¼ lb. dried apricots (stewed).
1 oz. margarine.	

RUB margarine into flour. Add sugar, beaten egg and milk.
Knead with hands. Divide paste into two portions, one
larger than the other. Roll out larger piece and line sandwich-
cake tin. Spread with sweetened stewed apricots. Cover with
rest of paste. Bake in moderate oven until lightly browned.
Turn out when cold. (Lovely if served with bowl of whipped
cream.)

From Mrs. E. Birkett, Cumberland.

AUSTRALIAN CHEESE SCONES

TAKE 2 cupfuls sifted flour, ½ cupful grated cheese, 2 teaspoonfuls baking powder, 1 cupful milk (or buttermilk),
a pinch of salt. Mix quickly and cut out. Bake in a hot oven.
These are very nice and tasty.

From Mrs. F. Stillborn, Australia.

BANANA FINGERS

MIX together ½ lb. rolled oats, ½ lb. sugar, ½ lb. wholemeal flour, ¼ lb. butter and ½ teaspoonful bicarbonate of soda or 1 teaspoonful baking powder. Mix to a stiff dough with 2 eggs. Divide in two portions, putting one in the bottom of a greased shallow tin, about 9 in. square. Slice 4 bananas on to this, then put the other half of the mixture on top. Bake a golden brown and cut into fingers. Walnuts or chopped almonds can be used instead of bananas. Excellent for school lunches or picnics.

From Miss H. Rowlinson, Cheshire.

BANANA TART

Flaky pastry.   Lemon juice.
Bananas.   Sugar.

FILL a greased pie-dish with bananas cut into thin rings. Add juice of half a lemon and about one to one and a half tablespoonfuls of sugar. Top with flaky pastry, decorate with leaf design. Bake until browned.

From Mrs. E. Birkett, Cumberland.

BANBURY CAKES

Flaky pastry.   ¼ oz. ground cinnamon.
¼ lb. butter.   ¼ oz. mixed spice.
½ lb. finely cut mixed candied peel.   A little lemon juice.
1 lb. currants.

MAKE the pastry and allow to stand for 1 hour. Beat the butter to a cream, mix in the candied peel, currants, cinnamon, mixed spice and lemon juice. Mix all well together.

Roll out the pastry about ½ in. thick and cut into pieces, then roll out again until each piece becomes twice the size, put some filling in the middle of one side, fold the other over it, and pinch it up into a somewhat oval shape.

Flatten at the top, letting the seam be at the bottom. Brush the tops over with white of egg and sprinkle on granulated sugar.

From Mrs. B. Manley, Oxfordshire.

BRAMBLE CAKES

Short-crust potato pastry:

8 ozs. self-raising flour.   2 ozs. cooking fat.
2 ozs. cold mashed potato.   Pinch of salt.
1 teaspoonful sugar.   Cold water.

RUB fat, then potato, into dry ingredients; add enough cold water to make a stiff paste. Roll into two squares of about 9 ins.

Filling:

½ lb. to ¾ lb. brambles (bottled).   Porage oats.
Honey or syrup or sugar to sweeten.

Place brambles in pan and stir over gentle heat; add sweetening and enough porage oats to make mixture fairly stiff. Allow to cool, then spread on one half of pastry, placing other half on top. Prick with fork and brush over with a little milk in which a little sugar is dissolved. Bake in hot oven for about 30 minutes.

When cool cut into 16 small squares.

From Mrs. R. Weir, Selkirkshire.

BRANDY SNAP

¼ lb. butter.   1 tablespoonful ground ginger.
½ lb. treacle.   Rind and juice of 1 lemon.
½ lb. sugar.   1 teaspoonful ground cinnamon.
½ lb. flour.

MELT butter in a jar with the treacle and sugar. Mix the flour with ground ginger, the grated rind and the juice of 1 lemon, and the ground cinnamon. Mix with the melted butter and treacle, beat together 5 minutes, bake in a very slow oven until a pale brown, roll quickly on small rolling-pin or handle of wooden spoon.

From Mrs. Edith Laughton, Lincolnshire.

BREAKFAST CHEESE ROLLS

4 teacupfuls sieved flour.   4 ozs. castor sugar.
2 tablespoonfuls wheatmeal.   3 ozs. butter.
2 teaspoonfuls cream of tartar.   2 eggs.
1 teaspoonful baking soda.   Milk.
1 teaspoonful salt.   Some finely-grated cheese.

MIX flour, wheatmeal, salt, cream of tartar, baking soda and sugar together. Lightly rub in the butter. Beat up 2 eggs: reserve some of the beaten egg and milk to brush the rolls. Roll out dough lightly on a floured board to ¼ in. thickness, cut into rounds and brush the edges with milk. Sprinkle on the finely-grated cheese, fold over double, brush with egg and milk. Bake on a buttered baking-sheet in a hot oven for 15 minutes.

From Miss Mary MacDonald, Inverness-shire.

BUTTER BISCUITS

11 ozs. plain flour.   4 ozs. icing sugar.
8 ozs. butter.

R UB all together to a stiff dough, then either make it into
a roll and cut off slices and bake in a moderate oven or
press through a cookie press and also bake in a moderate oven.

From Mrs. E. Hodge, Somerset.

BUTTERMILK BREAD

1 lb. flour.   1 teaspoonful baking soda.
1 teaspoonful salt.   1 breakfastcupful buttermilk.
1 teaspoonful cream of tartar.

M IX all dry ingredients, then add buttermilk and mix to a
light, elastic dough. Divide in two and shape into rounds.
Place on a greased tin, mark the top with a knife and bake
for 20 minutes in a quick oven. Delicious and easily made.

From Miss E. Walker, Lanarkshire.

BUTTERMILK CAKE

1 lb. flour.   A little cinnamon.
$\frac{1}{2}$ lb. brown sugar.   Mixed spice and ground ginger.
1 lb. mixed fruit.   1 tablespoonful black treacle.
$\frac{1}{2}$ lb. butter.   Nearly $\frac{1}{2}$ pint buttermilk or sour
1 teaspoonful bicarbonate of soda.   milk.

R UB butter into flour until dry and crumbly. Add sugar,
fruit and flavouring; warm the buttermilk and to it add the
treacle and soda. Mix this till it froths. Stir and bake in a brisk
oven.

From Miss K. Hall, Co. Down.

CARAWAY ANGEL CAKE

5 ozs. flour.   The whites of 2 eggs.
4 ozs. castor sugar.   1 teaspoonful baking powder.
2 ozs. butter.   2 ozs. candied peel.
1 gill milk.   1 large teaspoonful caraway seeds

B EAT the butter and sugar to a soft cream, stir in the milk
gradually, and when it is quite smooth add the stiffly-
whipped whites of eggs. Mix the baking powder and a pinch of
salt with the flour, and stir it in lightly, then the candied peel
thinly sliced and the caraway seeds. Pour into a well-greased
tin and bake $1\frac{1}{4}$ hours in a moderate oven.

This is a useful recipe when egg yolks are used to make a
custard.

From Miss J. Haile, Durham.

181

CHEESE BISCUITS

6 ozs. plain flour.	Pepper and salt to taste.
4 ozs. butter.	A little milk for mixing.
2 ozs. grated cheese.	

RUB fat into flour, add cheese, which must be finely grated, pepper and salt. Mix to a stiff paste with cold milk and roll to about ⅛ in. thickness. Cut into rounds about the size of the top of a tumbler, prick with a fork to prevent rising, and bake in a hot oven 7 to 10 minutes. The biscuits should be a light golden brown when done.

From Miss J. Griffiths, Montgomeryshire.

CHEESE MUFFINS

1½ cupfuls flour.	4 teaspoonfuls baking powder.
½ cupful grated cheese.	1 egg.
¼ teaspoonful salt.	¾ cupful milk.

BEAT the egg lightly, add the salt and milk. Sift the flour and baking powder together, and then put in the grated cheese. Make into a dough with the liquid, beat well and roll out. Cut into rounds, brush with beaten egg, and bake for 10 minutes in a sharp oven. These are delicious split, spread with butter and eaten hot.

From Mrs. G. Towler, Yorkshire.

CHERRY AND ALMOND CAKE

8 ozs. butter.	1½ teaspoonsfuls baking powder.
8 ozs. sugar.	6 ozs. cherries.
4 eggs.	4 ozs. candied peel.
4 ozs. ground almonds.	6 ozs. sultanas.
12 ozs. flour.	2 ozs. whole almonds.
Pinch salt.	

CREAM butter and sugar, add eggs, then ground almonds, flour sifted with salt, and baking powder, and lastly the fruit. Put in a lined 8-in. tin, placing the blanched almonds on top. Bake in a moderately slow oven.

From Mrs. R. A. Falkingham, Selby.

CHOCOLATE BUNS

RUB 4 ozs. margarine into ½ lb. flour, then add 2 ozs. cocoa; ¼ lb. sugar, ½ teaspoonful baking powder. Add 1 well-beaten egg and mix to a stiff paste. Roll out on a floured board, cut into large rounds, put a little jam in centre of each, damp the edge and draw up to the middle to form a round shape. Brush over with milk and bake in hot oven for 15 minutes.

From Mrs. Scarlett, Suffolk.

CHOCOLATE TARGETS

3 ozs. castor sugar.
1 oz. cocoa.
2 ozs. butter.
¾ lb. short crust pastry.

CREAM sugar, cocoa and butter together, warming the basin. Roll out about ¾ lb. of rather firm short pastry into a strip 12 in. by 9in., spread on the above mixture. Roll up as for a jam roll, wetting the last edge to hold it in place. Cut into 12 slices and lay flat on a baking-tin. Bake for about 20 minutes in a moderate oven.

From Mrs. W. Proctor, Norfolk.

COCONUT OAT BISCUITS

¼ lb. flour.
¼ lb. coconut.
2 ozs. lard.
¼ lb. sugar.
¼ lb. rolled oats.
2 ozs. margarine.
1 tablespoonful golden syrup.
2 tablespoonfuls water.
1 teaspoonful bicarbonate of soda.

MIX the dry ingredients together. Rub in the fat and dissolve the bicarbonate of soda in the water. Mix with the hand. Roll out on a floured board and cut into shapes with cutter. Bake in a cool oven until a nice biscuit colour.

From Martha Annie Bradley, Yorkshire.

COFFEE CAKE

½ lb. butter.
¼ lb. sugar.
3 eggs.
4 tablespoonsfuls coffee essence.
2 tablespoonsfuls golden syrup.
8 ozs. self-raising flour.

CREAM butter and sugar, add eggs. Beat until smooth. Add coffee essence and syrup. Add flour slowly. Divide into three sandwich tins and bake in a fairly hot oven for about 20 minutes.

From Mrs. Dearlove, Harrogate.

COFFEE WALNUT CAKE

8 ozs. self-raising flour.
3 oz. chopped walnuts.
5 ozs. butter.
6 ozs. sugar.
3 eggs.
1 dessertspoonful coffee essence.

SIEVE the flour and add the walnuts. Cream the butter and sugar till white. Stir in each egg separately and beat hard. Fold in the flour and add the coffee mixed with a little milk or water. Bake at 350 deg. F. for 1–1½ hours. When cold, ice and decorate with walnuts.

From Mrs. P. Hall, Selby.

183

CORN GRIDDLE CAKES

1 cupful flour.
½ cupful wheatmeal
1¼ cupfuls milk.
3 teaspoonfuls baking powder.

3 tablespoonfuls sugar.
1 egg.
¾ cupful drained canned maize.

SIFT together flour, meal, baking powder, sugar and salt. Beat egg, add to milk and stir in maize. Mix lightly with dry ingredients, then beat well. Bake in large tablespoonfuls on a greased girdle, keeping the batter as round as possible as you drop it.

When bubbles show on top and they are lightly brown underneath, turn cakes and cook lightly on the other side. Serve buttered, hot.

If preferred, you can omit the sugar, season with pepper and salt, and serve with hot bacon or sausages.

From Mrs. Mary Stokes, Caernarvonshire.

COVENTRY GODCAKES

12 ozs. plain flour.
12 ozs. margarine.
Pinch of salt.
Water to mix.

Mincemeat.
1 white of egg.
Castor sugar.

ADD a pinch of salt to the flour and sieve into basin, pour in cold water gradually and mix to a stiff paste. It should be neither sticky nor dry, just pliable. Turn on to a floured board and knead lightly until smooth. Roll out to an oblong shape. Press out the margarine until not quite half the size of the pastry, put on the one half and fold over the other.

Press edges well together, roll out to same thickness as before, fold into three; do this twice more, but the last time roll out to about ⅛ in. thick. Cut out three-cornered pieces of pastry and place mincemeat in centre, place another piece of pastry on top, press well together, and make one or two cuts on top and bake in a very hot oven for about 15 minutes.

When cooked, glaze the tops with the white of egg beaten to a froth and dust castor sugar over. Return to oven for 3 minutes. Place on a sieve until cold.

These cakes are sold round here for New Year's Day in most confectioners' shops, and they are also made at the old-fashioned farmhouses. They vary in size up to 18 in. per side. Jolly good they are. God-parents usually present one to their god-children for good luck.

From Miss N. Fennell, Warwickshire.

CREAM BASKETS

8 ozs. flour.
1 teaspoonful baking powder.
Pinch of salt.

5 ozs. lard or margarine (or half of each.)

MIX dry ingredients together. Rub in the lard or margarine, mix to a dough with cold water and roll out to a ¼ inch thickness on a floured board. Cut into rounds of 2½ ins. diameter. Use a smaller cutter to take the centres out of half the number of rounds, moisten the edges and stick on to each round, one from which the centre has been cut. Bake in a hot oven until golden brown.

When cold, place a teaspoonful of jam and a teaspoonful of whipped cream in the centre hollow of each.

From Mrs. Heydon, Co. Kildare.

CRYSTALLIZED GINGER CAKE

3 ozs. butter.
3 ozs. castor sugar.
6 ozs. self-raising flour.
1 dessertspoonful golden syrup.

2 ozs. crystallized ginger.
¼ teaspoonful ground ginger.
2 eggs.

BEAT the sugar, butter and golden syrup to a cream. Sift the flour and ground ginger together. Sprinkle a handful of flour over the mixture, add 1 egg and beat all well together. Add more flour and the second egg, and beat well again. If more moisture is needed, use a little milk or hot water: add the remainder of the flour. Finally, add the grated crystallized ginger and beat the mixture well. Put into a well-greased and lined cake-tin. Bake in a moderate oven until golden brown and firm (about 45 to 50 minutes). This is a delicious cake and one which does not go dry.

From Miss L. N. Wood, Oxfordshire.

CUP-OF-TEA CAKE

4 ozs. butter.
½ lb. mixed fruit (currants, sultanas, candied peel).
1 cup tea.
½ lb. self-raising flour.

4 ozs. sugar.
1 teaspoonful each of bicarbonate of soda and mixed spice.
1 egg.

MELT butter in pan, add fruit and tea. Bring to boil and simmer for 2 minutes. Cool. Sieve dry ingredients, add boiled mixture and egg, mix well. Bake for 1¼ hours at 350 deg. F. in a 7-in. tin.

From Mrs. Asquith, Harrowgate.

185

CUPID KISSES

½ lb. flour.
2 ozs. cocoa.
6 ozs. sugar.

Pinch of salt.
1 egg.
4 ozs. margarine.

SIEVE flour and salt and add the cocoa. Mix well over a bowl of warm water; cream together the margarine and sugar till light and fluffy. Beat up the egg. Add egg and flour alternately to the creamed mixture, beating each well in; if necessary add a spoonful or more of milk. The mixture should be a stiff paste. Roll out on floured board; cut in fingers 1 in. wide and 2 ins. long. Lay these on a greased baking sheet and bake in a moderate oven for 10 minutes. Cool off and when cold put together with:—

CHOCOLATE CREAM

1 dessertspoonful cornflour.
1 oz. sugar.
1 oz. cocoa or grated chocolate, and, if liked, a few drops vanilla.

¼ pint milk.
1 oz. unsalted margarine.

WITH a little milk mix the cornflour to a smooth paste. Set rest of milk in a small saucepan to boil and when boiling stir into the paste. Return to saucepan and bring back to boil for 3 minutes. Now cream together sugar and margarine and add to it the cocoa or chocolate. Drop a teaspoonful at a time of cold cornflour mixture into this and beat well with egg beater. This makes a most delicious thick chocolate-cream filling.

From Mrs. Betteridge, Herefordshire.

DATE CAKE (no sugar)

Short crust.
Dates.

Nuts of margarine.
Water to quarter-cover dates in basin.

PUT dates, water and margarine in basin. Heat in oven and mash well with wooden spoon. Line plate with short crust Cover with date mixture. Cover with crust. Bake in a brisk oven until browned.

From Mrs. E. Birkett, Cumberland.

186

DATE AND WALNUT CAKE

12 ozs. flour.
2 ozs. sugar.
1 teaspoonful baking powder.
2 ozs. butter.
4 ozs. walnuts, chopped.

1 lb. dates, cut small.
1 teaspoonful bicarbonate of soda
   in a large teacupful of cold milk.
1 egg.

CREAM the butter and sugar, add the egg, dates, walnuts and then stir in the flour and baking powder. Mix with the milk and bicarbonate of soda, beat well. Bake in a flat, well-greased tin for 1½ hours.

From Mrs. Bell, Northumberland.

DIGESTIVE BISCUITS

4 ozs. medium oatmeal.
1½ ozs. castor sugar.
4 ozs. wholemeal flour.
3 ozs. butter.

A pinch of salt.
A small pinch of bicarbonate of
   soda.
½ egg.

RUB butter into flour and oatmeal, add sugar, salt and soda. Bind with the beaten egg, put the dough on pastry-board sprinkled with oatmeal, and roll out. Sprinkle lightly with oatmeal, roll it in, and then cut in oval shapes. Bake in a tin in a fairly hot oven.

From Mrs. M. Ware, Gloucestershire.

DOUGHNUTS FOR LENT

1 large cupful granulated sugar.
1 large cupful milk.
2 ozs. butter.
2 small eggs.

A good sprinkling of currants.
1½ teaspoonfuls cream of tartar.
¼ teaspoonful bicarbonate of soda.
8 ozs. plain flour.

MIX all dry ingredients well, then add milk and beaten eggs and flour to make a nice soft, workable paste. Roll into small balls (they will double their size) and fry in deep fat till a nice nut-brown. Toss in sugar. This quantity will make a good number.

From Margaret Coleman, Hertfordshire.

DRUID'S CAKE

6 ozs. butter.
6 ozs. castor sugar.

8 ozs. self-raising flour.
3 eggs.

RUB the fat into the flour, add the sugar and the well-beaten eggs. The mixture should be soft—add a little hot water if necessary. Bake in a square tin in a moderate oven until golden brown.

Variations: Add cut cherries or any dried fruit or "polka dots" to the mixture. Ice, mark in squares, put a cherry, nut or piece of angelica on each.

From Mrs. E. Graham, Ripon.

DUTCH APPLE CAKE

½ lb. plain flour.
½ teaspoonful salt.
4 teaspoonfuls baking powder.
¼ lb. margarine (or margarine and lard.)

1 egg.
4 tablespoonfuls sugar.
6 tablespoonfuls milk.
2 apples.

SIFT together flour, salt and baking powder. Rub in the margarine and add the sugar. Mix lightly. Mix to dough with beaten egg and milk. Turn on to floured board and shape with hands and pat to about ½ in. thick and round. Put on greased sheet.

Pare and cut apples into eighths and press into dough in parallel rows. Sprinkle with sugar and cinnamon (in the proportion of 2 tablespoonfuls sugar to ½ teaspoonful cinnamon) and dot with margarine. Bake in hot oven—400 degrees F.—for 20 minutes.

From Mrs. E. Taylor, Lincolnshire.

EASTER NESTS

1 lb. pastry (any kind).
10 ozs. margarine.
Whites of two eggs.

Any jam without stones.
Little sugar.

ROLL out the pastry and cut it into rounds to fit your patty tins. Put a little rice in them so that the pastry does not rise too much. Bake until a nice brown, then take the cases from the tins, shake out the rice and put some jam in each. Take the whites of the eggs and beat to a stiff froth, add a little sugar to the meringue and put it in the cases to line them like nests. Take the marzipan and shape like eggs, roll them in cocoa and put them in the nest.

From Miss E. Bond, Somerset.

ECONOMICAL CHOCOLATE CAKE

2 ozs. margarine or lard.
One egg.
Pinch of salt.
½ teaspoonful bicarbonate soda.
6 ozs. plain flour.

2 ozs. sugar.
2 dessertspoonfuls of cocoa mixed
   to a paste with water.
½ teacupful of treacle filled up with
   warm milk.

CREAM fat and sugar, add beaten egg, then cocoa paste, then add alternately the rest of the dry and wet ingredients. Mix well and pour into a shallow greased tin or two sandwich-tins, and bake in a moderate oven from ½ to ¾ hour.

Do not have oven too hot as this mixture easily burns. When cooked and cold, melt a bar of chocolate with a little water and spread on top.

From Mrs. F. Cradock, Lincolnshire.

EGGLESS FRUIT CAKE

8 ozs. flour.
3 ozs. sugar.
6 ozs. fruit.
1 teaspoonful bicarbonate of soda.

3 ozs. fat, margarine, lard or
   dripping.
½ grated nutmeg.
½ pint milk.

RUB fat into flour and add the dry ingredients. Dissolve bicarbonate in a little of the milk, and add to mixture with the rest of milk. Leave standing all night, then bake 1½ hours in moderate oven. This makes a nice cake which keeps moist.

From Mrs. Rogers, Wrexham.

FAIRY MOUNTAINS

1 egg.
2 ozs. margarine.
2 ozs. sugar.

1 strawberry or raspberry blancmange powder made up in
   weight with self-raising flour
   to 2 ozs.

CREAM the margarine. Add the sugar and cream again. Beat egg and add to creamed mixture a little at a time, beating well between each addition. Lightly stir in flour mixture. Divide into eight greased patty tins and bake in a fairly hot oven for about 15 minutes. Before baking, hollow out the centres of the mixture in the tins as the tops are wanted as level as possible.

When cold, cut the tops off level and turn each cake over.

189

Make some butter-icing by creaming 1½ ozs. margarine and adding gradually 1½ ozs. sifted icing sugar, beating well. Add a drop or two of vanilla essence and colour pale pink. Pile up on top of each cake and slope the sides to make the mountains. Drop a teaspoonful of thick white water-icing on top of each cake to represent snow.

From Mrs. D. M. Sewell, Gloucestershire.

FAMILY SLAB CAKE

1 lb. flour.	½ teaspoonful mixed spice.
10 ozs. sugar.	2 tablespoonfuls syrup.
4 ozs. margarine.	1 teaspoonful bicarbonate of soda.
1 egg.	½ lb. mixed sultanas, dates or
1 oz. peel.	currants.
Milk to mix.	

SIEVE flour and spice, rub in fat and add dry ingredients. Beat the egg in milk and the syrup (warmed). Mix to a dropping consistency and spread in a Yorkshire pudding tin. Bake in a moderate oven for about 1½ hours.

From Mrs. L. K. Wilkinson, Leicestershire.

FARMHOUSE CURRANT CAKE

2 lbs. self-raising flour.	¼ lb. sultanas.
¾ lb. sugar.	¼ lb. peel.
½ lb. lard and butter mixed.	1 beaten egg with milk enough to
¼ lb. currants.	make the mixture stiff.

RUB the lard and butter into the flour, add the sugar and fruit, and mix with the beaten egg and milk into a stiff mixture. Put into 3 loaf tins and bake in a moderate oven for ¾ hour. Sufficient to make 3 cakes.

From Mrs. Joyce Noden, Warrington.

FARM POUND CAKE

½ lb. flour.	2 ozs. glacé cherries.
1 level teaspoonful baking powder.	1 lemon—grated rind and juice.
Pinch salt.	½ lb. butter or margarine.
1½ ozs. finely chopped peel.	½ lb. sugar.
½ lb. sultanas.	½ lb. eggs (equals 4 average size).

BEAT butter and sugar, add the rest of the ingredients and, if necessary, a wee drop of milk to required stiffness. Bake for 1¾ to 2¼ hours.

From Mrs. Cook, Northumberland.

FIG PARKIN GINGERBREAD

6 ozs. self-raising flour.
2 ozs. margarine.
2 ozs. oatmeal.
1 oz. sugar.
4 ozs. figs.

1 egg.
1 teaspoonful ground ginger.
2 tablespoonfuls syrup.
Pinch salt.
Little milk.

SIFT flour and salt into a bowl. Rub in fat, add sugar, ginger, oatmeal and chopped figs. Melt syrup and add with beaten egg and milk to make a soft dropping consistency. Turn into greased and lined tin and bake in a moderate oven for about 1½ hours.

From Miss E. Rutherford, Tweedmouth.

FIG SLY CAKES

6 ozs. cooked figs.
3 ozs. chopped walnuts.
1½ ozs. currants.

1½ ozs. raisins.
2 ozs. sugar.
Water.

Pastry:

8 ozs. flour.
3 ozs. lard.
3 ozs. butter.

2 ozs. castor sugar.
Pinch of salt.

MAKE filling by chopping figs and walnuts with currants and raisins. Add sugar and simmer, in sufficient water to cover, until tender and pulpy. Allow to cool. For the pastry, mix flour, sugar and salt, and light rub in the shortening. Mix to a paste with cold water. Put in a cool place for about 1 hour. Roll out pastry and line tin—a toffee-tray size is suitable. Spread in filling and cover with pastry. Seal edges and mark with back of knife, then brush with egg yolk and milk. Bake in a fairly hot oven for 20 to 30 minutes. When cool cut into squares.

From Miss E. Rutherford, Northumberland.

FRUIT CAKES

Filling:

½ lb. currants or seedless raisins.
½ lb. rhubarb.

1 cupful sugar.
Piece of butter the size of a walnut.

Put above mixture into a small pan and stew gently till soft. Allow to cool.

Paste:

½ lb. self-raising flour.
1 teaspoonful sugar.

¼ lb. butter or lard.

R UB the butter into the flour and sugar and make into a stiff paste with a little water. Roll out, divide into two and place one half on a shallow baking-tin (a roast-tin does quite well). Spread on the mixture and place other half on top. Brush with white of egg (or milk with sugar dissolved in it). Bake for ½ an hour in a brisk oven. When cool sprinkle with sugar and cut into 16 pieces.

From Mrs. R. Weir, Berwickshire.

FRUIT SQUARES

M AKE pastry or short crust, without sugar, to your plate size. Make fillings of mixed dried fruits heated together with 1 tablespoonful butter and one of sugar.

Put a layer of pastry on the plate (warmed), spread on the fruit and finish with a layer of pastry. Brush over with a little milk.

From Miss E. Walker, Lancashire.

GINGERBREADS

2 lbs. flour.	1 teaspoonful mace.
1 lb. moist sugar.	A little orange peel.
1 lb. syrup.	2 tablespoonfuls bicarbonate of soda.
1½ ozs. ground ginger.	
1 oz. cassia.	1 lb. butter.

M IX flour, sugar and spices all together. Rub butter in and mix with the syrup into a firm ball. Pinch off pieces the size of a walnut, and put on a sheet, about 12 at a time, and bake in a moderate oven. This amount will make about 7 or 8 dozen gingerbreads which are very tasty.

From Mrs. K. E. Mollard, Cornwall.

GINGER CAKE

1 lb. flour.	Pinch of salt.
6 ozs. lard.	1 teaspoonful bicarbonate of soda.
1 cupful sour milk.	1 tablespoonful boiling water.
¼ lb. granulated sugar.	1 cupful black treacle.
2 teaspoonfuls ground ginger.	

C REAM the lard and sugar together, add the treacle and sour milk, then the bicarbonate of soda dissolved in boiling water. Sift together the ginger, salt and flour; beat them into the mixture. Line a flat oblong tin with well-greased greaseproof paper, and bake in a moderate oven for 40 minutes.

From Mrs. Violet Cooper, Cornwall.

GINGER CAKE WITH PEANUT BUTTER

2 cups (small size) plain flour.
½ cup sugar.
Small ½ teaspoonful baking soda.
Pinch salt.
½ teaspoonful ground ginger.
2 eggs.

2 tablespoonfuls treacle or one each of treacle and syrup.
2 ozs. fat or 1 oz. fat and 1 oz. peanut butter.
Quantity of dried fruit as liked.

SIFT flour, salt, soda, spices and add sugar. Rub peanut butter into flour. Put fat, treacle or syrup with fruit into saucepan and melt, then pour into flour, add prepared eggs and mix, using a little warmed milk to make a soft, dropping consistency.

Turn into greased or paper-lined tin and bake in moderate oven until cooked. Leave for week before cutting.

From Mrs. McLennan, Argyllshire.

GINGER SHORTBREAD

2 breakfastcupfuls of flour.
1 breakfastcupful of *moist brown* sugar (this is important as white sugar won't make it).
¼ lb. butter.

2 teaspoonfuls ground ginger.
1 small teaspoonful bicarbonate of soda.
Pinch of salt.

MIX all dry ingredients together, work in the butter until the whole becomes crumbly. Spread evenly in a well-greased dripping-tin and bake in a moderate oven for ¾ hour. Cut into fingers while warm and lift gently from tin with knife-blade.

This is an economical shortbread which is quickly made, and is a good stand-by as it keeps well in tins.

From Mrs. M. E. Glover, Westmorland.

GINGER SNAPS

¼ lb. margarine.
¾ lb. self-raising flour.
6 ozs. sugar.
3 ozs. syrup.

1 egg.
2 teaspoonfuls ginger.
1 teaspoonful bicarbonate of soda.

BEAT together margarine, syrup and sugar. Add egg; beat again. Add flour gradually. Put on greased baking-tin in small round balls. Bake in moderate oven.

From Mrs. E. Birkett, Cumberland.

GINGER SPONGE SANDWICH

½ lb. self-raising flour.
2 ozs. margarine.
2 tablespoonfuls golden syrup.
1 tablespoonful black treacle.
2 eggs.

1 piled teaspoonful ground ginger
¼ pint milk.
4 tablespoonfuls icing sugar.
Preserved ginger.

SLIGHTLY melt and cream the margarine. Add the warmed golden syrup and black treacle. Blend thoroughly. Beat the eggs well, add alternately with the sieved flour. Mix to a smooth consistency with the milk. Put into two greased sandwich tins. Bake in a hot oven for 30—40 minutes.

When the cakes are cool, spread with the following filling: 4 tablespoonfuls icing sugar; enough syrup from preserved ginger to make a smooth cream with a sprinkling of chopped, preserved ginger. Place the second cake on top and dust with icing sugar.

From Miss K. Ashton, Shropshire.

GIRDLE SCONES

1 lb. flour.
2 good teaspoonfuls baking powder.
½ teaspoonful salt.
Water to make eggs up to ½ pint.

1 tablespoonful sugar.
2 ozs. lard.
2 eggs.

MIX flour, baking powder and salt. Rub in lard. Add sugar. Mix to stiff paste with egg and water. Chop paste vigorously with knife. Shape into cake. Handle very little. Cut into 6 pieces. Roll each into round, and cut into 4. Bake on fairly hot, well-greased girdle. Serve with jam.

From Mrs. E. Birkett, Cumberland.

GOLDEN BETTYS

3 ozs. sugar.
2 ozs. butter.
4 ozs. flour.
2 teaspoonfuls melted syrup.
1 teaspoonful ground ginger.

¼ teaspoonful bicarbonate of soda
¼ teaspoonful cream of tartar.
2 tablespoonfuls milk.
1 egg.

194

BEAT the butter and sugar to a cream, and add melted syrup, then the beaten egg; and beat well. Add the rest of the ingredients gradually. Half fill well-greased patty-tins, and bake in a moderate oven 15 to 20 minutes.

From Mrs. G. Thom, Aberdeenshire.

GRASMERE SHORTCAKE

½ lb. flour.
¼ lb. moist brown sugar.
¼ teaspoonful baking soda.

¼ lb. butter.
½ teaspoonful ground ginger.

Filling:

¼ lb. icing sugar.
2 ozs. butter.
½ teaspoonful ground ginger.

A small quantity of chopped preserved bottle ginger.
1 teaspoonful of the syrup.

PLACE the dry ingredients in a bowl and rub in the butter until it has the consistency of breadcrumbs. Have ready a shallow baking-tin lined with greased paper and empty the mixture into it. Spread evenly with the hand and press very lightly together. Bake in a very moderate oven until nicely browned. Turn out and trim the edges. Cut in two while still hot.

This can be kept in an airtight tin till required, when it makes a delicious and unusual cake with the filling.

To make the filling, beat the butter and sugar to a cream, and add the chopped ginger and syrup. Spread evenly on one of the pieces of cake and press the other into position on top.

From Mrs. J. Little, Cumberland.

GREAT GRANNIE'S GINGERBREADS

1 lb. flour.
½ lb. treacle.
¼ lb. sugar.

½ lb. fresh butter.
½ oz. ground ginger.

MIX 24 hours before baking, place a piece of candied peel on each biscuit, and bake in a quick oven. If preferred, add 1 or 2 drops of essence of lemon and a dust of baking powder.

From Miss N. I. Saunders, Suffolk.

HONEY BRAN KNOBS

2 cupfuls flour.
⅜ cupful butter.
½ cupful brown sugar.
½ cupful honey.
½ cupful stoned raisins.
Vanilla essence to taste.
2½ cupfuls bran.

⅜ cupful milk.
½ cupful chopped nuts.
2 eggs.
¾ teaspoonful bicarbonate of soda
½ teaspoonful salt.
1 teaspoonful baking powder.
1 teaspoonful cinnamon.

SIEVE together the flour, baking powder, cinnamon and salt. Melt the butter, add the sugar, honey and eggs (well beaten), mixing together in a bowl. Dissolve the soda in the milk, then to the mixture in the bowl add the sifted dry ingredients alternately with the milk. Stir in the raisins, nuts, bran and vanilla essence. Mix all well together and drop by teaspoonfuls on to a well-greased baking-sheet. Bake 10 minutes in a fairly hot oven.

From Mrs. V. Cantwell, Hampshire

HOT CROSS BUNS

1 lb. flour.
Pinch of salt.
¾ oz. yeast.
2 tablespoonfuls castor sugar.
1 level teaspoonful powdered cinnamon.

1 level teaspoonful mixed spice.
2 ozs. margarine.
2 ozs. currants.
1 egg.
About ½ pint milk.

SIEVE flour with salt and spices, rub in fat and add prepared currants. Cream the yeast with a little of the sugar, add a little warm milk and pour in centre of flour, sprinkle lightly over with flour and leave for 10 minutes. Mix to a stiff dough with the beaten egg, adding a little milk if required.

Allow to rise until the mixture doubles itself in size. Divide into portions, mould into small buns, mark with cross, and place on a greased and floured tin. Allow to rise until half as large again. Bake in hot oven 5 to 8 minutes. Melt a little sugar in 1 tablespoonful milk and brush over the buns. This is sufficient to make a dozen buns.

From Miss A. M. Foxley, Staffordshire.

JAM CAKE

8 ozs. flour.
2 ozs. sugar.
2 ozs. lard.

2 ozs. butter.
½ teaspoonful salt.
1 egg.

196

MIX the dry ingredients, rub in the lard and butter lightly and mix into a stiff paste with the beaten egg and a little milk if necessary. Divide into two parts and roll out thinly (both the same size). Cover one with raspberry jam. Place the other on top and nip together. Place on a greased baking-sheet and bake in a moderate oven for 15 to 20 minutes. When cool, cut into dainty shapes.

From Mrs. M. Stokes, Caernarvonshire.

LEMON BREADS

1½ ozs. margarine.
3 ozs. sugar.
6 ozs. flour.
1 egg.

Juice of lemon.
1 level teaspoonful bicarbonate of soda.

CREAM the fat and sugar, add beaten egg and lemon juice. Mix the flour, soda and a pinch of salt and add the fat mixture. Mix to a pastry consistency and then roll out *very thinly*. Cut into circles, placing two together so as to leave an air bubble in the centre.

Bake until light brown and crisp in a slow oven.

From Miss A. Coltman, Leicestershire.

LEMON CAKE

Short crust.
1 lemon (good sized).

3 ozs. sugar.
1 egg.

BEAT together egg, sugar and lemon juice. Line plate with pastry. Pour on mixture; cover with crust. Bake in brisk oven until nicely browned.

From Mrs. E. Birkett, Cumberland.

LEMON DIGESTIVE CAKE

12 ozs. any good cake flour (sweetened).
1 lemon.
2 ozs. each lard and butter.

2 eggs.
½ teaspoonful ground ginger.
½ gill milk.

SIFT flour and ginger, add grated lemon rind, rub in fats, add lemon juice, beat the yolks and 1 white of the eggs and stir into the flour with the milk. Then stir in the second egg white, beaten stiffly. Do not beat the mixture. Half fill a shallow tin, greased and lined with paper, and bake in a very moderate oven for about 1 hour. Cool on a sieve. This makes a very light cake.

From Mrs. Rogers, Wrexham.

MELTING SHORTBREAD

2 ozs. sugar.
6 ozs. flour.
Few drops of vanilla essence.
3 ozs. margarine.
1 oz. cornflour.

MIX dry ingredients together and work all to a dough with margarine. Press into shallow greased tin, mark with fork and cook for $\frac{1}{2}$ to $\frac{3}{4}$ hour in a moderate oven. Cut with knife after removing from the oven, and leave in tin until cold.

From Mrs. F. J. Sparey, Herefordshire.

NUTTY NIBBLES

4 ozs. flour.
4 ozs. small oats.
4 ozs. coconut.
4 ozs. sugar.
4 ozs. margarine, butter or lard.
1 egg.
1 small teaspoonful bicarbonate of soda.
1 saltspoonful salt.
1 level teaspoonful ground ginger.
2 tablespoonfuls syrup dissolved in 2 tablespoonfuls boiling water

MIX very well together with a wooden spoon, place in tiny heaps on a greased baking sheet. Bake in very moderate oven for about 15 minutes.

From Mrs. A. Gough, Yorkshire.

OAT CAKE

$\frac{1}{2}$ lb. bread dough.
$\frac{1}{4}$ lb. fine oatmeal.
2 ozs. good bacon dripping or lard.

MIX all together into a smooth paste. Roll out very thinly on to baking-tins. Mark into squares and prick well with a fork. Bake in a moderate oven until nice and crisp. This is delicious spread with fresh butter.

From Mrs. E. Moore, Cumberland.

OATMEAL BISCUITS

PUT $\frac{1}{2}$ lb. medium oatmeal and 1 teaspoonful salt into a basin. Add 1 oz. melted dripping, 1 large tablespoonful golden syrup and enough boiling water to form mixture into a soft dough. Knead well, roll out thinly. Cut into rounds. Bake in moderate oven. Serve with butter or syrup.

From Miss E. Rutherford, Northumberland.

OATMEAL COOKIES

2 cupfuls flour.
2 cupfuls oatmeal.
2 tablespoonfuls lard or margarine.
1 cupful brown sugar.
1 teaspoonful soda.
1 teaspoonful salt.
$\frac{1}{4}$ teaspoonful cinnamon and nutmeg.

R UB the lard or margarine into the flour and oatmeal. Mix all with a little water, not too soft, then roll out thin and cut into cake size. These cookies are good with a date filling.

For date filling, boil dates for 10 minutes in a little water and then put between layers of paste and bake quickly until browned. About ½ lb. of dates is sufficient.

From Miss Margaret Ferguson, Ireland.

OATMEAL SCONES

8 ozs. self-raising flour.
1 oz. fine oatmeal.
3 ozs. sugar.
3 ozs. margarine or dripping.

Good pinch of salt.
Milk to mix into a soft dough.
1 egg.

C UT into rounds and bake for 15 minutes in a quick oven.

From Mrs. Schoon, Yorkshire.

OLD ENGLISH CIDER CAKE

¼ lb. butter.
4 ozs. sugar.
2 eggs.
8 ozs. flour.

1 teaspoonful bicarbonate of soda.
½ a nutmeg, well grated.
1 teacupful cider.

B EAT the butter and sugar to a cream. Add the eggs, well beaten, then 4 ozs. flour sifted with the bicarbonate of soda and the nutmeg. Pour over all the cider beaten to a froth, and mix thoroughly. Stir in the other 4 ozs. flour and mix well together. Bake in a shallow well-greased tin in a moderate oven for 45 minutes. This cake when properly made is delicious with a distinctive flavour.

From Mrs. J. Preston, Oxfordshire.

ONE-EGG MOCHA CAKE

2 ozs. butter.
4 ozs. sugar.
1 large egg.
¼ teaspoonful salt.

4 ozs. self-raising flour.
⅛ pint milk.
1 dessertspoonful coffee essence.

C REAM butter and sugar, add egg. Beat until smooth, add coffee essence and salt. Add flour and milk. Put in an

199

8-in. greased and floured cake tin and bake in a fairly hot oven for about 20 minutes. When cool, decorate with coffee butter icing or split and fill.

From Mrs. B. Armitage, Otley.

ORANGE TEA BISCUITS

2 cupfuls flour.	1 teaspoonful baking powder.
½ cupful shortening (mixed butter and lard is best).	¾ cupful cold milk or half milk and half water.

SIFT together the dry ingredients, rub in the shortening and mix with the liquid to a soft dough. Toss the dough on to a floured board and handle as little as possible. Roll or pat to about ¾ in. thick and cut out with a floured biscuit cutter. Dip lumps of sugar into orange juice (or lemon juice) and press a lump into the top of each biscuit before putting them into a hot oven for 12 to 15 minutes. (Probably half a lump of cane sugar would be sufficient). Our beet-sugar lumps are smaller.

The biscuit recipe lends itself to infinite variety. Mix in grated cheese or diced crisped bacon for savoury biscuits—currants, raisins, dates, spices, fresh berries, etc., for sweet ones. A " pie " crust made of tiny round biscuits placed close together on top of the meat or fowl is dainty and economical.

From Mrs. Alan Cole, Canada.

PIKELETS

1 lb. flour.	Pinch of salt.
1 oz. yeast.	2 eggs.
1 teaspoonful castor sugar.	Rather more than 1 pint of milk.

MIX the sugar and yeast together until liquid; next add the warmed milk. Make a hole in the flour, add the salt, pour in the liquid and mix well; then add the beaten eggs and beat the batter well for 10 minutes. Put in a warm place to rise, which will take about 1 hour, then cook the pikelets either in the oven or over the fire.

If in the oven, heat the baking-tin and brush it over with melted dripping. Put 1 large tablespoonful of the mixture at equal distances on the greased tin, turn them once when holes have formed on the surface, butter them and serve hot.

To cook over the fire, melt some fat in the pan, then drop the mixture in tablespoonfuls at equal distances in the hot fat. Five or six pikelets can be cooked at once in this way. Turn over once and brown the other side.

These are delicious for tea, but any left over may be toasted and buttered the next day.

From Mrs. M. Lingard, Lincolnshire.

POTATO CHEESE CAKES

½ lb. mashed potatoes.	1 egg.
¼ lb. sugar.	Few chopped sultanas.
Grated nutmeg.	Pinch salt.

BEAT the potato with the back of a fork until smooth. Add the rest of the ingredients and stir well. Place in tins lined with thin pastry and bake in the ordinary way. These brown beautifully.

From Mrs. C. Smith, Yorkshire.

POTATO SCONES

3 ozs. cooked potatoes.	2 level teaspoonfuls baking powder
3 ozs. flour.	1 oz. butter.
A pinch of salt.	Milk (if necessary).

COLD cooked potatoes can be used, but better results are obtained if freshly-boiled ones are rubbed through a sieve before mixing the scones. No milk should be used with freshly-boiled potatoes.

Sieve the flour, salt and baking powder in a basin. Rub in the butter with tips of the fingers. Add the sieved potatoes and mix to a fairly soft dough, adding a little milk if necessary. Roll out very lightly to about ¾ in. thick; cut into rounds 2 in. in diameter and bake in a moderate oven until golden brown.

Serve hot on a napkin.

From Miss L. Newell, Belfast.

PRUNE CAKE

Prunes.	Pinch salt.
Short pastry made with 8 ozs. self-raising flour.	4 ozs. lard.
	Water to mix.

201

STEEP prunes and stew until tender. Stone and drain (use juice as family medicine). Cut into small pieces. Line plate with pastry. Sprinkle with flour and add prunes. Grate over rind of one lemon. Sprinkle with sugar and cover with pastry. Bake in a quick oven for 20—25 minutes.

From Mrs. Birkett, Cumberland.

QUICK MILK ROLLS

½ lb. flour.
2 teaspoonfuls baking powder.

¼ pint milk (sour will do).
A pinch of salt.

PUT flour, baking powder and salt in basin, pour in milk gradually, and mix into firm dough. Divide into small-sized rolls and brush over the tops with milk. Prick rolls with a fork and place them on greased baking-tin. Bake 10 minutes in a good oven.

From Mrs. J. A. Kimble, Bedfordshire.

RASPBERRY ROCK CAKES

½ lb. self raising flour.
2 ozs. clarified dripping.
Pinch of salt.

2 ozs. sugar.
1 egg.
1 dessertspoonful solid raspberry jam.

RUB fat into flour, mix in salt and sugar, add 1 beaten egg. Lightly stir in jam. Mix all stiffly, using a kitchen fork. Drop from 2 forks, in small rough heaps, on to a greased, floured baking-sheet. Bake in hot oven for 20 minutes.

2 ozs. sugar only is needed as jam provides sweetening. Any kind of jam can be used if it is not very syrupy, as the cakes do not require much moisture.

From Miss E. H. Hughes, Buckinghamshire.

RHUBARB SHORTCAKE

TAKE a few sticks of rhubarb and cook in a casserole in the oven with a tablespoonful of water and a little sugar till tender (but not broken).

Meanwhile you will need for the shortcake 12 ozs. flour, 3 to 4 ozs. fat, 2 ozs. sugar, 1 egg, 1 teaspoonful baking powder, and milk to mix. Rub fat into flour, add dry ingredients, and mix with egg and milk to a stiff mixture. Divide in two. Roll one half out to an oblong shape, ¼ in. thick. Place on a greased baking-tin. Spread with cooked rhubarb. Roll out other half and put on top. Bake in a hot oven for 25 minutes. When cool, cut in slices.

From Mrs. Erwen Thomas, Glamorganshire.

RICH BUTTER BISCUITS

1 lb. flour.	A pinch of salt.
½ lb. butter.	½ cupful milk.
¼ lb. sugar.	1 teaspoonful baking powder
2 eggs.	¼ lb. sultanas.

SIFT the flour, salt and baking powder into a bowl. Rub in the butter. Stir in the sugar and fruit and mix to a smooth dough with beaten eggs and milk. Roll out and cut with shaped pastry cutters. Bake in a hot oven. When cool, store in an airtight tin.

From Miss E. Tudor, Cheshire.

ROLLED OAT MACAROONS

4 ozs. margarine.	4 ozs. rolled oats.
4 ozs. sugar.	Almond essence.

CREAM margarine and sugar well together, then mix in the rolled oats and enough almond essence to taste. Form into small piles on a greased baking-tin with the aid of a teaspoon and bake in a moderate oven until nicely browned. Leave on tin until cold, then slide off with a knife.

From Mrs. Armisted, Lancashire.

SCRUGGIN CAKE

1 lb. self-raising flour.	½ lb. granulated sugar.
¾ lb. chopped scruggins.	Milk and water for mixing.

Scruggins are the small pieces of fat left after the flair of a pig has been melted down.

CHOP the scruggins into small pieces, then put in a basin the flour, chopped scruggins and sugar; mix all the dry ingredients together, then make into a soft dough with the milk and water. Roll out the dough about 1 in. thick and press into a square tin, well greased with lard. Cut the top of the cake into squares, and sprinkle with a little castor sugar, bake in a moderate oven for about ½ hour.

From Mrs. W. Sadler, Monmouthshire.

SEED BREAD

2 lbs. plain flour.	1 oz. yeast.
¼ lb. sugar.	2 ozs. mixed chopped peel.
¼ lb. lard or margarine.	2 eggs.
Pinch salt.	¾ oz. Caraway seeds.

Sufficient lukewarm milk and water for mixing.

PLACE flour, salt, sugar, peel and seeds in a bowl, rub in margarine. Cream yeast in a basin with a little sugar until liquid then add a good breakfastcupful of warm milk and water.

Make a well in the flour, etc., and into it drop the well-beaten eggs and the yeast mixture. Stir well together, drawing in enough flour to make a sloppy batter. Cover the bowl and put in a warm place until the sponge is risen and bubbly, then work in rest of dry ingredients adding enough warm liquid to make a kneadable dough. Put the bowl back for dough to rise again. When it has about doubled itself, form into loaves and place in well-greased bread tins and put back to rise again. When they have doubled themselves, bake in a hot oven. A few minutes before they are done, paint the top with a little sugar dissolved in milk and return to oven to finish.

From Mrs. E. Clifton, Lincolnshire.

SEMOLINA SHORTBREAD

4 ozs. flour.	4 ozs. semolina.
5 ozs. lard or margarine.	3 ozs. sugar or syrup.
A few drops of flavouring.	

MIX dry ingredients and rub in fat and syrup until free from lumps. Add flavouring, turn on to a board sprinkled with a little rice flour, and form into a round, marking edge with a fork. Place on greased tin and bake in a moderate oven 20 to 30 minutes, and allow to cool before removing from the tin.

From Miss E. Rutherford, Northumberland.

SHORT-'N'-SWEET

6 ozs. butter.	6 ozs. plain flour.
½ teaspoonful vanilla essence.	3 ozs. plain chocolate.
2 ozs. icing sugar.	

CREAM the butter and the icing sugar, add the vanilla essence and the flour. Pipe, on to baking sheet, in fingers.

Bake in a moderate oven until pale golden brown. When cool, sandwich fingers with melted chocolate and dip each end in melted chocolate.

From Mrs. J. Darnbrough, Nr. Harrogate.

SIMNEL CAKE

½ lb. castor sugar.
6 ozs. butter or margarine.
½ lb. eggs (weighed in their shells).

½ lb. flour.
6 ozs. currants.
2 ozs. shredded peel.

For the almond paste:

6 ozs. castor sugar.
1 small egg.

3 ozs. ground almonds.

CREAM the sugar and butter, add each egg separately and stir in the flour, candied peel and currants as lightly as possible. Work the ground almonds, sugar and egg to a stiff paste and roll out to the size of the cake-tin.

Put half the cake mixture into a lined cake tin, add the almond paste and lastly a second layer of cake. Bake in a moderate oven for ¾ to 1 hour.

From L. H., Berkshire.

" SINGIN' HINNY " or
NORTHUMBERLAND FARMHOUSE GIRDLE CAKE

¾ lb. flour.
2 ozs. ground rice.
2 ozs. sugar.
1 oz. lard.

3 ozs. currants.
1 teaspoonful salt.
2 teaspoonfuls baking powder.
1 gill liquid, half cream and half milk.

MIX flour, ground rice, salt, sugar and baking powder. Rub in lard. Mix in currants which have been previously washed and dried. Then add the liquid and mix to a moderately soft dough. Roll this out to a ¼-in. thickness. Prick all over with a fork and bake on a fairly hot girdle until nicely browned on both sides. It can be cut in halves or quarters for convenience in turning. This cake is delicious split and buttered and eaten hot.

From Miss Mary J. Bell, Northumberland.

SPECIAL FLOUR FOR SCONES, CAKES, ETC.

4 lbs. flour.
2 ozs. cream of tartar.

1 oz. bicarbonate of soda.

SIEVE all together: this makes an excellent self-raising flour and is easy to prepare at home.

From Miss Eleanor Atkinson, Yorkshire.

SPICED CAKE WITHOUT EGGS

1½ lbs. flour.
6 ozs. lard (or dripping).
8 ozs. sugar.
8 ozs. raisins, sultanas or currants.
1½ teaspoonfuls mixed spice.

1½ teaspoonfuls bicarbonate of soda.
1 tablespoonful vinegar.
6 tablespoonfuls treacle.
Enough milk to mix.

THIS quantity makes two good-sized cakes. Bake in a moderate oven for 2 hours. Once the dough has been mixed to a consistency which will drop slowly off mixing spoon, beat well till smooth before turning into greased and lined cake-tins.

From Mrs. C. McLennan, Argyllshire.

STEAMED CHOCOLATE CAKE
(*Without Eggs*)

WELL mix 2 cupfuls plain flour, ½ teaspoonful bicarbonate of soda, 1 tablespoonful sugar, 1½ tablespoonfuls cocoà or chocolate powder; rub in 2 ozs. fat, 2 tablespoonfuls golden syrup, milk (sweet or sour) to make into a stiff batter. Have ready a well-greased cake-tin, put in mixture, cover top with greased paper, place in steamer, cook 1¼ hours; then place in warm oven for 10 minutes to dry off the top. Not to be cut until next day.

From Miss J. Hocking, Hampshire.

TOFFEE TART

LINE a sandwich-tin with pastry made from 6 ozs. flour; 2 ozs. fat; 2 ozs. sugar; pinch of salt. Mix to a soft dough with milk and water. Cover pastry with minced dates and 2 dessertspoonfuls of golden syrup. Sprinkle with rolled oats and a small knob of margarine. Bake in a hot oven for ½ hour.

From Mrs. S. Allen, Warwickshire.

TREACLE SCONES

8 ozs. flour.
1 oz. sugar.
1 oz. treacle.
1 oz. margarine.

1 teaspoonful cream of tartar.
½ teaspoonful bicarbonate of soda.
Buttermilk or ordinary milk.

RUB the fat into the flour, add the sugar, cream of tartar and soda and mix to a rather soft dough with the treacle which has been dissolved in ½ cupful or more of buttermilk. Turn out on to a lightly floured board, stamp quickly into rounds and bake in a fairly hot oven.

From Mrs. E. Edwards, Merioneth.

THE WEIGHT OF AN EGG

1 egg and its own weight in sugar, self-raising flour and butter or margarine

CREAM butter and sugar; whisk in beaten egg and flour alternately. Divide into about 9 greased patty-tins. Bake in a fairly hot oven till well-risen and nicely browned.

A delicious alternative is made by mixing double the quantity and substituting one pint packet of strawberry blanc-mange powder for the equivalent amount of flour.

From Miss L. Bacon, Anglesey.

VINEGAR CAKE

1 lb. flour.
½ lb. sugar.
½ lb. butter and dripping.
½ lb. currants.

¼ lb. stoned raisins.
3 tablespoonfuls vinegar.
1 teaspoonful bicarbonate of soda.
Just over ¼ pint of milk.

RUB fat well into the flour, add fruit and sugar. Put the milk into a large jug, and add the vinegar. Mix the bicarbonate of soda with a little milk and pour it into the milk and vinegar quickly, taking care to hold the jug over the cake mixture, as it will froth up. Stir into the flour, fruit, etc., put into a well-greased tin and bake in a hot oven for the first ½ hour, then a cooler one.

From Mrs. H. Huggins, Norfolk.

207

WALNUT AND CINNAMON SCONES

1 lb. flour.	1 egg.
2 teaspoonfuls baking powder.	1 teaspoonful ground cinnamon.
2 ozs. butter.	Milk to mix.
1 tablespoonful sugar.	Pinch of salt.
2 tablespoonfuls chopped walnuts.	

MAKE a light scone mixture, roll out quickly. Sprinkle the cinnamon, sugar and nuts over it, fold in three; roll lightly to the required thickness. Cut into shapes and bake in a quick oven.

From Miss Agnes S. Robertson, Lanarkshire.

WELSH CAKES

1 lb. self-raising flour.	½ lb. currants.
¼ lb. butter or lard.	½ teaspoonful salt.
½ lb. castor sugar.	

MIX the butter, or lard, and the flour well together with the hands, then add the sugar and currants. Take 1 egg and beat it in a basin, then put in the salt and a cupful of milk. Mix into the dry ingredients (using a fork) until it is just stiff. Finish with the hands.

Then put your iron pan over the fire to get warm and rub it over with lard. While the iron is warming roll out your cakes and cut with a cup. Put them on the pan and leave until brown one side, then turn and leave them for 5 minutes and they will be done. The fire should not be too sharp.

From Mrs. L. K. Davies, Montgomeryshire.

WHEEL CAKES

THESE cakes are delicious for tea and may be served either hot or cold.

Put 1 cupful currants, 1 cupful sultanas, ½ cupful sugar, 1 teaspoonful mixed spice and a little water in a small pan, and simmer slowly for 10 minutes, stirring occasionally. Remove from fire to cool. Mix 2 cupfuls flour, 2 tablespoonfuls sugar, 1 teaspoonful each baking soda and cream of tartar, and rub in 2 ozs. margarine until like fine breadcrumbs. Mix with buttermilk to a soft dough. Roll out into a large piece, spread the mixture over evenly, roll up like a roly-poly, and use a floured knife to cut into slices $\frac{1}{2}$ in. thick. Place on a greased baking-sheet, brush over with milk and bake in a hot oven for 20 minutes.

From Miss Agnes Campbell, Co. Down.

WHEATEN FRUIT CAKES

Wheaten pastry:

$\frac{1}{2}$ lb. wheaten meal (finely ground).
Pinch of salt.
$\frac{1}{2}$ teaspoonful baking soda.
1 teaspoonful cream of tartar.

$\frac{1}{4}$ lb. butter.
Teaspoonful sugar.
Water to mix.

Filling:

$\frac{1}{2}$ lb. seedless raisins.
2 apples (about $\frac{1}{2}$ lb.).
Piece of butter the size of a walnut.

2 tablespoonfuls brown sugar.
1 teaspoonful ground cinnamon.
2 tablespoonfuls water.

MIX dry ingredients in a bowl; rub in butter and mix with a little water into short-crust pastry. Divide in two portions, and roll out each to form 9-in. square. Prepare the filling the previous day if possible so as to have it cold. Grate the apples or put them through a mincer, add other ingredients and simmer slowly till liquid is absorbed. Spread filling on one square of pastry and place other on top. Bake in moderate oven for $\frac{1}{2}$ hour after brushing top with milk in which a little sugar is dissolved. When cool, sprinkle sugar on top and cut into 16 small squares.

From Mrs. R. Weir, Berwickshire.

WHOLEMEAL SPLITS

TAKE 2 breakfastcupfuls wholemeal and 1 breakfastcupful white flour; 1 teaspoonful salt; mix thoroughly in a basin. Make a well in the middle and into this put 1 teaspoonful sugar, and 1 heaped dessertspoonful yeast. Melt a knob of lard the size of a walnut and mix this with 1 breakfastcupful tepid water to which has been added 1 tablespoonful milk, and pour over the yeast.

Allow to stand till the latter rises and bubbles. Do not

knead, but mix with a knife only to the consistency of a soft paste, adding more warm water if necessary. Dust over with flour and set in a warm place to rise well. Then turn out on to a well-floured board, and lightly roll out to less than $\frac{1}{2}$ in. in thickness. Place on a warmed greased tin and set to rise once more. Bake in a moderately hot oven. When cold cut into squares, split and butter and spread with chopped walnut and date, or chopped nuts and cream cheese; or, if preferred, with butter alone.

From Mrs. M. Johnstone, Northumberland.

WIMBLEDON CAKE

1 lb. flour.	1 teaspoonful mixed spice.
$\frac{1}{2}$ lb. butter.	$\frac{1}{2}$ pint sour milk.
$\frac{1}{2}$ lb. sugar.	1 teaspoonful bicarbonate of soda.
$\frac{1}{2}$ lb. currants.	1 tablespoonful syrup.
2 ozs. chopped candied peel.	

RUB the butter into the flour; add the sugar, currants, peel and spice. Warm the syrup and stir it into the milk, add the soda and mix all together. Bake in a greased dripping-tin in a moderate oven for $1\frac{1}{2}$ hours.

From Miss M. C. Utley, Somersetshire.

YORKSHIRE PARKIN

$1\frac{1}{2}$ lbs. medium oatmeal.	$\frac{1}{2}$ lb. butter and dripping.
$\frac{3}{4}$ lb. flour.	1 small teaspoonful salt.
1 tablespoonful sugar.	1 teaspoonful bicarbonate of soda.
1 teaspoonful ground ginger.	$\frac{1}{4}$ pint milk.
2 lbs. treacle.	

MIX all the dry ingredients together. Warm the treacle and dripping together and dissolve the bicarbonate of soda in the slightly warm milk and mix all well together. Grease a large pudding-tin or 2 smaller ones and bake in a moderate oven for about $\frac{3}{4}$ hour, or until it is just firm to the touch.

From Mrs. A. Cooper, Yorkshire.

YORKSHIRE TEA CAKES

1½ lbs. flour.
¾ pint milk and water.
½ teaspoonful salt.

1 oz. yeast.
2 ozs. sugar.
2 ozs. lard.

PUT the flour and salt into a warm bowl and rub in the lard. Cream the yeast and sugar and add them to the milk, slightly warmed. Pour on to the flour and mix well together. Stand to rise for about ½ hour.

Divide into 12 pieces, roll out lightly, set on warm, greased tins, prick with fork, cover with a light cloth and stand to rise for ½ hour. Bake in hot oven for 7 to 10 minutes.

From Mrs. Holden Sussex.

SWEETMEATS

APRICOT JUJUBES

1 lb. dried apricots.
Icing sugar.

2¼ lbs. granulated sugar.
Minced nuts.

SOAK the apricots for 24 hours. Put through a mincing machine twice. They should now weigh 2 lbs., but water may be added to make up the weight if necessary. Put the apricots and the granulated sugar together in a preserving-pan and cook over a gentle flame for 1 hour, stirring frequently to prevent sticking. Pour into shallow moulds or on to plates, and leave to cool. When sufficiently cool, it should cut cleanly with a knife that has been dipped in icing sugar. Roll the pieces in the minced nuts and icing sugar.

From Miss D. Hemus, Worcestershire.

BARLEY FUDGE

MIX together 1 teacupful of flaked barley; 2 tablespoonfuls chopped dates; 1 tablespoonful golden syrup; 1 dessert-spoonful cocoa; 1 oz. margarine; pinch of salt and 4 teacupsful water. Put into a well-greased pudding bowl and steam for 2½ hours.

From Mrs. Rogers, Northumberland.

CANADIAN PENOCHI

PUT together in a saucepan 3 cupfuls of light brown sugar, 1 small cupful of milk and 2 tablespoonfuls of butter. Bring the mixture to the boil, stirring all the time with a wooden spoon, then allow it to boil with an occasional stir for 5 minutes. Add 1 cupful of either chopped walnuts, almonds, peanuts **or a** mixture of desiccated coconut and chopped preserved ginger. Boil, stirring constantly, until a little dropped in cold water forms a soft ball. Then add 1 teaspoonful of vanilla essence. Remove the pan from fire, and beat until the mixture is creamy. Pour into a butter-tin and cut into cubes when almost cold.

A delicious variation of this can be made by substituting granulated sugar for the brown, and chopped pineapple (well drained) for the nuts. Essence of lemon should be substituted for the vanilla in this case.

From Miss M. Turner, Sussex.

CHOCOLATE FUDGE

2 cupfuls white sugar.
½ cupful corn syrup.
½ cupful milk.

2 squares unsweetened chocolate
(or tablespoonfuls cocoa).

COOK all together until it forms a soft ball when dropped in cold water. Then add 1 tablespoonful butter, 1 tablespoonful vanilla extract, 1 cupful chopped walnuts and a pinch of salt. Remove from the heat and beat well. Pour into a buttered pan and mark into squares.

From Mrs. L. Morrow, British Columbia, Canada.

CHOCOLATE TRUFFLES

One 4-oz. block plain chocolate.
2 ozs. icing sugar.
½ teaspoonful vanilla essence.

1½ tablespoonfuls unsweetened
evaporated milk.
Desiccated coconut.

MELT the chocolate, but do not allow to get hot, stir in the sieved icing sugar and add the milk. Now add vanilla essence and work all together well. No cooking is needed. Shape into balls, then roll in the coconut.

From Mrs. Rogers, Wrexham.

CLAGGUM

THIS is the old-fashioned "teasing" candy. We used to make a large potful at Hogmanay time and found long sticks of it tremendously popular with the village children.

Put 2 teacupfuls treacle, 1 teacupful cold water in a pan. Set at the back of the stove and permit to dissolve slowly. Now boil briskly until a little forms a soft ball when tested in cold water. Pour into a well-buttered dish. When cold enough to handle, flour the hands and form the candy into a lump. "Tease" or pull out and in until it becomes pale cream in colour. Twist into long sticks. Store on a clean baking-board in the meal girnal.

From Miss Christian Milne, Aberdeenshire.

COCONUT ICE (1)

3 lbs. loaf sugar.   ½ pint milk.
1 lb. desiccated coconut.

PUT sugar and milk in saucepan, bring to the boil, have all sugar dissolved, boil 3 minutes. Take off the fire, and stir in the coconut. Let one-half remain white and colour remainder with a few drops of cochineal. A baking-tin is best to put it in to cool. Line tin with buttered paper. When cold cut in squares.

From Miss E. J. Brake, Gloucestershire.

COCONUT ICE (2)

1 lb. castor sugar.   1 teacupful milk.
¾ lb. coconut.   1 saltspoonful cream of tartar.

PUT sugar, milk and cream of tartar into a saucepan, and let it come to the boil slowly. Boil 20 minutes, then stir in the coconut. Rinse the mould out with cold water, then put half the mixture into it, add a few drops of cochineal to the remainder to colour it, place this with the other in the mould. When cold it will turn out quite firm.

From Mrs. B. Tween, Essex.

COFFEE NUT FUDGE

2 cupfuls granulated sugar.   1 cupful clear strong coffee.
1 teaspoonful butter.   1 cupful chopped walnuts.

BOIL sugar, coffee and butter to a soft ball. Take from the fire, and beat to a cream. Stir in the nuts, pour into a greased tin, and cut into bars when cold.

From Miss Elizabeth Tudor, Cheshire.

COTTAGE CANDY

1 lb. brown sugar.   6 tablespoonfuls milk (tinned milk
1 tablespoonful (heaped) butter.   is splendid).

BOIL all together till the mixture thickens; remove from heat, and beat hard till creamy. Cool in buttered tray; and mark into squares while warm. Chopped dates, nuts, crystallized fruits, may be added for variety.

From Mrs. M. Wilson, Northumberland.

CRUNCHY CHOCOLATE SLAB

½ lb. broken biscuits.
2 ozs. sugar.
1 egg.

2 ozs. margarine.
1 oz. cocoa.

MELT margarine in enamel saucepan over slow heat, add sugar and cocoa and stir till dissolved, add beaten egg and stir slowly for 2 minutes, all over slow heat. Break biscuits, if not already of the broken variety, to size of a pea or smaller. Add to saucepan and mix thoroughly, turn out into greased tin, press level and when cool cut in fingers. This is a rich mixture, a special treat for children, delicious with tea or coffee.

From Miss E. Walker, Dublin.

DIVINITY FUDGE

2 cupfuls white sugar.
½ cupful water.
1 egg white.
⅓ cupful candied cherries.

1 cupful corn syrup.
2 rings chopped candied pineapple.
1 teaspoonful vanilla.

COOK the sugar, syrup and water till it forms a firm ball when dropped in cold water. Add the syrup to the beaten egg white, pouring slowly and beating constantly. When it begins to thicken, add flavouring and fruit. It may be dropped in spoonfuls on a buttered sheet or poured into a buttered pan and cut into squares.

From Mrs. L. Morrow, British Columbia, Canada.

FUDGE

1 large tin of sweetened condensed milk.

1 lb. Demerara sugar.
¼ lb. butter.

PLACE ingredients in a saucepan and cook until the mixture candies, then beat well after lifting from the fire. Pour into a well-buttered tin; and when cool, cut into squares.

This fudge is good plain, but chocolate, walnuts or vanilla flavouring may be added if preferred.

From Mrs. M. Peeling, Surrey.

215

LEMON AND ACID DROPS

1½ lbs. loaf sugar.   ½ teaspoonful cream of tartar.
½ pint water.

BOIL the loaf sugar, water and cream of tartar until the mixture acquires a pale yellow tinge. Add the essence of lemon to taste, and turn the preparation on to an oiled slab. Sprinkle on 1 dessertspoonful of tartaric acid; work it well in, and, as soon as it is cool enough to handle, form into thin rolls. Cut off short pieces with the scissors, and roll into shape under the hand. Coat with sifted sugar, dry well and afterwards store in an airtight tin.

From Miss Eileen Porter, Lincolnshire.

MARZIPAN POTATOES

MIX together 4 ozs. of sweet ground almonds, and 8 oz. of castor sugar with the whisked white of an egg and a few drops of vanilla essence until a stiff paste is formed. Take small quantities and shape into little "potatoes", then roll them in cocoa to make them brown. They can be varied by placing a small piece of sponge cake and just a little raspberry jam in the centre with the marzipan rolled around.

From Miss I. Turner, Somersetshire.

PEPPERMINT JELLIES

SOAK 1 oz. leaf gelatine in ½ teacupful of cold water for 2 hours; or, better still, all night. Boil 1lb. granulated sugar in ½ a cupful of cold water. When thoroughly boiling add soaked gelatine and stir until all are well mixed. Boil slowly for 20 minutes, watching the mixture carefully, as it quickly boils over. Then add ½ teaspoonful essence of peppermint and a few drops of green colouring. Stand a sandwich-tin in cold water for a few minutes, pour mixture into wet tin, then put away till next day. Turn out on to a sheet of paper covered with icing sugar, cut up into neat squares with scissors, and coat well with icing sugar.

This makes about 1½ lbs. of delicious sweets at a small cost. The flavouring and colouring may be varied.

From Mrs. E. A. Thomas, Surrey.

RICE AND NUT CANDIES

MIX equal quantities of boiled rice, and skinned and chopped nuts—walnuts, hazelnuts and almonds. Press into small balls, about the size of marbles. Drop them into boiling syrup, and then allow to cool and harden. The syrup is made by boiling 1 lb. loaf sugar with 3 gills water, and a good pinch of cream of tartar in the crock. It is then ready for dipping the sweets.

From Mrs. C. Gibbons, Stockport.

TOFFEE

1 lb. Demerara sugar.
½ lb. butter.

2 pinches flour.
2 dessertspoonfuls treacle.

BOIL well for about 20 minutes till it will set in water. Put in a buttered flat tin in a cool place till cold, then break into pieces and put into a tin.

From Mrs. Norris, Lincolnshire.

WALNUT FUDGE

1 lb. brown sugar.
½ pint thin cream.
1 tablespoonful syrup.

½ teaspoonful vanilla essence.
¼ lb. chopped walnuts.

PUT the sugar, cream and syrup into a saucepan. Stir well until it comes to the boil, then boil for 15 to 20 minutes. Remove from fire, stir in walnuts and vanilla, place saucepan in a pan of cold water, and stir quickly until toffee becomes thick. Pour into a buttered tin, mark into squares with a knife, and leave till cold.

From Miss Muriel Broad, Cheshire.

WALNUT TABLET

2 lbs. brown sugar.
1 cupful milk (creamy if possible).
1 tablespoonful syrup.

About 1½ ozs. butter.
About 2 ozs. shelled walnuts.
Vanilla.

PUT sugar, milk, syrup and butter in a pan. Stir over fire till it melts, then boil fairly hard for about 10 minutes. If, when tested in water, it is fairly firm, add vanilla to taste, then chopped walnuts. Remove from fire and beat till it "sugars." Pour at once into well-greased tin and when partly cooled mark in squares which can be easily separated when cold.

From Mrs. R. Weir, Berwickshire.

PRESERVES

APPLE AND APRICOT JAM

1 lb. dried apricots.
12 lbs. windfall apples.

Sugar.
Water.

CUT apricots in small pieces, soaking thoroughly in 1 pint of water, or as much as they will absorb. Wash and cut up apples without peeling. Boil till soft in enough water to ensure thorough cooking. Then strain, squeezing through all the pulp. Add apricots, weigh, and bring to the boil. To each pound of pulp allow ¾ lb. of sugar (or 1 lb. to 1 pint). Boil fast till it sets when tested. Stir well. The faster it boils the deeper the colour, and stronger the flavouring of the jam.

From Mrs. Daniels, Bedfordshire.

APPLE CURD

½ lb. margarine.
2 lb. apples.
2 eggs.

½ lb. sugar.
Juice of lemon (when obtainable)
or lemon flavouring to taste.

BOIL and pulp apples. Add sugar and melted margarine, then beat in the two eggs. Cook slowly for ½ hour; add lemon juice or flavouring, and bottle in the same way as for jam.

This will keep good for about 2 months.

From Mrs. Punter, Wiltshire.

APPLE GINGER

4 lbs. apples.
3 pints water.

4 lbs. granulated sugar.
2 ozs. ground ginger (or less, according to taste).

GOOD for using up apples that do not keep well. Golden russets make a beautiful-looking preserve of a golden red hue, equally popular at tea-time or for filling tarts or dumplings. Make a thick syrup of the sugar and water by boiling together. Peel, core and cut apples into thin slices and boil in the syrup until transparent, then add ginger, boil for another 5 minutes. Bottle and seal.

From Mrs. L. Fox, Norfolk.

APPLE AND GRAPEFRUIT MARMALADE

TAKE 3 grapefruits, cut into pieces. Put pips and cores into a basin and cover with boiling water. To each pound of grapefruit pulp add 1 pint of water and soak overnight. Next add same amount of apple juice as water (previously strained as for jelly), and bring to boil, adding ¾ lb. of sugar to each pint of liquid previously measured (grapefruit, water and apple juice together). Boil fast for about 1 hour (with the pips, etc., in muslin bag), when the marmalade should form a jelly when tested. Pour into warm jars, and seal with greaseproof paper while still hot. Pips boiled in the pan cause the jelly to form more quickly.

From Miss Geraldine Ward, Essex.

APPLE JELLY
(*Clove-flavoured*)

THE tiny rosy-cheeked apples will do for this jelly. Put apples in jelly-pan, and barely cover with water: boil till pulpy. Then strain all night through a jelly-bag. To every pint of juice add 1 lb. preserving sugar and 2 cloves; tie the cloves in a piece of muslin and lift out when jelly is ready. It takes about ½ hour boiling rapidly. Test on cold plate, then pot. This is a tinted and delicious jelly.

From Mrs. Wright, East Lothian.

APPLE AND PLUM CHEESE

3 lbs. apples.
1 lb. plums.

¾ lb. sugar to every pint of pulp.

PEEL, core and slice apples; and cook in a little water until nearly tender. Add plums, and cook until soft. Rub

219

through a sieve, and boil up with the sugar. Directly it sets, pour into jars. This is a good way of using up windfall apples.

From Mrs. L. Tyler, Yorkshire.

APPLE PRESERVE

Apples.
1 lb. preserving sugar to each pint of juice and pulp.

Water.
1 lemon to every 2 pints.

WIPE the apples, no matter how small, provided they are perfectly sound; pare and core and slice them as for a stew. Put the pieces into a preserving pan, adding sufficient water to keep them from sticking. Cook until quite tender, take out the pulp and place in a bowl.

Put all the cores and peel and thinly-pared lemon rind into the preserving-pan with sufficient water to cover, stirring occasionally; cook until tender. Then put into a muslin strainer or jelly-bag and leave for 24 hours.

Next day take the apple pulp and the liquid. Boil together, and to every pint add 1 lb. preserving sugar and the strained lemon juice. Boil the whole quickly until it coats the back of the wooden spoon with which it is stirred. Put into small moulds or jars and tie down, when cold, in the usual way. It is delicious for tea, or with roast pork, and makes a pleasant addition to a crust of bread and cheese.

From Mrs. Frank Carding, Nottinghamshire.

APRICOT CURD

½ lb. apricots.
1 lemon.
2 ozs. butter.

½ lb. castor sugar.
Very little water.
2 eggs.

WASH the fruit and put in a preserving-pan, or saucepan, with a very little water and cook until soft; then pass it through a sieve. Put the fruit into a double saucepan, with the sugar, butter, the juice and grated rind of the lemon. When the sugar has dissolved, add the beaten eggs and stir mixture until it thickens. Pour into hot jars and cover.

From Mrs. E. A. Thomas, Surrey.

APRICOT JAM

2 lbs. dried apricots.
6 lbs. preserving sugar.

3 quarts water.
1 oz. bitter almonds.

WASH the apricots quickly in warm water and then soak them in 3 quarts of fresh, cold water for 24 hours. Boil fast for ½ hour. Add the sugar and stir over a low fire until it has dissolved. Bring to the boil again and boil fast until it sets. Pour boiling water on to the almonds and rub off the skins. Put the almonds into the jam as soon as it has finished boiling. This makes about 12 lbs. of jam which is both good and cheap.

From Mrs. M. A. Armstrong, Co. Durham.

BITTER ROWAN JELLY

PICK the rowan berries clean from the stalks and stew them down to as near a pulp as you can, with enough water to cover them, and a tiny pinch of ginger. Crush and strain the pulp and boil it up again for ½ hour, with only ⅔ of its weight in sugar. Put into small jars. It will become firm as it cools.

From Mrs. E. G. Mactier, Wigtownshire.

BLACKBERRIES

2 lbs. sugar.
2 pints water.

8 lbs. blackberries.
1 teaspoonful salicylic acid.

THE following is an excellent method of preserving black-berries, being always ready to serve as stewed fruit, and can also be quickly made into jam by the addition of extra sugar.

Boil sugar and water for 15 minutes, add fruit and cook till it is soft, not "mushy." Put in a stone jar, sprinkle acid on top, tie down at once with brown paper.

This can be used as required and tied down again.

From Mrs. Bell, Cumberland.

BLACKBERRIES AND APPLES

BOIL and strain the blackberries as though you were going to make jelly. Cut up your apples in slices and put into bottles or Kilner jars and instead of filling up with water in the usual way, fill the jars with the blackberry jelly, using ⅔ jelly and ⅓ water. Seal and sterilize in the usual way. No sugar is needed, and these make delicious pies. You can also make jam with it later on.

From Mrs. J. W. Oglanby, Berkshire.

BLACKBERRY AND APPLE JAM

3½ lbs. apples (windfalls will do).
3½ lbs. sugar.

2 lbs. blackberries.

PEEL, core and cut apples into thin slices and put in pre-serving-pan with a teacupful of water. Let them simmer until tender; then add blackberries and boil together for 5 minutes before adding sugar.

Bring to the boil and boil well for 25 to 30 minutes. You will find this jam very economical.

From Mrs. C. Harper, Warwickshire.

BLACKBERRY AND ELDERBERRY JAM

TAKE equal quantities of blackberries and elderberries (stripped of the stalks), put in a preserving-pan, squeeze slightly, bring slowly to the boil and boil for 20 minutes. Allow ¾ lb. of sugar to each 1 lb. of fruit. Put sugar on a dish and place in the oven to get hot before adding it to the jam. Bring again to the boil and boil for 20 minutes. Cover while hot. This jam is cheap and will keep for 12 months.

From Miss F. McIntyre, Suffolk.

BLACKBERRY AND SLOE JELLY

2 lbs. sloes.   8 lbs. blackberries.
3 pints water   5 lbs. sugar.

BOIL fruit well until bleached-looking. Then squeeze through double butter muslin, or a sieve, or a jelly-bag. To 7 or 8 pints of the juice add 5 lbs. sugar and boil up as quickly as possible, about ½ hour or less. To test whether it is set, put a spoonful on a plate. These quantities make about 11½ lbs. of good, clear jelly.

From Mrs. Jerram, Devonshire.

BLACKCURRANT JAM

3 lbs. sugar.   To every 1½ lbs. of fruit.
1 pint of water.

STALK and cut brown ends off fruit. Boil fruit and water together for 20 minutes, then add the sugar and boil for 5 minutes. Made in this way, the preserve will keep for 2 or 3 years.

From Mrs. Ford, Gloucestershire.

BRAMBLE AND APPLE MARMALADE

BOIL together equal quantities of apples and brambles. The apples should be washed first, but they should not be peeled or cored. Cut them up roughly, add the brambles (washed) and barely covered with cold water. Bring very slowly to the boil, and when the apples are reduced to a pulp, rub the contents of the pan through a sieve, leaving only the skins and the seeds. To every pound of pulp add 1 lb. sugar. Boil together for ½ hour, stirring constantly, as, being thick, the pulp is apt to burn. If poured into moulds this marmalade will turn out quite stiffly. In any case, it cuts like blancmange and is delicious served with milk pudding.

From Miss Christian Milne, Aberdeenshire.

BRAMBLE CONSERVE

TO every 1 lb. ripe brambles put 1 lb. sour apples. Wash apples and cut up roughly, without peeling or coring. Place in the preserving-pan with about half their bulk in water, and bring slowly to the boil. Boil gently until apples are soft, then rub as much of the pulp as possible through a fine wire sieve.

Place the brambles in jars with 1 gill of water to each 1 lb. of fruit, and leave till juice flows freely; then pass through a wire sieve. Measure the juice of both fruits, allow 1 lb. of sugar to each pint, and put both kinds together with the sugar in the preserving-pan. Set pan on stove and bring gradually to the boil, stirring frequently till the sugar is melted. Then boil briskly until the conserve thickens—about 15 minutes or a little more.

From Mrs. M. S. McLaren, Scotland.

BRAMBLE JAM

LAST year my bramble-jam experiment was so successful I pass on the method—which is, actually, the one I use for raspberries. It is simplicity itself and the result is a delicious preserve with the full flavour of the fruit.

Into a bowl I place the well-picked blackberries, very ripe and free from stalks, etc. This I weigh (i.e., bowl and fruit), leaving on the weights while I put the berries into a preserving-pan. Into the bowl I now place sugar to equal weight of the fruit (or if the preserve is to be used soon, about $\frac{3}{4}$ of the weight) This I add to the fruit in the pan, bring it quickly to boiling-point, then boil it quickly for 3 minutes. With the equal quantities of sugar and fruit, the preserve has kept perfectly for a year, and has retained the full flavour of the ripe blackberries.

From Mrs. R. Weir, Selkirkshire.

CANDIED PEEL

TAKE 8 oranges or 8 lemons or 4 of each and wash them. Cut the lemons lengthwise and the oranges crosswise. Remove all pulp. Dissolve $\frac{1}{2}$ oz. bicarbonate of soda in a little hot water and pour it over the pieces of peel; then add sufficient boiling water to cover the peel entirely. Allow to stand for 20 minutes then rinse the peel in several waters. Cover the peel with cold water; bring to the boil and simmer until tender. Make a syrup of 1 lb. of sugar with $\frac{3}{4}$ of a pint of water; pour it over the peel and stand for 2 days. Draw off the syrup and add to it another $\frac{1}{2}$ lb. sugar. Bring to the boil and simmer the peel in it until it looks clear. Take out the peel and dry it in a cool oven. Reduce the syrup by boiling it for about $\frac{1}{2}$ hour. Dip the peel in it and once more dry in a cool oven. The syrup left over may be beaten up until it is cloudy and thick and then a little may be poured into each cup-shaped piece of candied peel.

From Mrs. E. Anderson, Kent.

CANDIED TOMATOES

4 lbs. yellow tomatoes.	1 lb. loaf sugar.
2 lemons.	1 pint water.

POUR boiling water over the tomatoes, then peel them. Boil the sugar in a pint of water. Remove any scum, slice the lemons and add them. Then put in the tomatoes and simmer slowly until they look clear. Take out with a slice and put on a sieve. Boil the syrup until quite thick, then put the tomatoes in again. Simmer slowly for about 1 hour, then take out on the sieve again. Repeat once more, then flatten the tomatoes with a wooden spoon and dry in a warm oven. When dry put in glass jars.

From Miss D. Jeans, Leicestershire.

CHESTNUT JAM

2 lbs. sweet chestnuts.
1½ lbs. loaf sugar.

1 teaspoon vanilla essence.
½ pint water to make the syrup.

BOIL the chestnuts until ready. Peel and skin them. Time can be saved both in boiling and peeling them if you first cut a cross on both sides of the chestnuts. They should boil for 20 minutes to ½ hour. Then crush through a wire sieve.

Make a syrup with ½ pint of water, sugar and essence. When it is ready put in the crushed chestnuts, and cook gently until fairly stiff. Put in hot glass jars and cover. Always store this jam in a dry place.

From Miss Alice Wakelin, Cambridgeshire.

COUNTRY MINCEMEAT

FOR mincemeat I choose a large brown crock and into it put all sweet dessert apples—windfalls or faulty—chopped up with spices and usually Demerara sugar; but this year it has had to be honey. I add to it more apples, currants, sultanas or raisins, or any nice things available, including finely-chopped orange and lemon peel and the kernels of stone fruits I have saved. A little later on a few quinces improve it, also a little home-made wine, and I continue adding to it until the whole jar is full.

This proves a good winter standby, usually lasting until Easter, by which time it has acquired a nice winey taste. If it gets rather thin at the bottom of the jar, a few cake crumbs, breadcrumbs, or a little flour can be added, like Banbury cakes. If this winey flavour is not liked, when all the ingredients are mixed, the mincemeat can be put in Kilner jars, sterilized, and sealed.

From Miss Elsie G. Cook, Oxfordshire.

CRANBERRY PRESERVE

CRANBERRIES can be covered with water, brought to the boil, boiled for 10 to 15 minutes, put in large jars and covered. Then you can boil them with sugar when convenient. You can have always fresh-boiled jam.

From Mrs. L. Ingram, Aberdeenshire.

DAMSON AND APPLE JELLY

USING equal quantities of damsons and apples, add ½ pint of cold water to 1 lb. of fruit. Boil until fruit is quite soft. Strain through muslin; weigh the juice, and allow 1 lb. sugar to 1 lb. of the liquid. Boil the juice quickly for 15 minutes, then add sugar and boil together for ½ hour. This jelly is perfectly clear, and will keep for 12 months at least.

From Mrs. M. F. Corfield, Montgomeryshire.

DAMSON CHEESE

PUT some sound ripe fruit into a stone jar (or casserole), cover it, and bake in a very cool oven until the damsons are tender. Then drain off the juice, skin and stone the fruit, and put it into a preserving-pan. Pour back on them from a third, to half, of their juice, and boil over a clear fire until they form a dry paste. Add fine sugar, in the proportion of 6 ozs. to each pound of the fruit. Then stir continuously over the fire until the sugar has dissolved, and the fruit comes away dry from the sides of the pan. Press it into small jars, or moulds, and when perfectly cold place on the top of each a round of paper that has been dipped in spirit. Fasten securely, and store in a dry place. Will keep for months.

From Miss E. Evans, Northamptonshire.

DAMSON JAM

4 lbs. damsons (ripe).   ¾ cupful (small) of vinegar.
4 lbs. sugar.   ¾ cupful of water.

PUT the vinegar, sugar and water into pan, and boil until it syrups; then put in ripe fruit and boil 10 minutes.

From Miss M. A. Hutchinson, Kendal.

EMERGENCY MARMALADE

8 sweet oranges.   10 pints water.
2 large grapefruits.   7 lbs. sugar.
2 lemons.

REMOVE the juice and pips from the fruit. Put the fruit through the mincer and soak with the juice and water for 48 hours. Tie up pips in muslin and add to the above. After soaking, boil until the fruit is tender (about 2 hours). Remove the bag of pips and add the sugar; boil fast until marmalade jellies. This quantity makes about 15 lbs.

From Miss E. Lenton, Huntingdonshire.

226

FIG AND LEMON PRESERVE

2 lbs. figs.
2 pints cold water.

4 lemons (rind and juice).
3 lbs. sugar.

WASH the figs, remove the stalks and cut into about 6 pieces. Put them into a basin with the water and leave soaking for 24 hours. Turn into a preserving-pan, add sugar and cook slowly until dissolved, then bring to the boil and remove the scum. Wipe lemons and grate rind finely, squeeze out juice and strain it. Add both these to the figs and boil all together until it will jelly when cold, keeping it stirred and skimmed as required. Cool, pot and when cold, tie down.

From Mrs. W. A. Francy, Leicestershire.

GLACÉ GRAPES

½ lb. green grapes.
8 ozs. golden syrup.

1 cupful Demerara sugar.
2 ozs. unsalted butter.

MELT butter in a pan, add golden syrup and sugar, then stir till boiling. Boil till a little tested in cold water hardens, then remove from heat. While the mixture is cooling, cut grapes from stem in clusters of 2 or 3 and suspend them on a string. Dip in one cluster at a time in the mixture, and hang up on string to set. Serve on a glass dish lined with leaves.

From Mrs. C. Gibbons, Cheshire.

GOLDEN APPLE MINCEMEAT

2 lbs. sweet apples.
1½ lbs. sugar.
Juice of 1 lemon.
1 teaspoonful of ratafia essence.
¼ lb. of lemon peel.

2 lbs. sultanas.
1 teaspoonful ground ginger.
½ teaspoonful mace.
1 pint of water.

THIS makes a delicious filling for flans, tartlets and biscuits, and as it is cooked, is always ready. It keeps splendidly. Pippins give a delightful flavour and make the mincemeat a lovely golden colour.

Peel and core the apples and cut into dice. Shred the lemon peel. Butter the bottom of a pan and put in the apples, sultanas and water. Cook gently for 20 minutes. Rub the spices into the sugar and add with lemon juice. Boil for 20 minutes. Allow to cool, then stir in ratafia and turn into small jam-jars. Cover.

From Mrs. A. Adlem, Dorsetshire.

GOOSEBERRY MINT JELLY

2 lbs. green gooseberries.
½ doz. stalks fresh green mint.

Sugar.

WASH the gooseberries and put them in a preserving-pan; nearly cover them with cold water, and cook until they are soft and pulpy. Strain the fruit through a sieve, being careful to extract all the juice. To each pint of liquid add 1 lb. of sugar, put in a preserving-pan with mint tied in a bundle. Boil gently until the jelly will set, stirring frequently. Remove the mint, pour the jelly into pots, and seal at once.

From Mrs. A. Jones, Flintshire.

GRAPEFRUIT MARMALADE

3 lbs. grapefruit.
2 small lemons.

4½ pints water.
7½ lbs. sugar.

SLICE the grapefruit finely, place the lemon and grapefruit pips in 1 pint of boiling water and soak. Grate the rind of the lemons, peel them, throw away the pith of the rind. Add the grated rind and the inside of the lemons, finely chopped, to the grapefruit, and cover with the remaining 3½ pints of cold water. Stand for about 24 hours. Place in the preserving-pan with the water strained from the pips and simmer for ½ hour. Be very careful not to let it boil. Then add the sugar and bring to the boil. Boil rapidly for about 1 hour, or until it sets when tested. Pour into hot jars and tie down when cold.

From Mrs. E. S. Willcocks, Cornwall.

GREEN TOMATO AND APPLE MARMALADE

TAKE 1 lb. tomatoes and 1 lb. apples. Slice the tomatoes thinly and cut the peeled and cored apples into small chunks. Place in an earthenware bowl; add 1¼ lbs. granulated sugar, 2 tablespoonfuls vinegar and 2 tablespoonfuls water. Stir well with a wooden spoon; leave for a day or two, stirring occasionally—it should soon become a syrupy mass. Turn into a preserving-pan and bring to the boil. Boil until the apple is transparent—about 40 minutes. Pot in the usual way. The apple chunks will be slightly tough, somewhat resembling "chunky" marmalade, though, of course, without the orange flavour. It is quite nice, and better for keeping a little while.

From Mrs. A. Adlem, Dorsetshire.

GREEN TOMATO JAM

4 lbs. tomatoes.   3 lbs. preserving sugar.
Flavouring.

BREAK up the tomatoes, put them into the preserving-pan, and let them come to the boil. Add the sugar, a few cloves, or a small piece of whole ginger, or the grated rind of a lemon for flavouring. Boil fast for 20 minutes. It will set when placed on a plate in a cool place. This is an excellent way of preserving outdoor tomatoes that do not ripen well.

From Mrs. Baker, Monmouthshire.

HAW JELLY
(*Excellent with Cold Meat*)

GATHER 3 lbs. haws, wash them well and put into a pan with 3 pints of water; simmer for 1 hour, then pour into a jelly-bag and leave to strain overnight. Next morning measure the juice and return to the pan with 1 lb. of sugar and the strained juice of 1 lemon to each pint of juice. Boil until the jelly will set when tested.

From Miss E. Rutherford, Northumberland.

HIP-APPLE JAM

COVER 1 lb. rose hips with 1½ pints of water and simmer for 2 hours. Strain juice through fine muslin and let stand all night to drip. Next day slice up 1 lb. apples and cook until they pulp. Add ¾ lb. sugar, and boil fast for ½ hour.

From Mrs. W. Barrett, Essex.

HOME-MADE PECTIN

APPLES contain a large amount of pectin, and those house-wives who are fortunate enough to have a good crop would perhaps like to try the following recipe.

Choose apples of the soft kind which "fall" when cooked. Prepare as for jelly making and when cooking barely cover the apples with water. Strain through a coarse jelly-bag, but do not squeeze. Several lots can be prepared in this way and bottled in one operation. Heat to actual boiling-point and have ready screw-topped bottles of the Kilner type which must also have been heated to prevent cracking when the liquid is poured in. Screw down at once as in fruit bottling and store away until next summer, and use in the proportion of 1 lb. fruit, ¾ lb. sugar, ½ pt. pectin.

A slight cloudiness need not cause anxiety as this automatically disappears in the process of jam or jelly making. Strawberry jam to which this apple pectin is added has a delightful flavour and sets beautifully, as also do the other fruits which contain very little natural pectin.

From L. Watson, Northamptonshire.

JAM AND JELLY FROM FALLEN APPLES AND PLUMS

JAM

3 lbs. apples.   3 lbs. plums.
Lump sugar.

PEEL and core the apples (save the peels and cores for making the jelly). Stone the plums, and cook the apples and plums with 1½ pints of water until soft. Then add sugar, and boil fast until it will set when tried on a plate. This will take about 20 minutes. Skim and put into jars, and tie down when cold.

JELLY

Having saved the peels and cores of the apples, put them into a large saucepan and just cover with water, cooking until pulpy. Strain through a jelly-bag; and measure. To every pint of juice add 1 lb. of lump sugar, and boil fast until it sets. This jelly is equal to that made from whole apples.

From Miss N. Fennell, Warwickshire.

JELLIED MARMALADE

USE 1 sweet orange and 1 lemon to every 4 Seville oranges. Allow roughly 1 pint of water to every pound of fruit. Grate off only the yellow rinds of fruit. Remove all the white pith. Slice the pulp and put it into a preserving-pan with the water. Boil for ½ hour. Stir occasionally. Strain through a sieve (hair) or clean scalded cloth. Measure the liquid, and allow 1 lb. of best sugar to each pint. Put the juice and sugar into a pan. Add the grated rinds of fruit. Stir until the sugar has melted. Boil fast from 10 to 15 minutes or until the mixture jellies when tested. Keep skimmed. Put into small pots and cover.

From Mrs. Letitia Davies, Carmarthenshire.

LEMON CHEESE

2 eggs.
2 lemons.

8 ozs. sugar.
5 ozs. butter.

PEEL the lemons as thinly as possible, and squeeze out the juice. Put both the rind and the juice in a saucepan with the sugar and butter and dissolve very slowly. Beat up the eggs, then stir the lemon, etc., on to them. Strain, return to the pan, and stir over a low burner until the mixture comes to the boil and is thick and creamy. The cheese may be made most satisfactorily in a double saucepan. The steaming ensures the slow melting of the sugar and butter which is so essential. I find this recipe most useful as a means of using up cracked eggs.

From Mrs. E. Beveridge, Fifeshire.

LEMON CURD

1 oz. margarine.
½ lb. sugar.

2 lemons.
2 eggs.

PUT the grated rind of lemons, the juice, margarine, and sugar either into a double saucepan, or a basin or stone jam-jar, and stand in a saucepan half full of boiling water. While this is getting hot, beat the eggs. Stir into other ingredients and cook till thick. This takes about ½ hour and keeps very well.

From Mrs. M. Humphries, Bedfordshire.

MARROW CREAM

2 lbs. marrow.
2 lbs. lump sugar.

¼ lb. butter.
2 lemons.

PEEL the marrow and boil until it is quite soft; strain well and beat to a pulp. Then put into a saucepan with the sugar, butter, and the juice and grated rind of the lemons. Boil slowly all together for ¾ hour. This makes a filling equally as nice as lemon cheese.

From Mrs. S. Mills, Warwickshire.

MARROW JAM

5½ lbs. marrow.
5½ lbs. sugar.
Salt.

3 lemons.
½ lb. crystallized ginger.

231

CUT up the marrow; place in a bowl; sprinkle ¾ of a teaspoonful of salt; leave for 12 hours. Then strain off the
salty water, and put the sugar on the marrow; allow to stand
for 12 hours or longer. Add the lemons and the ginger cut
small, and boil all together until the marrow is quite transparent.

From Mrs. H. W. Oglesby, E. Yorkshire.

MARROW AND PINEAPPLE JAM

PEEL a marrow, remove the seeds, cut into small pieces,
weigh, and to each pound of marrow add ¾ lb. sugar. Put
into a stone jar and leave overnight. Next day add the chunks
—1 small tin to each 2 lb. marrow (without the syrup). Cut
each chunk into 3 or 4 pieces. Boil for 2 hours or until the pine
is soft and the jam sets. This is delicious for pastry tarts.

From Mrs. F. Steward, Suffolk.

ORANGE AND APPLE CURD

1 orange; the peel from 2 more.	1 lb. apples when prepared.
1 lb. sugar.	1 pint water.
2 tablespoonfuls plain flour.	

PUT prepared fruit through the mincer; cover with the pint
of water. Let this stand overnight. Bring to the boil and
cook till tender. Add sugar and stir till dissolved.

Mix flour to a thin paste with a little cold water and add to
the boiling fruit and sugar. Keep stirring and simmer for
7 minutes. Pour in warm jars and seal. This makes about 4 lbs.
of a cross between marmalade and orange curd and will keep
for a month.

From Mrs. Bateman, Leicestershire.

ORANGE HONEY

1 orange.	1 small teacupful water.
1 lb. granulated sugar.	

DISSOLVE sugar slowly in the water, then boil briskly for
10 minutes without stirring. Take off the fire, add the
juice and rind of the orange—a fine bread grater removes the
latter in dainty fragments.

Allow to cool slightly, then stir with a wooden spoon until
it becomes creamy. Whilst it is still liquid, pour into a jar. It
will set to the consistency of honey.

From Miss C. Milne, Aberdeenshire.

PEAR PRESERVE

THIS preserve has been a great favourite in our family for years and is good eaten with blancmange, semolina, etc.

It is very useful because any kind of dry pear will do, such as the Blakeney or brown pear and, as it is cut in quarters, even smaller, damaged ones may be used.

To 1 lb. of pears, after being peeled and cored, take ¾ lb. of sugar. Boil for 1½ hours or until cooked. To every 6 lbs. of preserve add 1 teacupful of vinegar and boil for 20 minutes. Add root ginger, crushed, to suit taste.

From Mrs. H. M. Rooker, Gloucestershire.

PINEAPPLE MARMALADE

3 jaffa oranges.   4 lbs. sugar.
1 lemon.   1 pint water.
1 large tin of pineapple.

WASH and peel both the lemon and oranges; cut up the peel in thin shreds, and the fruit into small cubes; cover with pineapple juice and 1 pint of water, leaving to soak all night. Then simmer gently in a preserving-pan until tender, add sugar and cook for ¾ hour, put in glass jars and seal when cool.

From Miss M. Cooke, Lincolnshire.

POTTED BRAMBLES

4 lbs. of brambles.   4 lbs. sugar.
1 oz. butter.

PICK over brambles, using also bruised ones. Heat sugar in a bowl in warm oven. Rub butter round preserving-pan, put over low heat. Put berries in; and when they start to bubble, pour in warm sugar. Beat with a wooden spoon for 30 minutes. Put into pots and seal. This makes 8 lbs.

From Miss E. Rutherford, Northumberland.

POTTED RASPBERRIES

4 lbs. fine white sugar.   1 oz. fresh butter.
4 lbs. raspberries.

PICK over the berries, using also the bruised ones. Have sugar heated in a bowl in a warm oven. Rub butter round a preserving-pan, put over a very low gas, and place the berries in. When they start to bubble, pour in the warmed sugar. Beat with a wooden spoon for 30 minutes and put into pots and cover.

This will make 8 lbs. of a lovely preserve with real raspberry flavour and colour. There is no waste, and it will keep indefinitely.

From Mrs. J. A. Forbes, Co. Tyrone.

PRESERVING PLUMS AS PRUNES

GET a shallow wooden box and stack the plums close together, stalks uppermost. Cover with a sheet of kitchen paper. Place on a rack above the stove for 18 hours; and afterwards at every opportunity when the oven is not required allow it to cool and then place the box of plums in it, and leave the door open. As they shrink, place the plums closer together in the box.

When sufficiently dried, which will take 3 days, pack in airtight jars and store in a dry cupboard. If the box is placed in a hot airing cupboard, the final drying can be more quickly accomplished.

From Mrs. A. Shute, Dorsetshire.

PRESERVED CHERRIES

TAKE fine sugar, put a little water to it, and boil it. Stone your cherries, put them in the sugar, boil, and let them stand in the syrup 2 or 3 days. Boil the syrup again, pour it over the cherries, let them stand some time, then lay them on a sieve to dry.

From N. A. Robby, Cumberland.

QUINCE JELLY

PARE and slice the quinces, and put in a preserving-pan with sufficient water to float them. Boil until fruit is reduced to a pulp. Strain the clear juice through a jelly bag, and to each pint allow 1 lb. loaf sugar. Boil juice and sugar together for about $\frac{3}{4}$ hour, removing all scum as it rises; and, when the jelly appears firm, pot up at once into small jars.

QUINCE JAM
(From the pulp left over from the preceding recipe)

PUT the pulp through a sieve, or mash very finely with
wooden spoon. Put ½ lb. granulated sugar to each 1 lb. of
pulp, and boil till it sets. Keep well stirred to prevent burning.
Cover when cold.

From Miss H. Jenner, Kent.

RASPBERRY JAM

TO every ¾ lb. of raspberries, allow ¼ lb. rhubarb and 1 lb.
of sugar.

Remove stalks from raspberries; cut rhubarb into small
slices, about ¼ or ½ in. thick. Put raspberries and rhubarb into
preserving-pan and let them boil gently for about ½ hour,
stirring well with wooden spoon to prevent sticking. Add sugar
and boil again for another ½ hour. Pour into pots and cover
whilst hot.

From Mrs. L. D. Martin ,Berkshire.

RASPBERRY PRESERVE

4 lbs. raspberries.   5 lbs. sugar.

PLACE the raspberries on a large dish and put into a hot
oven. Then place the sugar on another large dish and put
that also into the oven. When they are very hot (not boiling),
beat the fruit thoroughly, then gradually add the hot sugar,
beating all well together until the sugar is dissolved. It is then
ready to be put in the jars. This jam will keep any length of
time, and has the flavour of freshly-gathered fruit. It is easily
made, as there is no boiling or simmering.

From Mrs. B. A. Moor, Yorkshire.

RHUBARB CONSERVE

TAKE as much rhubarb as you wish, when it is tender and
full grown. Cut off both ends of each stick, but do not peel
it. Rub with a cloth and cut in pieces about 1 in. long. To each
pound of rhubarb allow 1 lb. of sugar, and put alternately into

a dish. Let it stand 24 hours, by which time the sugar should be in a liquid state. Pour the liquid in a pan and boil briskly for ½ hour, then add the rhubarb with crystallized ginger (about 2 ozs. to 1 lb. rhubarb, or more if liked), boil for another ½-hour. Take off the fire and let it stand for ½ hour before putting into pots.

From Miss E. T. Daltry, Kent.

RHUBARB AND MINT JELLY
(*for serving with lamb*)

WIPE some rhubarb and cut into pieces. Stew until soft and pulpy, then strain through a fine sieve. To each pint of juice allow 1 lb. of loaf sugar. Put juice and sugar into a preserving-pan with some fresh clean mint tied into bundles.

Boil until the jelly thickens when tested on a cold plate, stirring often. Remove mint before pouring into small pots. Choose rhubarb that has pale pink stalks.

From Mrs. Foster, Sussex.

RHUBARB AND MIXED PEEL JAM

4 lbs. rhubarb.   ½ lb. mixed peel.
4 lbs. sugar.

WIPE the rhubarb without peeling, slice it the long way of the sticks, and cut into pieces about the size of a large pea. Put the rhubarb and sugar in layers with the mixed peel in a preserving-pan, and let it remain till the next day. Strain off the juice, and boil for ¼ hour. Then pour it over the fruit, covering the pan to keep in the steam. Next day boil jam quickly for about ½ hour, or till it jells. Many people who do not like rhubarb jam made in the usual way appreciate this recipe.

From Miss V. Wadman, Wiltshire.

RHUBARB AND ORANGE JAM

TO every pound of rhubarb, add 2 fair-sized apples and 2 sweet oranges, 4 ozs. sugar, ¼ teaspoonful each of mixed spice and ground ginger, ½ teaspoonful of salt. Bring slowly to the boil, then boil briskly for 20 minutes, or till the apple slices are clear.

From Mrs. E. Downes, Shropshire.

ROSE-HIP APPLE JELLY

4 lbs. windfall apples, after any bruised or damaged parts have been removed.

2 lbs. of firm, just ripe, rose hips. Sugar.

CUT up apples and put into a preserving-pan with enough water to cover, and one pint extra for rose hips. While apples are cooking to a pulp, put rose hips through coarsest cutter of the mincer.

Add minced rose hips when apples are cooked, draw pan from heat, and just simmer for 10 minutes. Move away to stop it simmering; and leave another 10 minutes before straining through a thick jelly-bag. Leave to drip overnight. Next day measure the juice and allow 14 oz. sugar to each pint of juice. Measure sugar and put in oven to heat through thoroughly, add to juice when it has boiled 3 minutes. Test for setting and when ready pour into warm jars and tie down.

This jelly is a most attractive rose colour and has a delicious flavour.

From Mrs. McLennan, Argyllshire.

ROSE-HIP HONEY

IN making preserve use a wooden spoon, or the jam will be darkened in colour.

Take 1 lb. of hips and cover with water and boil until tender. Strain through a jelly-bag one night. Next day pulp $\frac{3}{4}$ lb. of cooking apples in a little water. Add to hip juice and measure. Return to pan and add 1 lb. of sugar to 1 pint of fruit juice. Cook until it sets when tested. Put into hot jars and tie down.

From Miss M. Bond, Somersetshire.

ROSE PETAL JAM

ROSE petals make a delicious jam, the old-fashioned damask roses are the best and you may gather them over two or three days, putting them in a deep crock as you do so, squeezing a little lemon juice over them. Cover the crock.

When you have enough, measure by weighing and allow $\frac{1}{2}$ lb. of sugar and $\frac{1}{2}$ lb. of honey to each pound of petals, add a very little water, then boil gently till the jam sets. Bottle as usual.

From Mrs. Thomas, Sussex.

237

ROWAN JELLY

TAKE 3 lbs. ripe rowan berries; pick the berries over, wash them, place in a preserving-pan with just enough water to prevent burning. Cook slowly until the berries are reduced to a pulp. Strain through a jelly-bag.

Next take 3 lbs. crab apples, wash and quarter. Barely cover with water, then boil gently until soft and pulpy. Strain. Mix both juices, weigh, and to every pound of juice add 1 lb. sugar. Boil rapidly for 20 to 30 minutes, or until the jelly "sets" when tested on a cold plate.

This is a firm, bright pink jelly, with a delightfully piquant flavour. To those who think that equal quantities of fruit produce too acid a preserve, this jelly may be made with 2 lbs. of rowans to 4 lbs. apples.

From Miss Christian Milne, Aberdeenshire.

SLOE AND APPLE JELLY

STEW equal quantities of ripe sloes and green apples (skins and cores included) until soft, barely covering the fruit in the stew-pan with water. Strain through a jelly-bag. To each pint of juice add 1 lb. of sugar. Bring to the boil and boil until a little sets when tested.

This jelly has a piquant flavour quite its own, and is delicious with mutton, hare or rabbit.

From Mrs. F. B. Jacob, Co. Wexford.

SLOE AND APPLE CHEESE

MAKE exactly as previous recipe, but put fruit through a sieve when cooked instead of through a jelly-bag. Add 14 ozs. of sugar to each pint of pulp.

From Mrs. F. B. Jacob, Co. Wexford.

SLOE JELLY

3 lbs. sloes (very ripe).   1 lb. apples.
Sugar.

COVER sloes and apples with water. Bring to boil, and boil until fruit is soft. Strain. To every pint of liquid add 1½ lbs. sugar. Bring to boil. Boil gently until a trial sample skins over. Be careful not to boil too long, as the extra sugar may make the jelly sugary.

From Mrs. Birkett, Cumberland.

SPICED BRAMBLE JELLY

CAREFULLY pick over and wash brambles. Put into a pre-serving-pan and cover with water. Add nutmeg, mace and cinnamon in the proportion of a saltspoonful of mixed spices to 1 lb. of fruit.

Bring to the boil, and then simmer very slowly until all the juice is extracted from the fruit; pour through a jelly-bag. Next day, put the juice in the pan with 1 lb. of sugar to each pint of juice and boil rapidly for 30 minutes, or until it jellies when tested. Put into warm jars and tie down.

The flavour of this jelly is much appreciated by those who like something more than just a sweet taste. The spice gives an additional elusive flavour that charms.

SPICED BRAMBLE CHEESE

WITH the pulp left in jelly-bag, this delicious cheese can be made—and so all waste is avoided.

Rub pulp through a wire sieve and to each pound add ¾ lb. sugar and leave for some hours to melt. Add the juice and grated rind of a lemon; boil all together, carefully stirring all the time. Pot and seal. This makes a delicious preserve for breakfast.

Both recipes from Miss E. Rutherford, Northumberland.

SUGARLESS RASPBERRY JAM

3 tablespoonfuls boiled water.	16 saccharine tablets.
½ oz. powdered gelatine.	1 lb. raspberries.

SOAK the gelatine in the boiled water. Stew the raspberries gently until reduced to ⅔ of the original bulk. Grind the saccharine to a powder, and add a teaspoonful of water to them. Add this to the fruit, and stir in the soaked gelatine. Put into clean glass fruit-bottling jars; sterilize and screw up tightly.

This jam is appreciated by those who, for health reasons, are unable to eat ordinary jam. Make small quantities only at a time if gelatine is used, as it will not keep.

From Miss Christian Milne, Aberdeenshire.

SWEET SPICED APPLE PRESERVE

8 lbs. apples (weighed after being peeled and cored).	5 lbs. sugar.
½ pint water.	½ pint vinégar.
	12 cloves.

239

MIX all together, leave standing overnight. Next morning place in pan with cloves tied in muslin bag. Bring to boil, cook 45 minutes, keeping well stirred to prevent burning. Pot and cover.

This is good in tarts and puddings. A few currants, cinnamon or sultanas provide variety if desired. This also keeps well, will last till next year's apple crop comes along.

From Mrs. Lane, Kent.

TOMATO MARMALADE

7 lbs. tomatoes.	½ pint water.
8 lbs. loaf sugar.	6 lemons.

SKIN tomatoes and cut in halves. Peel lemons and cut in slices. Put sugar and water in a pan. Stir gently till the sugar is dissolved. Skim and boil to a syrup. Add tomatoes and lemons and boil, stirring all the time. Remove scum as it rises. When the marmalade is sufficiently cooked it will hang in thick gelatinous flakes. When done, fill into jars and store.

From Mrs. Smith, Yorkshire.

PIG CURING and BY-PRODUCTS

BEER AND JUNIPER CURE FOR HAMS

A ham of 16 lbs.
1 lb. soft brown sugar.
½ oz. bay salt.
3 pints of beer.

1 lb. salt.
¼ lb. juniper berries.
½ oz. saltpetre.

PUT all above ingredients into a saucepan and just let it boil. Leave the liquor to get cold and pour over the ham. Rub every day for first few days—then every 2 or 3 days for a month —then take out of pickle, hang up and dry.

From Miss L. A. Honour, Oxfordshire.

CUMBERLAND CURE

A 20 st. pig.
¼ lb. saltpetre.

1½ st. salt.
1 lb. brown sugar.

LAY hams, flitches and shoulders on a stone slab, rind to the top. Rub salt into rind until moisture forms. Turn over, take out all blood veins and sprinkle all over with saltpetre and brown sugar (more so about the bones and veins), then cover

241

with salt. Leave 1 day, when salt will have moistened. Cover again, and do so each day for 3 or 4 days.

Take out flitches at the end of 14 days, shoulders and hams at the end of 21 days. Wash all pieces with a cloth dipped in lukewarm water and hang to dry. Curing time from November until March.

From Mrs. T. Fox, Cumberland.

HOME FREEZING OF PORK

To Home Freeze Pork

INSTEAD of pig-curing today many farmer's wives get a pig killed and put the meat into the deep freezer. Here are some short notes on packaging the meat after cutting up, which is best done by the butcher.
Packaging.

Use only special quality moisture-vapour-proof polythene paper and bags.

1. Select best cuts of meat, hung for the required time.
2. Freeze joints of sizes suitable for use on one occasion.
3. If convenient, freeze boned joints—they take up less space. If bones are not removed, wrap any sharp ends with several thicknesses of greaseproof paper to avoid the wrapping being pierced.
4. Wipe meat with a clean cloth.
5. Wrap in polythene paper or bag—exclude as much air as possible.
6. Seal and label.
7. Chops or steak. Wrap each separately in polythene or transparent paper and place in polythene bag, then the required number can be easily removed.
8. Thaw joints of meat slowly if possible, in refrigerator overnight—as there is less loss of juices. Cook immediately. On no account should thawed meat be refrozen, unless it has been cooked.
9. Pork will keep up to 4 months in a home cabinet but it should be looked at occasionally and if the fat is going at all yellow it should be used at once.
10. Pork offal can be deep frozen but should be used within 2 months.

DEVONSHIRE CURE

7 lbs. of bay salt.   2 ozs. of saltpetre.
1 lb. of treacle.

HAVE in a vessel 8 quarts of boiling water, add the above ingredients and stir until all are dissolved. Place freshly-cut hams in an earthenware standard, then, when pickle is cold, pour over them. After 6 weeks, take hams out, thoroughly dry them, put in muslin bags and store in malt dust or wood ashes. Better still, if an open fireplace is available, hang hams in the chimney for a fortnight before storing.

From Mrs. M. Tuckett, Devonshire.

HEREFORD HAM AND BACON CURES

For each stone of pork you will need:
1 lb. salt.   6 ozs. moist sugar.
1 oz. saltpetre.   ¾ pint pickling vinegar.

TO prepare: remove the backbone and ribs from the flitches and cut off the feet. Cut off the thick shoulder end as it takes longer to pickle than the rest of the flitch. Saw into the hip joints of the hams and remove the head of the thigh-bone. Sprinkle all the pieces of meat with plenty of salt and lay them on sloping boards for 24 hours to drain. Then wipe with a cloth.

To pickle: First rub in the saltpetre, then the salt. Lay the pieces skin down on a little salt in a pickling trough, and spread the sugar on top. Leave for 3 days, then pour the vinegar into the trough.

Bathe the pieces with the pickle several times a day and turn them every other day. Bacon and cheeks will take 10 to 14 days. Hams and shoulders from 3 weeks to a calendar month according to the size.

Pork so cured will keep perfectly through the hot weather, if hung in a dry place and protected from flies. If liked, smoking is an advantage. If the above are found too salt, it is a good plan to soak the bacon for 12 to 24 hours before using.

From Mrs. M. Wilsdon, Herefordshire.

LEICESTERSHIRE METHOD

THE usual way to cure and preserve bacon is with salt and saltpetre. The method I adopt is, first to prick the hams and shoulders with a sharp pricker on the rind side—in about a score of places—then rub the rind with a small amount of saltpetre, finishing off with salt until it sweats. I don't use much saltpetre except round the bone of the hams and shoulders, as too much saltpetre has a tendency to make the meat hard.

Put on plenty of salt and then change the meat round in 3 days' time, adding more salt; about 3 weeks is the time I allow for curing.

When cured, I dry the meat well with a brush and cloth. I do not wash it as I think it causes reast. I then dredge it well with flour; this helps it to dry. When dry, I paint the meat side with paraffin wax—melt the wax and paint the meat side with a small brush. This has no taste or smell and will keep the meat from reast and also keeps out the flies, as it seals the meat. I have used this method for some years and have not known it to fail.

From W. M. Booth, Leicestershire.

LINCOLNSHIRE CURE

WHEN the pig is cut up ready for curing, I have ready 2 lumps of salt (about 3 to 3½ stone) cut up fine, and ½ to ¾ lb. of saltpetre. This quantity is for about a 30-stone pig.

Place the flitch in the salting tub and rub the rind well with a little saltpetre, paying particular attention to the shoulder part and where the bone has been cut off, putting a little extra saltpetre into the pocket part and filling it with salt. Rub all over with salt.

Turn the flitch over and leave it the meat side uppermost, then sprinkle it with saltpetre, rub all over with salt, and leave nicely covered all over with salt.

The ham is cured in the same way, but using a little more saltpetre as the ham is thicker. Let there be plenty of fresh air in the place where it is cured. After a day or two, if the salt has run into the meat and left bare places, cover them again with salt.

After about a month it is cured and should be taken out and the salt rubbed off and the meat hung up to dry. When dried a little, it will then be ready to put into a bacon bin or clean bacon bags to keep the flies from it.

I have used this method for 30 years and have never had

any go wrong. I put ¼ lb. brown sugar on the ham and shoulder, for moistness, but it cures without.

From Mrs. Mason, Lincolnshire.

NORTHAMPTONSHIRE HAMS

FOR a ham of 18 or 20 lbs. Rub well with salt and leave until the next day, then wipe dry with a cloth. Rub in 1 oz. of saltpetre. Mix together 1 lb. salt and ¼ lb. of pepper, rub with this each morning for 3 days, then pour over 1 lb. treacle, baste, turn each day for 1 month, from first putting in salt. Allow to drain for 1 day, then hang in a cool, dry place. When dry, tie up in ham bags, let hang for at least 3 months.

From Mrs. F. Cooch, Northamptonshire.

NOTTINGHAMSHIRE SWEET METHOD

THE following method has been used in my family for many years, and it is believed to be an old Nottinghamshire recipe.

Strew common salt over the meat and let it drain for a day and a night.

To every 5 lbs. of meat allow ¼ lb. of salt, 2 ozs. saltpetre, 1 oz. salt prunella, ¼ lb. sugar (coarse brown sugar if possible).

Pound the saltpetre and salt prunella very finely and mix with common salt and sugar. When well-blended, rub the bacon well; turn and rub every day for 3 weeks.

From Miss M. Neville, Essex.

OLD DERBYSHIRE CURED HAM
(*For a ham weighing* 10-12 *lbs.*)

1 pint old ale.	¾ lb. bag salt.
1 pint of stout.	¾ lb. coarse salt.
1 lb. treacle.	¼ oz. saltpetre.

PUT the ingredients into a saucepan, boil for about 5 minutes. While the mixture is boiling, rub the ham with coarse salt and put it in a large pickling-pan. Then pour over the mixture while it is hot. Keep the ham in pickle for 3 weeks, turning and rubbing it every day. After this, take out, put it into a thin cotton bag, and hang it up in the kitchen.

From Mrs. M. Johnson, Nottinghamshire.

PICKLING BACON

8 lbs. of salt.
¾ lb. brown sugar.
¼ lb. saltpetre.
4 gallons of water.

BOIL for 20 minutes and keep scum removed. When cold put the bacon in and leave about 10 days; turn every day. It does not need to be rubbed.

From Mrs. Sealey, Somersetshire.

PICKLING HAMS

A 20-lb. ham.
2 lbs. common salt.
1 oz. saltpetre.
1 lb. bay salt.
2 ozs. of mustard.
2 ozs. black pepper.

POUND all the ingredients and mix together, rub the hams with the mixture and let them lie in it for 4 days, rubbing them well every day. Then pour over them 1¼ lbs. of treacle. Keep them in the pickle for a month or 5 weeks. It is best to turn them and throw the pickle over them each day.

When taken from the pickle, put them in cold spring water for 24 hours, then hang them up to dry. When cooked the hams must not be soaked first, but put over the fire in cold water.

From Mrs. Sazley, Somersetshire.

ROCK SALT AND RED PEPPER

THOROUGHLY rub the fresh hams with a mixture of 4 lbs. good rough salt and 1½ ozs. saltpetre. Fine salt is of no use for curing hams. Place in a trough, rind downward; and allow to drain for 48 hours, by which time all impurities will have been forced out. Then the curing proper begins.

Make up a mixture of 4 lbs. crushed rock salt, 1½ ozs. saltpetre, 2 lbs. brown sugar, and 2 ozs. red pepper for 100 lbs. meat. Thoroughly rub in; then pile the hams in a tub, and cover the whole with ½ in. of salt. All the liquor now collecting should be poured over the meat. In 10 days' time, repeat the rubbing, and pile in the tub as before.

At the end of another 10 days the hams can be removed, the salt, etc., can be brushed off, the rinds thoroughly washed with warm water. They can now be rolled up, and the pieces tied in cloths, and hung up in a cool place ready for use.

From Miss Eliza Walker, Lanarkshire.

ROXBURGHSHIRE METHOD

TAKE ¾ lb. of brown sugar; ½ oz. of pepper, and mix together, in a basin. As hams are put into hogshead separately put a small quantity over each one. I have a hogshead kept specially for the purpose and I put a layer of salt in the bottom. I take hind quarters first and rub salt well into skin, then I turn it over and put a generous supply of salt thickly over fleshy parts. Where bones are taken out, I push salt well in, also in the shank ends.

Next, I take shoulders and do exactly the same as above. Lastly, the sides; rub skins well, also ends of each, turn skins and cover shoulders with salt. Cover with a clean cloth to exclude the air, and finally cover with a board to keep clean. After 12 days I take all out of hogshead, clean it out, and put shoulders in first, this time with a little fresh salt; repeat with hams next until all is done. I take sides out after about 3 weeks and roll, leave the hams another fortnight and hang them up.

I may add that I have salted all our pigs for years and never had a scrap of bad meat.

From Mrs. J. G. Martin, Roxburghshire.

SPICED AND ROLLED BACON

A 15-score pig.	28 lbs. salt.
2 lbs. brown sugar.	2 ozs. mixed spices.
2 ozs. Jamaica pepper.	1 oz. saltpetre.

I HAVE all the bones removed, even the ham ones, and cut the sides into halves. I take about 2 lbs. of salt and ½ oz. of saltpetre and rub the skin side until it sweats, putting a little of the remaining saltpetre into the places where the shoulder and loin bones came from, and giving the bacon a good rubbing all over the flesh side with whatever saltpetre I have left. Then I cover the pork completely with salt, about 7 lbs. to each piece.

I lay the meat in the salting trough, one piece on top of the other, and turn every second day for 12 days, putting the top one at the bottom, by which time the salt is absorbed. I brush off any surplus and sprinkle over with brown sugar, ½ lb. to each piece, and let it stand for 2 days more.

Then the bacon is ready for rolling. I put the spices and pepper into a dredger and give a sprinkle to each piece, then take a good strong twine or cord (not too thin), and tie round the roll every 2½ ins. till I come to the end. I make a strong loop to hang the rolls up by, and in a few days I can begin to use the bacon.

I've always done mine this way since coming to England from Scotland, and have never had a piece go wrong yet.

From Mrs. Jean A. Bryers, Northamptonshire.

SUFFOLK SWEET CURE

Here is a method of curing bacon and hams which was passed on to my husband and we have found it very successful:

1 qt. beer.	1 qt. best vinegar.
1 lb. gran. sugar.	½ oz. saltpetre.
1 lb. bay salt.	1 lb. cooking salt.
½ oz. peppercorns.	½ oz. cloves.

BOIL all together. Take 2 ozs. hops and boil in a quart of water for ½ hour, strain and add to liquid above. Pour over meat when cold.

The container should be shallow, and the meat should be baled over with the liquid daily. Hang up thin parts after 3 weeks and the hams and thick parts after 6 weeks.

From Mrs. E. J. Clarke, Suffolk.

SUFFOLK TREACLE CURE

RUB the meat well with salt and leave for 3 days in earthen pots or a slate tank. Then, take out and empty the brine away and wipe the vessels out clean and dry.

Now, having made the pickle the day before (consisting of 4 gallons of water; 8 lbs. of black treacle; 2 small bars of cooking salt; 4 lbs. of brown sugar and about 2 ozs. of black pepper), bring all this to the boil and let it simmer for about 20 minutes. Remove from the fire and when cold pour over the meat, which should be well covered.

Hams up to 20 lbs. need to be in pickle about a month; if larger, about 6 weeks; breasts and hands and rib spears about 3 weeks, according to thickness. Turn these in the pickle every other day, then hang them up to dry slowly.

The meat is ready to eat in about a month or 6 weeks and will keep good for 12 months and over, and the longer hams are kept the better, anything from 1 to 2 years.

From Mrs. G. Keeble, Suffolk.

SWEET PICKLED PORK

One small leg or a small hand of
pork.
3 ozs. coarse salt.
3 ozs. bay salt.

½ oz. saltpetre.
⅛ pint ale.
½ pint stout.

PUT the leg or hand of pork in a crock, after rubbing it well with coarse salt. Break up fine 3 ozs. of coarse salt, 3 ozs. of bay salt, and the ½ oz. of saltpetre, and mix the three together. Put them into a saucepan with the ale and the stout, bring to the boil, stirring often; and pour the mixture over the pork, boiling hot. Turn the pork over in the pickle every day for 14 days. It is then ready to cook—and it may be either boiled or baked and is delicious hot or cold.

From Mrs. A. Shute, Dorsetshire.

TWO ABERDEENSHIRE WAYS

For our hams, we use one of two cures. Here is the first:

2 lbs. salt.
2 ozs. pepper.
2 ozs. mustard.

2 ozs. saltpetre.
3 lbs. treacle.

MIX all the dry ingredients together and rub the hams well with them, then pour the treacle over them, turn and rub them every day for 5 weeks. This is enough for 2 good-sized hams.

When they have been in a fortnight put 2 tablespoonfuls of essence of smoke over them.

N.B.—Essence of smoke may be bought from the chemist; its trade name is crude pyroligneous acid.

Now this is our second method:

2 lbs. bay salt.
2 ozs. saltpetre.
2 lbs. brown sugar.
1 oz. cloves.
1 oz. pimento.

4 lbs. common salt.
2 ozs. salt prunella.
1 oz. whole pepper (black and
    white).
1 pint stout.

MAKE a pickle of above ingredients with water. It must be strong enough to float an egg. Bring to the boil, then strain. When stone cold pour over the hams. Leave for a fortnight then remove from brine and hang in the rafters to dry. Enough for 2 good-sized hams.

Both from Miss Christian Milne, Aberdeenshire.

WILTSHIRE
(*Wet method*)

Mix together:

1½ lbs. cooking salt.	2 lbs. treacle.
4 ozs. saltpetre.	½ lb. bay salt.
2 ozs. salt prunella.	1 oz. black pepper.
½ oz. juniper berries.	2 quarts beer.

BOIL all together, and cool slightly before putting over hams; which should have been sprinkled first with cooking salt and left for 12 hours to draw out blood, and wiped dry. Turn hams daily for a month, rubbing pickle well in. Dry well before storing. When cooking pickled hams, allow them to stay in the water in which they are boiled for 2 hours after cooking.

To pickle 2 sides of bacon in 3 weeks, mix together:

5 lbs. cooking salt.	4 ozs. saltpetre.
8 ozs. bay salt.	2 lbs. brown sugar.
2 ozs. salt prunella.	

1st day: Sprinkle with cooking salt to draw out blood.
2nd day: Wipe dry, rub well with pickle.
3rd day: Leave untouched.
4th day: Rub in pickle.
5th and 6th days: Leave untouched.
7th day: Rub in pickle.
For the next 2 weeks, rub in pickle every third day.

From Miss Susan Fisher, Wiltshire.

YORKSHIRE METHOD

FOR salting or curing a pig from 20 to 25 stones, I generally allow 3 large bars of salt; ½ lb. of saltpetre; 1 lb. of Demerara sugar (if not obtainable, white sugar will do).

Lay the pig on a cold slab with the skin on top. Rub the shoulders and hams well with salt, leave for 1 day. Next day cover the slab well with salt and lay the pig on it, skin downwards. Rub salt well in and cover well. Sprinkle with saltpetre and sugar and leave for 3 or 4 weeks. Then take out of salt, wash well with cold water, and hang up to dry in a dark room with a good draught. Put hams and shoulders into a bag or pillow-case to keep dust and flies away.

From N.B., Yorkshire.

BY-PRODUCTS

ABBEY FARM BRAWN

TAKE half a pig's head, which has been salted for 3 or 4 days. Soak for 1 or 2 hours in water and wash all the salt off. Cook gently in just enough water to cover, with a few peppercorns added, until the meat can be slipped easily from the bones. Remove the rough skin (the fine skin may be left on, particularly if it is a young pig); and skin the tongue.

At the same time, but in a separate receptacle, cook an old fowl—no matter how old—in water to which has been added 1 medium-sized onion, 1 or 2 leaves of parsley, 1 small teaspoonful of salt, ½ teaspoonful of pepper and the giblets. Boil very gently until the bird is thoroughly tender; and while still warm, cut up the meat in neat slices, removing all the bones, and using the breast meat to place in the bottom and sides of the moulds or pie-dishes.

Place a layer of pig meat next, and alternate with fowl until all the meat is used up; seasoning with pepper to taste between the rows. This quantity fills 2 large pie-dishes or 3 moulds. Mix the 2 liquors the meats have been cooked in, and strain it —this will make a clear jelly—and with it fill up the dishes and leave in a cool place to set.

The secret of the goodness of this dish, and the attractive appearance, lies in the very slow cooking (so that the meat has no trace of "ragginess"): and in the separate cooking of the meat to retain the distinct red and white flesh.

From Mrs. C. Harrison, Bedfordshire.

AYRSHIRE BACON DUMPLINGS

TRIM ¼ lb. bacon and chop finely. Mix well ½ lb. flour; 1 teaspoonful baking-powder; 1 saltspoonful salt; 1 saltspoonful pepper; 1 teaspoonful mixed herbs; 1 dessertspoonful chopped parsley.

Rub in 2 ozs. chopped suet (or dripping); make into a firm dough with cold water and cut into eight pieces.

Roll each piece into a ball, flatten and place some chopped bacon on each. Damp edges, nip together firmly, roll into ball again and dust lightly with flour. Boil about 1 hour with close-fitting lid on saucepan.

Mrs. J. B. Lindsay, Kirkintilloch.

BLACK PUDDINGS

1 quart of fresh pig's blood.	1 cup of barley.
1 quart of new or skimmed milk.	1 lb. fresh beef suet.
½ loaf of bread cut into cubes.	2 or 3 handfuls dry oatmeal.
1 cup of rice.	Pepper, salt, black pepper and dried mint.

PLACE the bread in a large pie-dish; pour the milk over this and set in the oven to warm gently. Do not make too hot. Have ready the blood in a large bowl, and pour into this the milk and bread when warm. Prepare the rice and barley beforehand by bursting with water and cooking well in the oven. Add this to the blood as well. Then grate into this the beef suet, stirring up with the oatmeal. Season with the pepper, salt, black pepper and dried mint. Put into well-greased dripping-pans about ¾ full, and bake in a moderate oven until cooked through.

This is much easier for the busy farmwife than filling into skins. They last quite a long while and when warmed up in the frying-pan or oven are grand for breakfast or supper. They are even eaten for dinner with mashed potatoes up north. These puddings are always delicious, and as light as a feather.

From Mrs. M. E. Glover, Westmorland.

BLACK PUDDINGS

FIRSTLY, the blood must be saved when the pig is killed. This is done by catching the blood in a handbowl and placing in a bucket, stirring with the hand while still hot to remove the veins (which will adhere to the fingers, and be easily removed). Then proceed as follows:—

Place 1 lb. of groats in a cloth and boil for 20 minutes. Take 1 lb. back fat (or leaf) and cut into small dice. Peel 1 lb. onions and pass through the mincer. Mix the fat, groats and onions together in a large basin or bowl; add blood and ¼ lb. flour. Season with 2 ozs. salt, 1 oz. pepper, ½ oz. sage and a pinch of Pennyroyal (if available). Mix all ingredients together and fill in sausage skins. Simmer at 180 degrees F. for 25 minutes.

Mrs. Thorpe, Northamptonshire.

BLACK PUDDING TOAST

½ lb. black pudding.	A little dripping.
1 onion.	1 small cupful oatmeal.
Seasoning.	

HEAT the dripping in a pan and add the black pudding. Mash well and add chopped onion and oatmeal. Stir for a few minutes and cook gently till onion is tender. Serve on hot toast.

From Mrs. Rogers, Wrexham.

BRAWN

INGREDIENTS: Half of a pig's head pickled. Thoroughly clean the head, then put to soak overnight in cold water. Next, put into a large pot, cover with cold water, and bring to the boil. Pour off this water, rinse head and pot. Return to pot along with 2½ quarts of cold water. When at boiling-point, remove any scum that rises and add a blade of mace, 3 or 4 cloves, bunch of herbs, and a teaspoonful of white peppercorns. Simmer gently for 4 hours.

Strain off the stock from the head and allow to become quite cold, when it will jelly. Remove fat from jellied stock. Take out the tongue, skin it, and cut it into neat square pieces, also trim all the meat from the head and cut into small cubes. Put the meat into a basin and add enough of the jellied stock to make it a nice consistency. Allow to get cold and almost set.

Have ready some small bowls and pour the mixture in. When set and firm, turn out. If brawn is preferred without so much stock, put the mixture into a cake-tin with a movable bottom and only enough stock to moisten it. Put something flat with a weight on top. When well pressed, turn on to a dish and serve garnished with parsley.

From Miss Christian Milne, Aberdeenshire.

COOKING INTESTINES

THE intestines (or tripes) are cut in pieces, say 3 ins. long. Then let a running spout of water through them, and wash every sign of dirt away—repeating this 2 or 3 times until they are quite clean. Then place them in a boiler with hot water for about 30 minutes, over a good fire, to be scalded.

Then they are taken out with a long spoon and rinsed thoroughly in cold water. Afterwards they are left in cold water with a handful of salt, changing the water and salt daily for a week. After this, boil them until they are quite tender. (They are called tripes after this process.)

By this time they are well purified, and fit for cooking. The tripes can now be cut up into small pieces about 1 in. long and fried with onions, pepper and salt to taste, and breadcrumbs. Sprinkle oatmeal over them when frying until they are looking nice and brown.

From Mrs. Reynolds, Carmarthenshire.

ELIZABETH PASTY

LINE a fairly deep tin or plate with pastry and fill with the following mixture:—

Take of the "scratchings" left over from lard-making about 1 lb., the tongue of the pig, the heart, and about 8 ozs. of liver, which must be rather more than half boiled; 1 small teacupful of well-washed currants; 1 teaspoonful of chopped mixed herbs; 1 onion, which must be part boiled, and cut in rings, not chopped; salt and pepper as liked; 1 teaspoonful Demerara sugar; 2 ozs. breadcrumbs; 2 hard-boiled eggs.

Place part of the "scratchings" smoothly on the bottom of the pastry in the tin, then cut tongue, liver and heart in slices; place on top the mixed breadcrumbs and sugar, currants and herbs, together with a little stock (in which tongue, etc., was cooked); spread this smoothly over meat, season well, place alternate rings of onion and hard-boiled egg on top, taking care not to separate the yolk from the white; cover with the remainder of the "scratchings" and pastry and bake in a medium oven until thoroughly cooked—about 1 hour.

This old recipe was given me some years ago by an old Herefordshire lady, and it has been used by her family for several generations, handed down from mother to daughter. I have never seen it published in any book or magazine.

From Mrs. F. Preston, Oxfordshire.

FAGGOTS

1 lb. pig's fry (lites, liver, heart, melt, etc.).	5 parts of salt.
1 pig's caul.	1 part ground white pepper.
3 small onions.	1 part ground ginger.
3 oz. breadcrumbs (or boiled potatoes).	1 part ground sage.
	1 part ground pimento.
	(About 1 oz. seasoning will be required.)

SOAK caul in tepid water. Cover fry and onions with water and simmer ¾ hour. Drain off liquid, pour a little on crumbs, keep remainder for gravy. Mince fry, onion and breadcrumbs, add seasoning to taste and beat to smooth paste with a fork. Cut caul into 4-inch squares. Form meat into balls and place caul on top of each. Place in greased tin and brown quickly in a hot oven. Cool and freeze in packs of 4 or 6. Use within 4 months.

GRANNY MORGAN'S BRAWN

CLEAN a pig's head and soak in brine for a few days. Before using, wash in clean cold water. Boil until the meat drops from the bone. In a separate saucepan cook the liver, heart and tongue, until very tender. Strain the stock in which the head was cooked, then turn this stock into that in which the remainder of the meat was cooked; add to it 6 black peppercorns, and an equal number of whole cloves, and boil until it is reduced to 1 pint. Strain again, add 1 cupful of good vinegar and re-heat.

In the meantime, chop the meat or put it through the mincer, add seasoning of chopped onions or sage if desired. Add salt and pepper if needed. Pack into stone crocks, pour the stock over it, cover with a plate, weight well, cover with a cloth and set aside for a week before using.

From Mrs. Jones, Shropshire.

HARVEST-TIME MOULD

1 cow's heel, or 2 pig's feet.	Cut vegetables.
1 lb. of shoulder steak.	Pepper.
Ham scraps.	Salt.

STEW the cow's heel or pig's feet very slowly with the shoulder steak and ham scraps. Season with pepper and salt, and add the vegetables. When thoroughly well cooked cut up the meat into small pieces, and pour with the liquor into a mould that has been well rinsed in cold water. Then leave to set, and turn out next day. This is excellent served with a nice green salad and a few cut hard-boiled eggs, making quite a good meal if all have been out in the fields during the day.

This dish is economical and easily prepared—which is what we require in these days when, as farmers' wives, it is necessary to consider expenses and our time.

From Mrs. H. M. Dirmond, Worcestershire.

HEART AND KIDNEY PUDDING

For the crust:

½ lb. self-raising flour.	Salt.
¼ lb. shredded suet.	Cold water.

For the filling:

1 pig's heart.	1 tablespoonful flour.
2 pigs' kidneys.	Salt and pepper.
	Water.

MIX together flour, suet and salt, and make into a soft dough with cold water. Roll out, and line a basin with part of the dough; leaving enough over for a lid. Cut heart and kidneys into small pieces, after removing all deaf ears and skin; roll in seasoned flour and add enough water to cover. Roll out remainder of the dough to make the lid. Cover with grease-proof paper and steam for 3 hours.

From Miss M. R. Whittall, Salop.

MEAT LOAF

1¼ lbs. pork scraps.	1 oz. salt.
1 lb. "skretchings" (or "scratchings").	¼ oz. ground white pepper.
1¼ lbs. bread (3 days stale or rusk).	¼ oz. ground parsley.
2½ pints water.	¼ oz. ground pimento.
	Amount to taste.

SOAK bread or rusk. Mince meat and skretchings. Add seasoning and mix all ingredients thoroughly (minced onion can be added if desired). Pass mass through the fine plate of the mincer. Press into well-greased tins. Bake in a moderate oven for 2 hours. Cool, remove from tins, pack into polythene bags and freeze. Use within 3–4 months.

From Kathleen Thomas.

MEAT PUDDING

MY mother always made a meat pudding the day after we killed a pig; with the trimmings of meat, and half a kidney, with a piece of skirting. For the crust of pudding (which was made in the old-fashioned way and boiled in a cloth) we used the caul, the laxy part which covers the intestines. Cut up fine, and used like suet, it makes a lovely light crust.

From Mrs. Philpott, Sussex.

MY OWN RECIPE FOR BRAWN

THE day we cut up the pig, I bring together all the pig's head which has been cut up and the trotters. I have ready by my side a good-sized crock and a good supply of crushed salt. Then I rub each piece well with salt and fit them as neatly as possible into the crock. I leave it like this for 2 or 3 days. I then wash all the pieces in cold water and place in a big boiler, covering them with water. Bring to the boil and simmer gently for 3 to 4 hours until the meat leaves the bone.

Lift all the pieces on to a large tray (a crock will do) and leave liquor to cool. Mince all the meat in a large bowl and add to this 8 medium-sized onions, minced; 2 tablespoonfuls dried sage and pepper. Add salt according to taste.

Remove fat from the surface of the liquor. Strain liquor into a crock and have boiler free from all tiny bones. Then replace 4 quarts of the liquor into the boiler and add to this all the mixture in the bowl. Place over fire and simmer for about 15 minutes, turning frequently. Have ready about a dozen good-sized basins and pie-dishes; fill them with the mixture. Leave till cold. When turned out it looks a lovely glossy jelly and tastes delicious with apple sauce.

From Miss H. Slaymaker, Carmarthenshire.

OATMEAL AND PIG'S LIVER PUDDING

THIS makes a very satisfying meal served with a vegetable and potatoes. Any left over can be fried and helps to eke out the bacon.

Put into a large saucepan 1½ pints of water, ½ lb. liver, ¼ lb.

pot barley and a teaspoonful of salt. Bring to the boil and simmer for 1 hour; lift out the liver, allowing barley to simmer a little longer. Pour barley and liquid into a large bowl; add ½ lb. dripping, lard or suet and stir in the grated liver, adding gradually 1 lb. medium oatmeal, a little grated onion (if liked), and a seasoning of salt and pepper to taste. Grease a pudding bowl and fill up to the top with the mixture, cover with butter paper. Steam for 2 hours.

From Mrs. A. W. Dickman, Northumberland.

OATMEAL PUDDINGS

2 lbs. oatmeal.	1¼ lbs. finely chopped onion.
5 tablespoonfuls salt.	1¼ lbs. fat or cracklings, also finely
3 tablespoonfuls pepper.	minced.

HAVE the ingredients for filling thoroughly mixed. Fill the skins with the mixture, leaving space for the oatmeal to swell. Tie securely. Plunge puddings into a large pot of boiling, salted water, pricking for the first few minutes to prevent bursting. Simmer for 1½ to 2 hours. Drain puddings. Allow to become quite cold and store.

To cook puddings, put in boiling, salted water for about 20 minutes, then fry until lightly browned with a little butter. Serve very hot.

From Miss Christian Milne, Aberdeenshire.

PIG'S BRAIN AND KIDNEY

WASH the kidneys and cut into slices; boil 1 egg for 10 minutes, and chop finely with a handful of parsley, also chop the brain finely. Mix together and sprinkle with salt. Pour a little hot water over and cook for 1 hour or more.

From Mrs. Bailey, Cheshire.

PIG'S FEET AND EARS

CLEANSE the feet and ears very thoroughly, soaking for some hours. Boil them in salted water until tender. Take out of the water and dry them; cut the feet in two, slice the ears then dip in frying batter and fry in hot fat. Serve with a little melted butter seasoned with mustard, and vinegar poured over.

From Mrs. O. Stirzaker, Lancashire.

PIG'S FEET AND PARSLEY SAUCE

WASH thoroughly 4 pig's feet. Put them in a saucepan with enough water to cover. Bring to the boil, skim, and simmer gently for 2½ hours.

Make a parsley sauce with ½ pint milk, 1 tablespoonful chopped parsley, 1 tablespoonful cornflour (or plain flour), a piece of butter or margarine, salt and pepper. Serve with the pig's feet. This is sufficient for 6 people.

A good soup can be made with the addition of vegetables to the stock in which the feet were boiled.

From Mrs. G. E. Jones, Hampshire.

PIG'S FRY AS MOCK GOOSE

1 lb. pig's fry.
1 onion.
A little powdered sage.

3 lbs. potatoes.
1 apple.
Pepper and salt.

BOIL the potatoes until half cooked. Then cut them and fry in slices. Chop the onion and apple in small pieces. Grease a pie-dish and put a layer of sliced potatoes at the bottom, then a layer of pig's fry; sprinkle it with the onion, apple, sage, pepper and salt. Then cover again with potatoes fried, and so on until the dish is full, ending with a layer of potatoes. Pour over ½ pint of water, cover with greaseproof paper and bake in a moderate oven 1½ hours.

From Miss O. Stirzaker, Lancashire.

PIG'S HASLET

WASH and dry some liver, heart, lights, and sweetbread, fat and lean bits of pork, beating the latter with a rolling-pin to make it tender. Season with salt, pepper, sage, and a small, finely-shredded onion. When mixed, put all into a caul and fasten up tightly with a needle and thread. Roast it on a hanging jack or by a string.

This is a very old recipe of my mother's, which she used when they killed pigs. She used to serve the haslet with a sauce of port wine, water, and mustard just brought to the boil. Served in slices, with parsley sauce, it is also very good.

From Mrs. Rogers, Wrexham.

PIG'S-HEAD PUDDING

½ pig's head.
3 eggs.
Any available cooked beef.

½ lb. breadcrumbs.
½ nutmeg.
Pepper.

SOAK the head, nose and ears overnight; having first soaked them in salt for a fortnight or more. Then boil for 2½ hours. When cold, put through a mincer with the cooked beef. Add the grated nutmeg, breadcrumbs and pepper to taste. Then mix in the eggs and make it into a firm roll. Tie in a pudding-cloth like a roly-poly; place in boiling water, and boil for 2 hours. Serve cold.

From Mrs. Parsons, Cornwall.

PIG'S PUDDING

Blood from 1 pig.
½ lb. rough fat cut in small pieces.
1 tablespoonful of chopped onion cooked.

½ lb. groats or pearl barley previously cooked.
1 dessertspoonful of dried sage.
Saltspoonful of pepper.

PLACE a heaped-up tablespoonful of salt in a clean bucket and catch the blood from the pig. Stir until quite cold. Empty into a large bowl and add all the above ingredients to the blood and mix well. Take sufficient skins to hold the mixture, turn them inside out and scrape quite clean with the back of knife. Wash in salt and water; then fill. Tie with string in convenient sizes and put in a pan of boiling water and boil for 20 minutes. Take out, and let cool. They can be fried when required.

From Mrs. Heath, Cheshire.

PORK SAUSAGES

2 lbs. lean pork.
1 lb. breadcrumbs.
½ oz. pepper.
Pinch of nutmeg and pinch of mace.

1 lb. fat pork.
1 oz. salt.
¼ oz. sage.

REMOVE crust from bread and crumb. Mix in with meat, having first removed bone and rind, and pass through the mincer. Add seasoning and pass through the mincer a second time; and fill into skins from pig.

How to prepare entrails for sausages: Remove small entrails from intestines when taking away apron fat. Run out and place in water; scrape away all slime until transparent. Skins are then ready for use.

From Mrs. Thorpe, Northamptonshire.

SAUSAGE MEAT

9 lbs. lean pork.	3 ozs. salt.
3 lbs. firm pork fat.	1 oz. white pepper.
3 lbs. bread.	¾ oz. mace.
	½ oz. ginger.
	¼ oz. sage.

TRIM off burnt portions of bread crust, cut into large cubes and place in water to soak. Separate lean and fat and weigh out correct quantities. Run the meat and fat through the coarse plate of the mincer and thoroughly mix the seasoning with it. Squeeze out excessive moisture from the bread (it should absorb its own weight of water). Thoroughly mix all the ingredients and run the mass through the fine plate of the mincer. This freezes well and should be packed into 1 or 2-lb. packs, use within 2 months.

PREPARATION OF TRIPE

WHEN you get the intestine from the newly-killed pig, cover it up well and keep in a warm place until you are ready to attend to it; but the sooner you start work on it the better. Lay it on the table, and unravel it with your fingers until it is one long tube, separating the small intestines from the fat and placing it on a bowl as you go along. Then take a fairly blunt round-ended knife, and scrape the fat off the large intestine; keeping it on a plate (afterwards it can be melted into lard). Be very careful not to break the wall of the intestine, lest any of the contents should come out.

When finished, take it out to some running water and have another clean vessel ready to hold it. Cut the large intestine into 6-in. lengths, hold under running water until all contents are washed away, turn inside out, wash again and throw into a clean receptacle. Draw your thumbs through small intestine, cutting it into 2- or 3-ft. lengths.

Open the stomach from end to end, scrape well to get rid of the slime, place all together and well wash in cold salty water; then wash once in boiling water; and draw through the fingers into clean salty water again. Leave until next day, then change the salty water every day for a week—drawing it through the fingers each time, so that all the slime is taken off.

At the end of a week boil for 1½ to 2 hours. Leave to cool. Cut into chunks; fry with onions—and it is delicious.

From Mrs. Jones, Carmarthenshire.

RENDERING THE LARD

R EMOVE the two large sheets of fat from the ribs. Cut into small pieces and place in a baking-tin in a moderate oven. Strain the fat into earthenware jars. If you are the fortunate possessor of a roaster, use it in place of the baking tin, and you will get lard of special purity. This lard is invaluable for pastry, etc. When most of the fat has been expressed, the "cracklings" are turned into a dish and kept until required for making puddings.

From Miss Christian Milne, Aberdeenshire.

STUFFED HEART

T AKE the heart and slice deep cuts each side to drain away the blood, then wash well and stuff with sage and onions and fine breadcrumbs. Sew up and place in a casserole and cook for 2 hours. This is nice cut in slices and eaten cold.

From Mrs. Philpott, Sussex.

SUSSEX BRAWN

T HIS is a very old recipe. Cut off the ears from a pig's head take out the brains and clean the head well and cut into halves. Prepare the feet and ears of the pig and rub in a mixture of 6 ozs. sugar and 1½ ozs. saltpetre into the parts; let them remain for a few hours and then rub in 6 ozs. salt. After 12 hours pour over a gill of vinegar, and leave for a week, turning the pieces daily.

Then drain the pieces and wash and cook gently until all the bones can be easily removed. Flatten the halves of the head, keeping them as much in the proper shape as possible sprinkle over a little salt and mixed spice. Place the ears, feet and tongue in the centre and roll into a long shape. Tie round tightly and fasten in a cloth; cover with water and boil for 4 hours, adding onions, carrots and celery for flavour. Let the roll cool in the liquor, drain off, and press between weights for a day or two. Take off the cloth, trim, and it is ready for the table.

From Mrs. B. Shillets, Cambridgeshire.

WHITE PUDDINGS

THIS recipe for "White Puddings" was always used at pig-killing times in a Northumbrian farmhouse of last century. Take half a pig's head, brain, tongue, lights, heart, kidneys and rinds, also any odd pieces of pork. Boil together all except brain and rinds. Boil brain separately in a piece of muslin. When well cooked take meat from bones, and pass all through a mincer. Boil ¼ lb. pearl barley and add to other ingredients. Mix well together and season with salt and pepper. Use stock from boiling to moisten, but do not make too damp. Fill well-scraped skins and fry in a little lard.

From Mrs. M. J. Wilson, Essex.

WHITEMEAT PUDDINGS

THESE are made by boiling a quantity of pot barley and mixing it with scraps of boiled spare rib meat or other white meat from the pig. No liver, heart, or dark meat must be added. A proportion of lard or fat is added, but very little if the rib meat is fatty. The skins are filled with this mixture, thoroughly seasoned, and then boiled. These puddings are of much softer consistency than the meat puddings, but are really delicious. Serve fried or baked in the oven with plenty of dripping.

From Miss Christian Milne, Aberdeenshire.

WINES and MEADS

AGRIMONY WINE

A good bunch of agrimony.
2 gallons water.
7 lbs. sugar (Demerara or white).

3 lemons.
6 oranges.
4 ozs. root ginger.

CRUSH ginger, put with agrimony, and boil in the water until a good colour. Pour liquid on to the sugar, lemons and oranges (sliced), and allow to stand 2 or 3 days. Strain, put into a big jar, and leave to work. The wine, which is exceptionally good for severe colds, can be used after 6 months.

Agrimony can be used freshly gathered or dried. Gather when in full flower. This is in July in the Leicestershire district, where it grows abundantly. Some people may not be acquainted with its name, but no doubt have noticed it in the grass-fields. The plant grows between 1 and 2 ft. in height, and has small yellow flowers growing closely together up the whole of the slender but hard stem.

From Mrs. A. Macer, Leicestershire.

264

BALM WINE

4 gallons water.
8 lbs. loaf sugar.
Juice of 6 lemons.

Whites of 4 eggs.
1 peck balm leaves.
Slice of toast spread with yeast.

BOIL together the water, sugar, lemons and white of eggs, well beaten, for ¾ hour, skimming well. Then take the balm leaves, put them in a tub with the thin peeling of the lemons; pour the boiling liquor on, stirring well until almost cold. Put on top the toast spread with yeast. Let it work for 2 or 3 days, then strain off, squeezing the leaves through a cloth and afterwards through a flannel bag into a cask. Stop lightly until it has done hissing, then bung down close. At the end of 3 months, bottle. July is the best time for making this tonic drink.

From Mrs. M. E. Moulam, Derbyshire.

BLACKBERRY WINE

PLACE alternate layers of ripe blackberries and sugar in wide-mouthed jars; and allow to stand for 3 weeks. Then strain off the liquid and bottle; adding a couple of raisins to each bottle. Cork lightly at first and later more tightly. Nothing could be more inexpensive and the wine will keep in good condition for a year, having a flavour rather like that of good port.

From Mrs. A. Clayton, Yorkshire.

BURNET WINE

TO every quart of burnet heads add 2 quarts of boiling water. Let stand 24 hours. Strain and to every quart of juice add 1 lb. sugar. Boil well for 20 minutes. Pour into a jar and to every 3 quarts of juice add 1 lemon and 1 orange sliced. Let stand until lukewarm. Toast and put on the top a thick slice of bread, spread with 1 oz. yeast. Stand 24 hours, strain again, then stand it in a warm place 6 weeks before bottling. Keep 12 months before using.

From Mrs. T. Coulthard, Cumberland.

BLACKCURRANT WINE

4 gallons ripe currants.
2½ gallons water.

6 lbs. loaf sugar.

PUT the currants into a large earthenware jar with a cover to it. Boil the water with the sugar, carefully remove the scum as it rises on the liquid, and pour, still boiling, on the currants. Let it stand for 48 hours. Next strain the whole through a flannel bag into another vessel, return it thence into the jar, let it stand a fortnight to settle, then bottle off. Excellent for colds and coughs in winter.

From Mrs. T. J. Mayne, Buckinghamshire.

BROOM WINE

1 gallon water.	Rind and juice of 2 lemons and
3 lbs. lump sugar.	2 oranges.
1 gallon broom flowers.	2 tablespoonfuls yeast.

BOIL sugar and water together with the lemon and orange rinds for $\frac{1}{2}$ hour. When lukewarm pour over the flowers, picked from the stalks, and the juice of lemons and oranges. Stir in the yeast and allow to ferment 3 days. Put into a clean dry cask and allow to work for about a week or ten days, filling up as required. Then stop up close and keep for 6 months or longer when an excellent drink will be found. This is a very old recipe given me by my grandmother, and the wine should be made during May.

From Mrs. N. Fennell, Warwickshire.

CELERY WINE

THERE is always a waste of the outside pieces of celery: here is a recipe which makes from them an excellent wine, and is also good for those who suffer from rheumatism.

To each pound of green or outside stalks of celery allow 1 quart of water and boil all until tender. Then strain the liquid off and allow 3 lbs. Demerara sugar and $\frac{1}{2}$ oz. of yeast to each gallon put into the cask. Keep the cask well filled up until all the yeast has worked out, and close the bung lightly until the wine is quite still. Then close firmly, leave for a year and bottle off, when it will be ready for use.

From Mrs. Scarlett, Suffolk.

CHERRY WINE

I MAKE this from the cracked and windfall Morella cherries that are unsaleable.

After stalking and washing the fruit, place in a crock and add cold water, allowing 1 pint to each pound of fruit. Stir each day for 10 days, then mash well with the hands and leave another 10 days, stirring daily. Then place muslin over another pan. It is a good plan to tie this on. Then, by standing a colander on 2 laths over this, the bulk of the fruit is retained in the colander and enables the liquid to strain through the muslin more easily.

Do not squeeze or hurry it: when all is strained, measure, and to each quart of liquid add 1 lb. granulated sugar. Stir well and leave till dissolved; then put into big stone bottles, filling to the top. Leave to ferment, filling up as the liquid lowers in the bottles. When quite finished fermentation, cork tightly and let stand at least 6 months before using. It is not so good if used earlier, though a nice drink.

From Miss H Jenner, Kent.

CLEAT WINE

TO every quart of cleats put the same quantity of water. Stir well every morning for ten days then strain and to every gallon put 3½ lbs. coarse sugar, 2 bitter oranges and 1 lemon. Spread brewers' yeast on both sides of a piece of toast and stand on the liquid for three days. Put into a barrel for four months and then bottle.

From Yorkshire.

HOME-MADE CIDER

TAKE all the fallen apples, the smaller the better; cut up, and place in an earthenware jar. Cover with cold water, protect with muslin and let stand for 10 days, giving an occasional stir daily. When fermentation has ceased, strain; and add 1⅜ lb. sugar to each gallon. A slice of beetroot improves the colour. Bottle and let stand uncorked for 14 days. It should then almost cease working. Cork securely (not screw stoppers) and in two or three months' time you should have lovely sparkling cider.

From Miss E. Rutherford, Northumberland.

RED CLOVER WINE

2 quarts of purple blossom.	2 oranges.
4 quarts boiling water.	4 lbs. white sugar.
3 lemons.	1 oz. yeast on toast.

267

POUR the boiling water over the blossoms. Stand until lukewarm. Slice lemons and oranges, add sugar and the yeast on toast. Put all together in a bowl, stand for 5 days and stir twice each day. Next strain, and stand for another 5 days. Strain again, leave for 3 days, then bottle, leaving corks loose for 10 days. Then cork up, and it will be ready in a month.

From Mrs. W. Skelton, Cumberland.

COLTSFOOT WINE

To each gallon of water allow:

2 quarts coltsfoot flowers.	1 lemon.
3 lbs. sugar.	1 orange.
½ lb. raisins.	A little yeast spread on toast.

MEASURE the flowers, put into pan or tub with the right proportion of raisins and rind of the lemon and orange. Put the sugar and water into a saucepan with the lemon and orange juice, bring to the boil, and while boiling pour over the flowers and stir well. Cover and leave till lukewarm. Add a little yeast spread on toast. Leave to ferment for 4 days. Strain into cask, reserving some for filling up. When fermentation subsides, cork down and leave for 6 months.

From Mrs. W. Fennell, Warwickshire.

COUNTRY WINE

I START by mashing over-ripe plums, greengages, and so on in a china or enamel pan, covering them with water and adding any surplus that wants dealing with, such as over-ripe pears, damsons, and sloes—the last two are best scalded before adding—blackberries, too, and even the pulp left from blackberry jelly making. They will all add colour and richness to the messy-looking mass which will ferment itself without yeast.

More water may be added; but the more fruit juices and the less water, the richer the wine.

Strain off the liquor in about a fortnight (starting another lot if you have the fruit); using 3 lbs. of sugar to a gallon of liquor.

Miss Elsie G. Cook, Oxfordshire.

COWSLIP MEAD

TO every gallon of water allow 2 lbs. of honey: and boil ¾ hour, skimming well. Take 1 pint of the liquor and slice into it 1 large lemon, then pour remainder into an earthenware bowl and put in 1 gallon of cowslip heads. Stir well, cover, and set in a warm place for 24 hours.

Stir in the lemon liquor, 2 sprigs of sweet brier (optional), and ¼ oz. yeast, dissolved in a little of the honey. Let it work for 4 days, then strain into a cask. Keep in a cool place for 6 months, then bottle.

From Mrs. E. Symes, Northumberland.

COWSLIP WINE

4 quarts freshly-picked cowslip flowers, free from stalks and bits of green.
4 quarts boiling water.
3 lbs. loaf sugar.
1 lemon.
1 juicy orange.
2 tablespoonfuls yeast.
A little brandy, if liked.

PARE the rinds very thinly from the orange and lemon, halve the fruit and press out the juice. Put this with the rinds into a tub or pan, and pour on the boiling water in which the sugar has been simmered for ½ hour. (Any scum rising to the top while simmering should be carefully skimmed off.) When the liquid is lukewarm, stir in the flowers and yeast, and leave the tub covered with a cloth or flannel for 3 days, stirring twice a day. Then strain the liquid off, and pour it nearly all into a cask, leaving the bung loose till all working has stopped. Full up with liquor kept over for the purpose, and bung up close. Leave undisturbed for 3 months before using. A little brandy will greatly improve it, but it is not necessary.

From Mrs. A. E. Brooker, Berkshire.

CRAB APPLE WINE

PUT 1 gallon of sliced crab apples into a gallon of water, and let them soak for a fortnight. Strain and add 3 lbs. of Demerara sugar to each gallon of liquor. Stir well and frequently until fermentation takes place, which should be in a day or a day and a half. Leave for 3 days, and then put wine into cask or jar. Lay muslin over the opening until the hissing noise (which tells that the wine is working) has ceased. Then cork tightly, and bottle after 3 months.

This wine is one of the most delicious of our country wines, and improves with keeping.

From Mrs. C. Butchart, Lancashire.

DAMSON WINE

CARE must be taken that the fruit is ripe, sound and unbroken. Wipe and pick over 12 lbs. of damsons, and pour over them 1½ gallons of boiling water. Cover over immediately with a heavy cloth and leave for 4 days, stirring occasionally with a wooden spoon. Strain the fruit from the juice and add to every gallon of the latter 3½ lbs. of loaf sugar; then pour the wine into a cask, covering the bung-hole with some thick material until fermentation is over, when the bung should be inserted.

In a year the wine may be bottled. I have some of this wine which is 2 years old and is nearly equal to port.

From Mrs. G. Dams, Rutlandshire.

DANDELION WINE

3 quarts flowers.	The rind and pulp of 2 lemons and
1 gallon water.	1 orange.
3 lbs. sugar.	1 oz. yeast.
	1 lb. raisins.

THE flowers must be freshly gathered, picked off their stalks, and put into a large bowl. Bring the water to the boil, pour over the dandelions, and leave for 3 days, stirring each day. Cover the bowl with butter-muslin. After the third day, add the sugar and the rinds only of the lemons and orange. Turn all into a pan and boil for 1 hour. Put back into the bowl and add the pulp of the lemons and orange. Allow to stand till cool, then put in the yeast. Let it remain covered for 3 days, when it will be ready to strain, and put into bottles. The bottles should not be quite filled, and the raisins should be equally divided amongst them. Do not cork tightly till fermentation ceases. This wine, if made in May or June, is good at Christmas.

From Miss L. Kent, Cheshire.

ELDERFLOWER WINE

2 breakfastcupfuls loosely-packed elderflowers freed from stems.	3¼ lbs. loaf sugar.
	1 white of egg.
1 lb. raisins split but not stoned.	1 gallon water.
juice of 1 large lemon.	1 oz. yeast.

DISSOLVE the sugar in the water, stir in the well-beaten white of egg, bring to boil, boil 30 minutes, then skim. Have ready in an earthenware bowl the prepared elderflowers, the raisins and the lemon juice. Pour over the water mixture. Stir thoroughly; and when a little more than milk warm, add the yeast.

Stir once a day for 10 days, then strain and put into a clean dry stone jar, setting the cork in loosely. When the mixture has done working, cork very tightly; and bottle in six months, taking care to strain through flannel and making sure that the bottles and corks are thoroughly sterilized and dry to receive it.

From Mrs. Whiteborn, Surrey.

ELDERBERRY WINE

TAKE 7 lbs. berries and 2 gallons of water. To each gallon of liquid add 3 lbs. best loaf sugar, 1 lb. raisins, ½ oz. ground ginger, ½ oz. whole ginger, bruised, 6 cloves, ½ stick cinnamon, 1 lemon.

Strip the berries from the stalks; pour boiling water over them. Let them stand for 24 hours, then bruise them well and strain through a hair sieve or jelly-bag. Measure the liquid, put into an earthenware pan and add sugar and the lemon cut in slices. Boil the cloves, ginger, raisins and cinnamon in a little of the liquid. Strain and add to the rest of the wine.

Allow to stand for a few days, then take off the cap. Strain again and pour into stone jars or casks. Leave open for a few weeks, continually adding more wine until fermentation ceases. Bung tightly and let it remain for 6 months, then bottle.

From Mrs. F. E. Carter, Devonshire.

GINGER BEER

(Without the bitter taste which is apparent if all the white pith of the lemons is not removed)

5 quarts boiling water.	¼ oz. cream of tartar.
1¼ lbs. sugar.	Good tablespoonful yeast (about 1 oz.).
1 oz. whole ginger, bruised.	
2 lemons.	

R EMOVE rinds of lemons as thinly as possible. Strip off
every particle of white pith. This needs a very sharp knife.
Cut lemons into thin slices, removing pips. Put the sliced lemon
into an earthenware bowl with sugar, ginger and cream of
tartar, and pour on the boiling water. Leave until blood heat,
stir in the yeast, and leave, covered with a cloth, in a moderately warm place, for 24 hours. Skim yeast from the top, strain
ginger beer carefully from the sediment. For bottling screw
stoppers are best; if corked, tie corks securely. In 2 days the
beer will be ready for use.

From Mrs. Margaret Patrick, Surrey.

GOOSEBERRY WINE

8 lbs. gooseberries.   3 lbs. sugar to each gallon of juice.
2 gallons water.

WASH, top and tail the gooseberries, which should have
been picked before they began to change colour. Bruise
them well, either with a rolling-pin or wooden vegetable
presser. Put them in a wooden tub or unglazed earthenware
crock. Add water, and mix and mash well. Leave covered with
a cloth for 2 days. Then strain and measure the liquid. Put this,
together with the proper proportion of sugar, into the vessel.
Let it stand until the sugar has dissolved, stirring often. Pour
into a cask, and leave in a warm place until the fermentation
has ceased; this will probably take about 3 weeks. Then drive
in the bung securely. Fit a peg into the vent hole, and every day
pull it out to allow any gas to escape. When all seems quite still,
close up tightly, and leave in a cool place for 8 months. It will
then be ready for bottling.

From Mrs. W. Scott, Essex.

GORSE WINE

½ gallon flowers.   3 lbs. Demerara sugar.
1 gallon water.   1 orange.
2 ozs. root ginger.   1 lemon.
1 oz. compressed yeast.

SIMMER flowers, water and ginger together for 15 minutes,
stir in sugar till dissolved. Slice orange and lemon and add
to cooling liquid, and when just warm float yeast on a piece of
toast on top. Cover with a folded blanket, leave undisturbed
for a week, then skim off the head. Strain into a jar, allow to

272

work for another week before corking tightly. A few raisins and a lump of sugar candy keep it lively. Bottle off in November.

From Miss N. Johnson, Ayrshire.

GRAPEFRUIT CHAMPAGNE

CUT up 7 grapefruit in a pan. Pour over 1 gallon of cold water. Let it stand 10 days, then sieve over 4 lbs. of sugar, and leave another 8 days, stirring every day. Strain into another pan, and remove all scum: let it stand a few more days, remove scum as it rises. Bottle off; ready for drinking in 3 weeks. It is also a good tonic and pick-me-up.

From Mrs. S. Allen, Leicestershire.

HONEY BEER

4 quarts water.	4 ozs. clear honey.
1 oz. ground ginger.	Juice of 3 lemons.
1 lb. white sugar.	Large teaspoonful fresh yeast on
2 ozs. lime juice.	bread.

BOIL 2 quarts of the water with ginger for $\frac{1}{2}$ hour. Put in a pan with the white sugar, lime juice, honey, lemon juice, and the remaining 2 quarts water (cold). When just at blood heat, add the yeast spread on a piece of bread. Let it remain for 12 hours, then strain through a muslin bag. Allow to settle for an hour or two, and then bottle.

From Mrs. M. Machin, Yorkshire.

MANGOLD WINE

5 lbs. mangolds.	2 lemons.
1 gallon water.	2 oranges.
3 lbs. lump sugar.	$\frac{1}{2}$ oz. yeast.

WASH the mangolds but do not peel. Cut into pieces and boil until tender. Strain, and to every gallon of liquid add sugar and rinds of lemons and oranges, boiling for 20 minutes. Allow to cool. Add juice of lemons and oranges. Stir in the yeast mixed with a little castor sugar. Stir all well together, and put into a clean dry jar or cask. Allow to work for about a week, keeping the jar well filled up while working. When finished working, cork down tight and keep for at least 6 months; but the longer it is kept the better.

From Miss N. Fennell, Warwickshire.

MILD BROWN ALE

5 ozs. hops.
8 gallons water.
2 ozs. yeast.

3 lbs. brown sugar, more or less
to taste.

BOIL the hops and water together slowly for 40 to 50 minutes, strain over the sugar; add yeast when the liquor is lukewarm, turn into a pan or tub to ferment for 4 days, then cask or bottle for use as wanted.

From Mrs. F. L. Saunders, Berkshire.

MULLED ALE

3 eggs.
1 quart milk.
1 pint ale.

¼ lb. castor sugar.
¼ nutmeg (grated).

BRING the ale to the boil in a saucepan, then set aside. Beat the eggs well and stir into the milk. Mix together and pour into the ale. Add the sugar and nutmeg and heat slowly. Stir constantly until the mixture thickens but do not allow to boil. Pour into a jug and stir for two minutes.

From Mrs. C. Utley, Somerset.

NETTLE BEER

2 gallons nettles.
½ oz. root ginger.
4 lbs. malt.
1 oz. yeast.

2 ozs. hops.
4 ozs. sarsaparilla.
2 gallons water.
1½ lbs. castor sugar.

CHOOSE young nettles. Wash and put into a saucepan with water, ginger, malt, hops and sarsaparilla. Bring to the boil and boil for ¼ hour; put sugar into a large pan or earthenware jar; strain nettle mixture on it. Stir until sugar has dissolved. Beat yeast to a cream, and add, leaving until it begins to ferment; then put into bottles. Cork and tie down with string. This may be used at once.

From Mrs. J. Blackford, Worcestershire.

ORANGE WINE

FOR 26 oranges allow 2 gallons boiling water, and to each gallon of liquor allow 2 lbs. sugar. Wipe the oranges and cut in slices, removing the pips. Place in a tub and cover with the boiling water. Cover up and leave for a week, stirring every day with a wooden spoon. Then strain through a fine sieve, allowing the liquid to drip through on its own accord. Measure and add sugar in proportion. Put in a cask and bung up after a week. This will be ready in 3 months.

From Mrs. R. Walker, Gloucestershire.

PARSLEY WINE

TO every pound of parsley add 1 gallon of boiling water. Let this stand for 24 hours, then strain and boil the liquor for 20 minutes with 1 oz. of lump ginger, the rinds of 2 oranges and 2 lemons. Then pour the liquor on to 4 lbs. of sugar and add the juice of the oranges and lemons. When nearly cool put ½ oz. of yeast on to a slice of toast, and let stand for 4 days. Strain and bottle but do not cork down until the wine has stopped working.

This makes a delicious wine, and is better for keeping.

From Mrs. F. Eyre, Derbyshire.

PARSNIP WINE

TO each gallon of water take 3 lbs. parsnips cut into pieces ½ in. thick, 2 lemons and 1 orange cut small. Boil until the parsnips are soft, strain and pour over 3 lbs. white sugar; stir till dissolved and bottle while warm, adding to each bottle a small piece of German yeast (about the size of a marble). Keep the bottles full while fermenting; after fermentation has ceased, cork and wire. This is an excellent imitation of champagne.

From Miss S. Jarrett, Montgomeryshire.

PEAR WINE

ALLOW 1 gallon of sliced pears to each gallon of water, and leave to soak for a fortnight, stirring every day. Strain off and add 3 lbs. of sugar to every gallon of liquor. Stir frequently until fermentation takes place, in a day or two. Leave for 3 days: then pour into a cask, lightly covering the opening until fermentation ceases. Bung tightly and bottle in 3 months. Small hard pears are suitable for this.

From Miss E. Rutherford, Northumberland.

PLUM PORT

1 gallon water.   4 lbs. damsons.
4 lbs. sugar.

BOIL water and pour over damsons. Leave until next day. Squeeze and stir daily for 5 days, then strain through a jelly-bag. Stir in the sugar, and add 1 breakfastcupful of boiling water, and leave to ferment for 8 days. Then skim, and bottle.

From Miss P. Hutchinson, Durham.

POTATO WINE

TAKE ½ gallon of small potatoes, wash them well and cut them in half. Put them into a pan with 1 gallon of fresh cold water with 3 pieces of root ginger, bring to the boil, boil for 10 minutes.

Have another pan ready, into which you have put 3 lbs. of granulated sugar and 2 sliced oranges and 2 sliced lemons. Strain the potato water on to the sugar, etc., and boil again for ½ hour. When cold, bottle, and as soon as the wine has finished working, cork tightly. No yeast is required.

From Mrs. W. H. Charlwood, Sussex.

PRIMROSE WINE

1 peck primroses.   2 gallons water.
3 lb. lump sugar.

BOIL the water and sugar together, pour over the primroses and when cold stir in two spoonfuls of yeast to ferment. Strain and bottle.

From Yorkshire.

RHUBARB AND BALM WINE

WIPE and cut up 2 lbs. of rhubarb, put it into a large saucepan, with ½ lb. balm leaves (well washed), and 4 quarts cold water. Bring to the boil and boil 30 minutes. Strain and when lukewarm add ½ oz. yeast, ½ oz. citric acid and 1 lb. to 1½ lbs. Demerara sugar, according to taste. Cover, and let it work for 24 hours, then skim and bottle. It is ready for drinking the same day. This makes a most refreshing and health-giving drink.

From Mrs. Vincent, Devonshire.

ROWANBERRY WINE

WHEN the berries are perfectly ripe is the time to make this delicious wine. To each quart of berries add 1 quart boiling water and a small piece of bruised whole ginger. Let them steep for 10 days; well stir each day, then strain, and to each quart of liquid add 1 lb. of loaf sugar. When dissolved, bottle up. Do not cork tight until fermentation has ceased.

From Mrs. E. Westcott, Devonshire.

TREACLE ALE

TAKE 5 quarts boiling water, 2 lbs. treacle, 2 ozs. yeast, sugar if required. Melt the treacle with the boiling water in a crock: if not sweet enough add sugar accordingly. When cold, add 2 ozs. yeast (on toast). Cover closely and leave for 3 days. Then bottle and cork tightly, and tie down, as this ale becomes very strong.

This recipe was handed down from my great-grandmother, and it makes a very good drink. In the lean years of part of last century, this ale was used in many Highland homes instead of milk, with porridge (served in separate bowls): and a very excellent substitute they considered it.

From Mrs. J. Neil, Perthshire.

CHEESE MAKING

CHEESE MAKING has become big business and is seldom
done in the farmhouse today largely because of the
demand for liquid milk and the regulations concerning the
production and sale of Farmhouse Cheese.

But this does not mean that some of these old recipes cannot
still be used today if you have a house-cow or for some reason
a quantity of milk is unexpectedly available. Some of the
small, soft and lactic acid cheeses are in demand in high-class
shops or on local market stalls and we give here the basic
method which must be followed if the cheeses are to come up
to the standard required for up-to-date marketing. This
method can then be adapted to produce the regional cheeses
such as Coulommier or the Nottingham-Colwick.

SOFT CHEESES

VERY little equipment is needed for the making of soft
cheese, so it is particularly suited for the farmer's or
smallholder's wife. A room with a constant, not too hot or
dry, atmosphere is needed and good level table space; much

of the other apparatus can be adapted from ordinary utensils.

Choice of milk.—Unless you are sure that the source of your milk supply is absolutely safe it is best to heat-treat milk for soft cheese making, as deterioration can occur very rapidly because of the high moisture content. To heat-treat the milk, place it in a bucket or container and bring to 150 deg. F., then cool at once by putting the bucket into running water as cold as you can get it. When cooled to about 95 deg. F. the starter can be added as given in the directions. Starter is always required if milk has once been heat-treated.

As in the making of semi-hard varieties, certain processes must be gone through; they are given here in the order in which they must be undertaken.

Milk must be treated, rennet added, curd sliced and dipped, drained, salted, then drained again.

The treatment of milk.—Evening milk is best and it should be cooled and kept overnight at a low temperature. This will allow a little acidity to develop, but on no account should it be allowed to sour, as this will spoil the cheese. It is not necessary to use starter unless the milk has been heat-treated or you wish to heat-treat it yourself. To do this, proceed as given above. If raw milk is used, raise the temperature directly to 95 deg. F.

Addition of rennet.—This can be added as soon as milk is at the right temperature; it must be cheese making rennet and not that used for junket. The amount used is smaller than for semi-hard cheese, and as the milk is "sweet" the curds take longer to form. A drachm glass measure is best used for measuring, and the rennet should be diluted to 6 times its volume in water to ensure thorough mixing. Mix this into the milk and top-stir until coagulation takes place. Then cover your bucket and leave until the curds can be handled, the times will vary according to your recipe. Sterilize the boards, hoops (or tins) and mats which you propose to use and leave them standing in hot water until the curd is ready to handle.

Slicing of curd.—Fairly large pieces of curd are permissible for soft cheese as they do not require a lot of drainage, the pieces must pack down slowly into the hoops. Scoop the curd direct from the bucket using a skimmer or scoop, do this gently, being careful not to break the curd more than necessary. Temperature is all-important in the making of soft cheese, and during this time it should be maintained at about 65 deg. F. If too much heat is lost the whey is not expelled quickly enough and the curd does not sink in the hoop.

To make.—Remove the equipment from the hot water and set up as required. The curd is ready if it will leave the side of the bucket when a little is pulled away with the finger. Some cheeses of the soft variety are given "tops"; to do this press the hoop which you propose to use on the surface of the curd to give you the size, then scoop this piece out very carefully without breaking and slide it on to a clean plate. Make enough "tops" to have one for each cheese you propose to make. Then ladle out the rest of the curd in the bucket, into the hoops which you have placed on mats, the mats themselves being on boards. Go on filling up the moulds till the curd reaches the top, then let it shrink a little. You can hasten this process by dipping out the whey from the top. Go on until all the curd is filled into the mould, then as soon as possible slide the "top" on to the curd and leave the moulds in a warm place for 12–14 hours for the whey to drain.

To drain out-of-mould.—If you are using double moulds, then the top half can be removed as soon as the level has sunk sufficiently, otherwise you are faced with the more difficult task of turning out the cheese without breaking or spoiling it. If tins are being used from which the bottom has been cut and holes pierced in the side, remember that on no account must there be a rim at either end, as if there is, it will be quite impossible to remove the cheese.

Twenty-four hours after making, have ready boards and mats, one set for each cheese; they should be boiled and then allowed to dry. Put a mat over the top of the cheese in the hoop, then a board over the mat, and invert the whole thing, keeping one hand firmly over each end. Then leave to drain for another 24 hours.

By this time the cheese should be firm enough to remove the hoop and turn it out on to a clean straw mat, some salt can be sprinkled on the exposed surface if liked. Turn the cheese each day now, keeping it in a cool, dry atmosphere meanwhile. Salt can be added while the cheese is undergoing the process of draining, but be careful not to use too much, a little sprinkled on the exposed surfaces for the first two or three turnings is enough.

If a mould begins to grow on the surface of the cheese, wipe with a damp cloth, using cold water, and put the cheese into a colder place, as dry as possible.

It is best not to wrap this type of cheese unless you are going to market it, and a wrapping is then necessary as a hygienic precaution. If the cheese is to be eaten at home a greaseproof paper lightly covering it is all that is required.

STARTER

STARTER is a growth of special cultures in sterile milk and is advised as a means of ensuring the correct proportions of lactic-acid-producing organisms. It can be bought from most dairy schools, agricultural colleges which maintain instructional dairies, and many of the commercial dairies to which farmers send their milk. Quite a number of these will by arrangement deliver a bottle of starter by the lorry which takes away the milk churns. Starter can be safely used over a period of 3 days provided it is kept in a cool place. A refrigerator is suitable.

BUTTERMILK CROWDIE

IN Aberdeenshire a delicious crowdie is made from buttermilk. Raise the temperature of the buttermilk to 140 degrees F., holding it at this for 15 minutes and stirring continuously. Cool to 90 degrees F. Settle for 20 minutes and then run off the whey.

Ladle the remaining curd into a cheese cloth on a draining rack and tie cloth, tightening as drainage takes place. This is usually complete in 6 to 8 hours. When ready it should cling together when pressed in the hand.

Mix with a small quantity of good cream, and add salt at the rate of $\frac{1}{4}$ oz. to the pound of curd. This is ready for use immediately.

If the buttermilk is of good quality—as it is when the cows are luxuriating in the clovery meadows—this cheese should prove delicious.

From Miss Christian Milne, Aberdeenshire.

CORNISH CHEESE

TO make our good Cornish cheese, first clean out your bath or pan and place in it on the stove, to bring to a milk temperature of 94 degrees. Then put in a cool place to lower the temperature to 88 degrees for renneting. You will need the special cheese rennet in the following proportions: 1 dram of rennet to 2 gallons of milk, 2 drams to 5 gallons, 3 drams to 9 gallons, 4 drams to 12 gallons.

Put every 2 drams of rennet into four times as much water and pour into the milk when the latter is at 88 degrees. Deep stir for 3 minutes; then top stir till set. Take count of the time the curd takes to set (counting from the time it starts to turn), and when it has set, leave exactly 4 times as long for the whey to rise. If setting has taken 10 minutes, for example, leave for 40 minutes.

Now cut the curd into $\frac{1}{4}$-in. cubes, and leave for 10 minutes. Next, put on the stove and bring to a temperature of 98 degrees, stirring till this has been reached. Leave for another 10 minutes. Then dip off the whey, take up the curd and squeeze it in strainer-cloth; fix on a plate, and put a heavy weight on top. Squeeze like this for 15 minutes, and then cut into 6 large pieces. Squeeze again 3 times, for 15 minutes at a time, and keep turning the pieces in between.

After this, break into small pieces and once more get the temperature up to 78 degrees. Now mix salt in thoroughly, using 1 oz. salt to every 4 lbs. curd.

Put in strainer-cloth, and keep in a mould for 2 hours. Then put into muslin, and leave for 24 hours. After this, butter the outside of the cheese, bandage, and keep in a cool place; turning every day. It will take 6 weeks to ripen.

From Mrs. Stuart Hicks, Cornwall.

COTTAGE CHEESE

PLACE a jugful of sour milk in a warm place until the milk is quite thick, then salt should be added in the proportion of $\frac{1}{2}$ small teaspoonful to a pint. Stir well, and place in a muslin bag. (Well-washed flour bags do excellently for the purpose.) Hang it up to drain overnight, press between two plates for an hour, then work up with fresh cream and make into a pat.

From Mrs. Robert Thompson, Dumfriesshire.

COULOMMIER CHEESE

THE Coulommier cheese is a small, flat, circular cheese and may either be eaten fresh, i.e., from 3 days to a week old, or left to ripen for 2 or 3 weeks.

Take ½ gallon of fresh, clean milk (this quantity is most essential) and heat to 88 degrees. Add ½ dram rennet, which has been diluted with 4 times water. Stir into milk until it just thickens. Test by water in glass.

Leave for 40 minutes and skim off cap. Place the mould on a straw mat on a board, and when the curd is quite ready, ladle out a little; leave for 10 minutes, then ladle out a little more. This should be repeated until the mould is full. Then slide on the cap. The cheese should be turned in about 6 hours.

Second day: Turn out and salt on straw mats; when quite firm, slide off mould. If the cheeses are to be ripened it is necessary to keep them in a dry, airy room at a temperature of about 62 degrees for a few days, until a white mould begins to appear; then remove to cellar for a while to ripen. It is advisable to turn the cheese daily at this stage.

From Mrs. E. Wareham, Wiltshire.

CUMBERLAND CHEESE

TO make 14 lbs. of cheese, add 8 tablespoonfuls of rennet to 8 gallons of new or separated milk (heated to 90 degrees C.). Add butter colouring to colour the mixture; and allow to set. Then put it in a muslin with holes in the bottom to allow the surplus whey to escape.

Break the mixture up with the fingers, adding salt to taste. Put the muslin into a round cheese press. Change the muslin every third day. Leave in the press for a fortnight, then take out to harden.

From Mrs. Roper, Cumberland.

DOUBLE CREAM CHEESE

ONE gallon of double cream will make 2 dozen cheeses of 4 ozs. each.

Steam-heat the cream by placing container in a pail of hot

water until it reaches 60 degrees F. Add 4 tablespoonfuls of starter. Ripen for 2 hours. Ladle into twill cotton cloth over bowl. Gather corners of cloth and tie with string. Suspend in a cool atmosphere for a few hours.

Unfasten occasionally, and scrape cream from sides of cloth to assist drainage. When changed from liquid consistency, transfer to a closer-textured material—a piece of old hucka-back towelling is excellent.

Press with a 7-lb. weight until the cheese becomes pasty (usually about 2 hours). Carefully work in a small quantity of fine salt ($\frac{1}{2}$ oz. per gallon). Press into special moulds lined with greaseproof paper.

Balls of cream cheese are delicious with salad, and with bread and butter form a tempting and satisfying meal for a summer day.

From Miss Christian Milne, Aberdeenshire.

GOATS' MILK CHEESE

THE milk from the previous evening's milking is first skimmed, the cream then being warmed by standing it in a vessel in hot water. When warm, the cream is thoroughly mixed into the morning's milk, this is then strained into the evening's milk from which the cream was skimmed. Heat to 84 degrees F., by the same method as heating the cream. Add rennet at the rate of 1 drachm to each gallon of milk and stir for five minutes.

Cover and leave for about $\frac{3}{4}$ hour when the curd will break clean over the finger. Cut the curd into $\frac{1}{2}$ inch cubes, stir for ten minutes and slowly raise the temperature to 98 degrees F.

Continue stirring for another 40 minutes or until the curd becomes springy, when the whey can be run off. Line a small cheese mould with calico and pack the curd in gently. Cover and put on 10 lb. pressure for about $\frac{1}{4}$ hour. It must then be reversed in the mould and 20 lb. pressure applied for an hour. It is then reversed again, a clean calico put on and 30 lb. pressure applied for 4 hours. Leave all night with 5 lb. pressure and next morning rub in a little salt.

Put in a cool airy dairy and turn daily for three weeks or until thought ready.

From Mrs. C. McLennan, Argyllshire.

LINCOLN CHEESES (SOFT)

TAKE 1½ gallons of new milk and 2 pints sour milk or buttermilk. (Buttermilk is best if available.) Heat to 70 degrees F. and add 2 c.cm. of rennet. Leave for 2 hours to set, then cut the curd and ladle into cloths to drain.

This will make about 12 cheeses, which will be ready after maturing for 2 days. *Note.*—1 cubic centimetre of rennet means 15 drops and 4 cubic centimetres of rennet are 1 teaspoonful.

From Miss F. S. Smithson, Lincolnshire.

NOTTINGHAM-COLWICK

TO 1 gallon of new milk, at a temperature of 85 degrees F. add 17 drops of rennet which has been diluted with 3 times its own bulk of water. The rennet should be carefully stirred into the milk for 3 minutes, after which the vessel is covered up with a lid or cloth to retain as much heat as possible during coagulation.

While coagulation is going on, the moulds should be placed on racks or a slightly sloping draining table. The moulds are then lined with butter muslin of sufficient size for the corners to reach well over the cheese and, if necessary, to hasten the process, to be tied up Stilton fashion.

The curd should be ready to ladle into the moulds in 1¼ hours from the time of renneting the milk. This is done by using a ladle or saucer. Large, clean-cut slices are taken until the moulds are full.

Drainage may now be left to take place of its own accord. In about ¼ hour's time, the ends of the cloth should be folded over the top of the curd. This will cause the curd as it drains to fall inwards. In 10 minutes' time—and if a quick cheese is required—take the 3 corners of the cloth and tie them round the fourth. As soon as the cheese is firm, the cloth may be removed and the cheese placed on a shelf till required. 1 gallon will produce 2 cheeses.

From Mrs. A. E. Coombe, Leicestershire.

A NOVICE'S METHOD

BEING an amateur I used "make do" utensils when I made over 80 lbs. of cheese last season with our daily surplus milk from one Guernsey cow. It was cheddar type and the cheeses averaged 2½ lbs. each.

285

For each cheese I used about 3 gallons hand-skimmed milk, from 3 consecutive milkings, warmed to 80 degrees. Then I added rennet ($\frac{1}{2}$ teaspoonful and 2 drops per gallon), stirring it well into the milk. When the junket had set I cut it into large dice with a knife, and put it to warm again slowly till the whey had risen well. Then I cleared the whey from the curd by baling it gently with a cup; also, by pouring it off.

Now, with a milk skimmer, I put the curd (with about a tablespoonful of salt mixed with it) into a steamer top (the part with the holes in it) lined with muslin, filling the steamer to the brim with the curd, then covering the curd with a fold of the muslin. On top of this I placed a cake-tin pierced with holes (the cake-tin must be an easy fit into the steamer), and set a heavy flat iron in the centre of the cake-tin.

Leave this overnight for the whey to drain away. Next morning replace muslin with a dry piece. Next day again, take cheese out of steamer, wrap it in dry muslin, replace it between two boards with the weight on top. Dry it with a rough cloth and turn it daily until dry. If the cheese is inclined to crack, rub it with salt and then once more rub it with a cloth to dry.

About the fourth day, bind the cheese tightly round the edge with a strip of calico or bandage. This will keep it from becoming too flat under the weight. Leave bandage on till the cheese is matured.

From Mrs. K. Churchill, Dorsetshire.

OLD ENGLISH HERB CHEESE

TAKE 4 ozs. grated cheese, 2 tablespoonfuls cream, 3 tablespoonfuls sherry; pepper, salt and a little butter and as many varieties as possible of finely minced herbs—tarragon, chives, chervil, sage, parsley and thyme. Put all into a double saucepan over a gentle heat and stir till creamy and a pale green colour. Turn into small pots and allow to cool before spreading.

From Miss E. Rutherford, Tweedmouth.

"PICKING" CHEESE

THIS is, I think, a purely local speciality; always given the same name.

Heat the quantity of sweet milk available to 86 degrees F.

Add 1 teaspoonful of rennet to each 2 gallons of milk used. Set aside in a warm place until curd forms. Then cut curd into cubes and drain off whey.

Set aside the curd *without salting* until next day, when it should be broken up and set outside where it can get really warm in the sun. Take it inside at night; and repeat this process of heating for at least 4 days. By this time the curd should have quite a strong smell. (If a very strong cheese is required, the heating process may be continued for a week.)

Now salt curd. (About 1 oz. to 3 lbs. of curd, or rather more according to taste.) Pack in chessel and press for at least a week (the best picking cheese I ever made was pressed for a month, but as it was the last cheese for the season, the chessel was not required so it could be left).

Remove cheese from chessel, put a piece of cotton round it in the form of a bandage, and set on a piece of slate or wood in an airy place to dry. Daily turning of the cheese is recommended to ensure equality in the drying process.

From my experience, I find that the whole secret of success in making this particular cheese lies in exposing the curd to heat. One person I know who is very successful in making it often hangs her pail of curd under a roof-light, so that the heat given off by the sun may be intensified by the glass. It is a very old-fashioned type of cheese such as our grandmothers in this part of the country would have pressed under a huge stone—many of which can still be seen hereabout.

From Mrs. J. Murray, Banffshire.

PONT L'EVEQUE

THIS is a variety of cheese which, owing to its firm character, is only ready after ripening. ½ gallon of clean, fresh milk makes 1 cheese.

Warm the milk to 90 degrees and add ¼ dram of rennet which has been diluted with 4 times its volume of water. Stir into the milk in the usual way and leave for 50 to 60 minutes.

When the curd breaks into a clean fracture over the finger, cut with an ordinary knife into 2 squares and leave for 5 minutes. Then ladle the curd into a coarse straining cloth laid over wooden frames with latticed bottoms, through which the whey may escape, and cover with hot cloths.

In 15 to 20 minutes cut into squares. Cover and leave to drain. Leave until the curd is quite firm and fairly dry, which can be detected by its falling away from the side of the cloth. Care should be taken that the curd does not get too dry or it will not unite when placed in the moulds.

When firm, break up the curd and fill in the moulds. Place on a straw mat with a board underneath. When the mould is ½ full sprinkle a little salt and fill in the curd. As soon as the mould is full, place a straw mat and board on the top, and reverse the cheese. In 10 minutes turn cheese again as before.

This should be done several times during the next few hours, and then the cheese should be left until the next day, when salt should be sprinkled all over and the cheese placed on a clean straw mat.

This should be done twice a day until the cheese is quite firm, when the mould may be removed. It is best to keep the cheese in an airy room for a few days, then remove it to the cellar. Turn the cheese daily. It should ripen in about 3 or 4 weeks.

Mrs. E. Wareham, Wiltshire.

SHROPSHIRE SAGE

MY cheese is very suitable when only a small amount of milk is available. To every 5 gallons of milk use 1 teaspoonful of rennet mixed with 4 teaspoonfuls of cold water. Strain 2 gallons of night's milk into a clean scalded wooden tub. Next morning add 3 gallons of new milk and warm it all to 88 degrees F. Stir well, add the rennet and with skimmer stir it for 3 minutes. Cover and leave to set. In ½ hour it should be a solid mass, and breaking away from sides of tub.

With long-bladed knife cut into ½-in. strips. Leave 10 minutes, then break up carefully with the hands, stirring the whole mass carefully. Warm some of the whey and add to bring temperature up to 90 degrees F.; keep on stirring till curd falls into cubes, smooth and firm. Cover; leave ½ hour (when curd should have shrunk into solid mass).

Push curds to sides and drain off whey; cut curd into 6-in. cubes, leave 10 minutes; turn over and cut again—and again

Blanching is carried out by means of putting the vegetables in a special blancher, or a wire basket or muslin bag, and leave 8 pints of water, which should be brought to the boil, the ...

Corn on the Cob.—Use fresh young co... 8 minutes, according to size. Pack individually in freezer paper or foil. Kernels can be scraped from blanched cobs and packed in cartons.

306

DAIRY PRODUCE

Butter.—Freeze in original wrappings, putting packages in bags for easy storage. Salted butter stores for three months, unsalted butter for six months.

Milk.—Milk should be pasteurised and homogenised and packed in cartons leaving 1 in. headspace. Only small quantities should be frozen which can be used quickly at one time.

Cream.—Cream should be pasteurised and cooled rapidly and packed in waxed containers leaving 1/4 in. headspace. 1 tablespoon sugar to each pint of cream will improve keeping time. Cream must contain 40% butterfat.

Cheese.—Freeze in small quantities (i.e. 8 oz. or less). Divide pieces with Cellophane and wrap in foil or freezer paper. Hard cheese crumbles; blue cheeses, Camembert and Port Salut tend to crumble. All cheeses should be carefully wrapped and sealed to avoid drying out and cross-flavouring.

Cream and Cottage Cheese.—Soft cheeses that break up during thawing. Cream cheese is best blended with heavy cream to be used as a cocktail dip, and should be packed in rigid containers. Cottage cheese must be frozen quickly to prevent water separation on thawing.

Eggs.—Eggs cannot be frozen in the shells. Whole eggs should be lightly mixed together and frozen in cartons in small quantities, adding 1 teaspoon salt or 1 tablespoon sugar to 5 eggs. Yolks should be lightly mixed and seasoned with 1 teaspoon salt or 1 tablespoon sugar to 6 yolks. Whites need no special preparation. Label eggs for the freezer very carefully, with details of seasoning.

Ice Cream.—Make ice cream with any recipes and see it is smooth and well-beaten before packing. Pack in small usable quantities in cartons, and cover surface with foil to prevent ice crystals forming.

PUDDINGS AND CAKES

All items made with flour freeze very well. It is usually easier to freeze them when baked, but some items may be prepared and frozen until to be cooked immediately before use. *Steamed and Baked Puddings.*—Make standard sponge and Cakes, scones and allow it to get cold. Sauces and cakes may be poured over sweetened fruit such as gooseberries, and may be frozen raw or cooked.

291

FOR YOUR CORNER CUPBOARD

TONIC DRINKS

AN ANCIENT BARLEY DRINK

(Suitable for invalids: a very effective and nourishing drink for feverish ailments)

2 ozs. pearl barley.	2 ozs. stoned raisins.
5 pints boiling water.	2 ozs. sliced figs.
1 oz. liquorice root.	

WASH and blanch the pearl barley. Add 4 pints of the water and cook until reduced one half. Strain, and to the barley water add the raisins, figs and the other pint of water. Simmer again until reduced to 2 pints, adding the liquorice root just before cooking is completed, then strain. This compound concoction is to be used, diluted, for drinks, and is suitable for mixing with plain barley water. It can also be given in small quantities.

From Mrs. E. Farrington, Worcestershire.

BLACKBERRY CORDIAL

POUR 1 pint of white wine vinegar over 1 quart of ripe blackberries. Let it stand in an earthenware jar for 7 or 8 days, stirring the mixture to extract the juices. Strain off when ready, and put the liquor in an enamel saucepan with 1 lb. of loaf sugar and 1 lb. of honey. Bring to the boil, then remove from the heat and allow it to get cold. Bottle and cork and keep it in a dark place. This is an excellent winter remedy for colds and sore throats, a tablespoonful in a glass of hot water making a pleasant bedtime drink.

311

From Mrs. A. D. Underwood, Essex.

for 15 minutes. Strain free of petals and boil till syrup thickens, when it will be a rich red colour. Pour into clean, dry, warmed jars and seal very securely. To make a good drink, put a teaspoonful into a milk beaker and dissolve in a tablespoonful of boiling water. When cold, fill up with milk. This is an excellent cure for sore throats and is also a splendid pick-me-up.

From Miss E. Rutherford, Northumberland.

½lb. quick macaroni.
¼ lb. grated cheddar cheese.
1 thick slice stale bread.
1½ oz. margarine.

A small amount of milk.
Salt and pepper.
Tomatoes (if available).

BOTTLED TOMATO JUICE

COOK the macaroni as directed on the packet. Grease a large ovenproof dish, and cover the bottom with a layer of macaroni. Season and sprinkle with a generous layer of cheese and a few breadcrumbs. Continue with alternate layers, ending with cheese and breadcrumbs. Dot with margarine and pour on most of the milk. Garnish with sliced tomatoes and bake in a moderate oven for 20–25 minutes. This dish is ideal for high tea or supper.

WIPE and stem ripe tomatoes; cut them in halves and put them, cut side down, in a saucepan, standing it at the back of a warm stove until the juice begins to flow. Press down frequently with a wooden spoon and boil them for 30 minutes. Strain through a fine colander—a soup strainer is ideal—pressing all the juice and most of the pulp through, leaving only skin and pips. Put the juice back on the stove, add salt, sugar and pepper to taste, boil for 15 minutes. Pour into hot sterilized jars or bottles and seal at once. Don't season the juice too highly, as more can be added when served. This makes a most healthful and refreshing drink. It will keep good for 12 months.

From Mrs. D. Esme Booker, Bedfordshire.

PHEASANT IN WINE

1 pheasant, ready for the oven
5 oz. tin tomato purée
¼ pint white wine.
¾ lb. onions.

½ lb. parsnips
½ lb. carrots.
Seasoning.

SLICE all the vegetables and place in a large casserole. Put in the pheasant. Mix together the tomato purée and wine. Season well and pour over vegetables and pheasant. Cook in slow to moderate oven, turning and basting the pheasant for 2 hours, or until tender.

TONIC STOUT

8 ozs. black (or burnt) malt.
1 oz. hops.
2 oz. black liquorice.

2 medium-sized potatoes
2 oz. brown sugar.
10 pints water.

WHEN the water is at boiling-point add herbs, malt, hops, liquorice, and the potatoes (well washed but not peeled, and perforated by a fork or darning needle). Simmer gently for 1 hour, then strain into a pan, earthenware, if possible. Add sugar. When about 95 degrees F. stir in the yeast, which has been dissolved in a little of the warm liquid. Cover up, and stand for 24 hours. Skim off yeast and put in jars or bottles; corking lightly at first, tightening up 12 hours later. Leave for 2 days. You will then find it a beautifully creamy stout, with remarkable tonic properties.

From Mrs. A. Foster, Hampshire.

APPLE CRUNCHIE

1 lb. cooking apples.
3 heaped dessertspoons soft brown sugar.

PEEL and slice the apples and put in a pie dish. Sprinkle with sugar. make a firm mixture. Spread over the apples and bake in a moderate oven for 20 minutes. Serve with cream.

294

From Mrs. J. Walker, Hampshire.

Recipes 1967–71

TREACLE POSSET

1 pint milk.
2 tablespoonfuls treacle.
The juice of 1 lemon.

PUT milk into a saucepan and bring almost to boiling-point. Add the treacle and lemon juice and boil slowly until the curd separates. Strain, and serve hot as a remedy for a cold.

From Miss E. Taylor, Cheshire.

MARROW AND APPLE CHUTNEY

4 lbs. well-ripened marrow.
4 lbs. Bramley apples.
8 ozs. onions or shallots.
8 ozs. seedless raisins.
1½ lbs. sugar.
Cayenne pepper.
¾ pint vinegar.

THIS is a very sweet chutney, very similar to mango chutney. Boil apples, chopped onions, raisins and sugar until quite pulped, stirring continuously. Add marrow cut into ½-in. cubes, and continue to simmer until marrow is quite transparent and apples are thoroughly pulped. Add salt, pepper and ginger to taste, citric acid and vinegar, and continue to simmer for further 15 minutes. On no account should iron or chipped enamel pans be used. Let mixture cool slightly, stir and pour into hot jars. Tie down when cold.

From Mrs. Wilson, Suffolk.

WINTER CORDIAL

4 dessertspoonfuls fine oatmeal.
1 lemon.
½ teaspoonful ground ginger.
1 quart boiling water.
2 dessertspoonfuls Demerara sugar.

MIX oatmeal, sugar and ground ginger together in a basin. Grate the rind of the lemon and add. Gradually pour on the boiling water, stirring the while. Put in saucepan, add lemon juice and simmer for 10 minutes. Strain and serve hot.

From Mrs. Westwood, Warwickshire.

SALVES AND COUNTRY CURES

PICKLED BEETS

Uncooked beetroot.
1 pint vinegar.
¼ oz. mace.
¼ oz. cinnamon stick.
Allspice.
A few peppercorns.

WASH and peel the uncooked beetroot, shred finely using a grater. Pack into clean, glass-topped preserving jars and cover with cold spiced vinegar. Make this by tying spices in a muslin bag and adding to the vinegar. Bring to boiling point and leave to stand for 2 hours. Use a saucepan with a tight fitting lid. Remove the bag and the vinegar is ready for use.

From Mrs. G. Edwards, Denbighshire.

BUTTERCUP OINTMENT

PUT 1 lb. pure vaseline into a pan with as many buttercup flowers (without the stems) as can possibly be pressed into it. Allow to simmer (not boil) for ¾ hour. While still hot, strain through muslin into small pots. It is ready for use when cold and is very good for all skin troubles.

From Miss E. Rutherford, Northumberland.

COLD CREAM

STAND 4 ozs. white wax in a warm place and when soft beat in 8 ozs. almond oil and 4 ozs. elderflower water. Add a little perfume to scent it if you like.

From Mrs. Dowson, Yorkshire.

PICKLED MUSHROOMS

Button mushrooms.
Salted water.
Vinegar.
Pickling spice.

CLEAN mushrooms with a cloth dipped in salt and water, and boil them in salted water for 5 minutes. Put on a cloth to cool. Pack into jars and cover with vinegar which has been boiled with pickling spice. A spoonful of olive oil on the surface will preserve them, but don't use them for a few days.

CUCUMBER LOTION

(For weather-roughened skins)

CUT 6 ripe cucumbers into slices about ½ in. thick. Steam till soft enough to pass through a colander, then press again through a piece of butter muslin. Measure the pulp, and for

295

From Miss R. Roberts, Merionethshire.

The top should be put on lightly. While still hot, strain the mixture through butter-muslin and bottle in jars. This very greasy cream is excellent for dry skins, or to rub into the hands after rough work.

CLOTTED CREAM

Use new milk and strain at once, as soon as milked, into shallow pans. In winter let the milk stand 24 hours; in the summer 12 hours at least. Then put the milk pan on a hot hearth if you have one, or in a wide brass kettle of water, large enough to receive the pan. It must remain on the fire till quite hot, but on no account boil, or there will be a skin instead of a cream upon the milk. You will know when done enough by the undulations on the surface looking thick, and having a ring round the pan the size of the bottom. The time required to scald cream depends on the size of the pan and the heat of the fire; the slower the better.

Clotted cream is best done over a stick fire. Remove the pan into the dairy or larder, where care must be taken in moving it, so as not that the cream is not broken both in putting on the fire and taking off; stand in a cool place, and next day take off the cream with a knife, laying it in a glass dish, or for a table, taking care to have a good crust all over.

From Mrs. Rawson, Brockwell, Yorkshire.

GRANDMOTHER'S EMBROCATION

TAKE ½ pint of turpentine and 1 egg; put them together into a large bottle. Cork it and shake it till it becomes a cream; then add gradually 1 pint of vinegar and a small tablespoonful of liquid ammonia, and bottle for use. This embrocation keeps years in well-corked bottles.

From Mrs. A. D. Jones, Cheshire.

FOR GREASY SKINS

A SIMPLE habit to improve a greasy skin is washing the face always with very hot water and stiffing afterwards with cold. Then, after drying, sponge well with this lotion: Four tablespoonfuls elderflower water, half a teaspoonful simple tincture of benzoin added drop by drop, stirring all the time; five drops of glycerine and five drops tincture of myrrh. This is very soothing and refreshing especially in hot weather.

From Mrs. C. H. Andrews, Norfolk.

HAIR-SETTING LOTION

MIX one teaspoonful of glycerine, very gradually, with six tablespoonfuls of elderflower water, one teaspoonful rectified spirit, and half a teaspoonful of fluid ammonia. Damp hair well with this before putting it in waving pins and it will be effective even in wet weather.

From Mrs. C. H. Andrews, Norfolk.

HAND CREAM

BEAT up well together 2 tablespoonfuls glycerine, an equal quantity of methylated spirits and of milk, and the white of one egg. Bottle, and use after washing hands and before going to bed. Rub well in.

From Miss F. Lucas, Yorkshire.

298

HONEY COUGH MIXTURE

PUT into a bottle 4 ozs. pure cod-liver oil, 1 oz. of glycerine, 4 ozs. of honey (pure), and the strained juice of 3 lemons. Shake well.

This mixture should be taken 3 times a day after meals, and shaken well always before pouring.

A GOOD LINIMENT

1 pint of vinegar, 1 oz. of camphor.

A GOOD old-fashioned liniment for sprains and chilblains can be made from the above ingredients. Mix all together well in a bottle until the resulting liquid is white and creamy. It is then ready for use.

MEDICINAL JAM

1 lb. prunes.
1 lb. seedless raisins.
1 lb. Demerara sugar.
1 lb. whole almonds.

REMOVE the stones from the prunes. Chop prunes and raisins very finely, together with the blanched almonds and the kernels from the prune stones. Soak all overnight in 1 pint of water. Next day add the Demerara sugar, bring to the boil and cook for ½ hour; boiling not too fast. Pour into hot jars and seal down immediately. You will find this jam delicious on brown bread, and is a mild, natural laxative for children.

SOFTENING SKIN LOTION

WHEN you have grated and squeezed lemons for other purposes, steep the husks in 4 ozs. boiling water. When cool, pour off this lemon water and dissolve in it 1 oz. powdered borax. Add 2 ozs. glycerine and pour lotion into a bottle.

into the pan, cover with cold water and bring to the boil. After boiling for 20 minutes, stand the pan by the side of the stove and simmer for 3 hours. Strain off the leaves and to every pint of liquid, add 1 tablespoonful of liquid ammonia. Put into a bottle and cork, and for safety label "Poison". It keeps indefinitely.

Spread the garment to be cleaned on a table, and with a cloth (preferably a piece of old blue serge), sponge, giving extra attention to the most soiled patches. Press with an iron afterwards.

From Mrs. Kate Carding, Nottinghamshire

SCOURING POWDER

SHAKE up 1 lb. whitening, 1 lb. pumice powder and 1 lb. soap powder to make a good cleanser economical to prepare and to use.

From Mrs. A. Hartley, Co. Derry

SCRUBBING SOAP

½ pint soft water twice (1 pint in all).
1 teaspoonful olive oil, coconut oil or similar oil.

MELT 1 lb. ... Put in an enamel pan. Dissolve soda in warm water, add to the fat while warm, stir thoroughly. Leave until next day, but stir it occasionally at first. Next day re-melt mixture, add the other ½ pint water and the oil. Let it boil and stir to mix thoroughly. Pour into a small wooden box (such as a small seed box) lined with wet cotton cloth. Allow to set and dry.

From Miss Ruy Cooper, Hampshire

SOFT SOAP

TAKE 1 lb. of stone potash ... by ... any kind of rendered fat. Crush the potash well, then place in a large pot with 2 gallons of water. Let boil until dissolved, then add the fat and when it is all melted pour into a large jar. Full up with boiling water. Stir every day for a week for ten minutes. It will gradually become a jelly. This soft soap keeps well and has many uses.

From Miss Christian Milne, Aberdeenshire.

TOILET SOAP

To make 6 lbs. you need
2½ lbs. well-clarified fat.
1 lb. caustic soda.
½ lb. coconut oil.
2 tablespoonfuls glycerine.

ALLOW the dissolved caustic soda to cool until just warm. Use an earthenware jug or vessel. Melt the fat until just warm, then pour soda solution in a thin stream into the fat, stirring one way for 2 minutes, add other ingredients while stirring. Pour soap into a wooden box lined with damp cotton. Put into a warm place for 24 hours. Cut with wire and store.

From Miss S. Elliott, Northumberland.

THREE-IN-ONE CLEANER

SHRED into a pan ¼ lb. white Castile soap, and pour on 2 quarts boiling water. Simmer until soap dissolves. Add ½ oz. saltpetre. Stir well: strain. Now add (carefully) ¼ pint ammonia. Bottle and cork tightly.

Damp your *carpets*, brush in some of the cleanser, and clean off with a sponge and clean water. Add enough whitening to make a thin cream, and you have a wonderful cleanser for *white paint*. Make the cream a bit thicker, and it cleans *silver*.

From Miss M. Scarlett, Suffolk.

WASHING SOAP

6 lbs. fat.
2½ pints of water.

BOIL fat for 10 minutes in pan, then pour kettle of boiling water over to clarify. Weigh 6 lbs. fat and then melt again. Put caustic soda into a bowl, pour to this 2¾ pints of cold water and stir. It will become very hot. Have fat in one bowl and soda and water in another. When both are lukewarm, slowly pour the soda and water into the fat together with paraffin oil. Keep stirring for 2 minutes until the mixture looks like honey. Have a wooden box ready lined with damp cloth. Pour the mixture in and cover. Leave until the following day, then take out and cut into pieces. Store for 1 month before using. While making this soap keep away from fire.

From Miss M. Rutherford, Northumberland.

BASIC FOOD FREEZING

FREEZING is an easy way of preserving both raw and cooked food. Good food will keep its quality and nutritive value in the freezer.

All food for freezing must be processed quickly as soon as it has been gathered and/or cooked and chilled, and it must be frozen quickly at the recommended low temperature, preferably against the cold surfaces of the cabinet. Food must be carefully packed to exclude air, labelled for identification, and recorded to encourage a steady turnover. Frozen cooked food should never be thawed and then refrozen; raw materials may however be thawed, then cooked and refrozen.

Packaging Materials

Waxed tubs and rigid plastic containers are useful for liquid cooked dishes, and for fruit and vegetables, and some fragile baked goods. Heavy duty polythene bags are useful for almost all freezer foods. Polythene sheeting or heavy duty foil can be used for wrapping, or specially prepared freezer paper. Bags can be closed with wire fasteners, but boxes and packets must be sealed with special freezer tape treated with gum which is resistant to low temperatures. Freezer labels also incorporate this gum.

Packaging Methods

Containers with lids should be packed so that headspace from $\frac{1}{2}$ to 1 in. is left above the surface of the food to allow for expansion. Sheet wrappings or bags must have the air released.

Foods Unsuitable for Freezing

Almost all food can be frozen, except salad dressings and mayonnaise, meringue toppings, custards, milk puddings, salad vegetables (tomatoes, celery and onions can be frozen for cooking, but not to serve raw), and hard-boiled egg whites.

VEGETABLES

Vegetables must be frozen when young, tender and at the peak of perfection. They should be prepared for freezing in small quantities, and are best prepared immediately after picking, preferably in the early morning. They must be blanched before processing, as the heat stops the chemical action of enzymes which affect quality, flavour and colour and nutritional value.

Blanching is carried out by means of putting the vegetables in a special blancher, or a wire basket or muslin bag, and plunging it into boiling water. The saucepan should contain about 8 pints of water, which should be brought to the boil, the vegetables lowered in, the pan covered tightly and the heat kept high. Blanching time is calculated from the time when water returns to boiling point. Vegetables should then be removed immediately, drained and cooled by plunging into iced water, then drained again, packed and frozen quickly.

Artichokes (Globe).—Remove outer leaves, wash thoroughly, trim stems and remove 'chokes'. Blanch for 7 minutes in water with lemon juice added. Cool and drain, and pack in boxes.

Asparagus.—Remove woody portions and small scales and wash well. Grade for size and blanch 2 minutes for small spears, 3 minutes for medium spears, 4 minutes for large spears. Cool and drain and pack in boxes or freezer paper or foil.

Beans (Broad).—Shell beans, blanch 1½ minutes. Pack in bags.

Beans (French).—Top and tail and leave small beans whole, but cut larger ones in 1 in. pieces. Blanch whole beans 3 minutes, cut beans 2 minutes. Pack in bags.

Beans (Runner).—Cut beans in pieces, but do not shred. Blanch 2 minutes and pack in bags.

Beetroot.—Use beet under 3 ins. diameter for freezing. Boil until tender, skin and pack in cartons.

Broccoli.—Use compact tender heads, trim and wash in salt water. Blanch 3–5 minutes according to thickness of stems and pack in bags.

Brussels Sprouts.—Clean and wash small compact head and blanch 3–4 minutes according to size. Pack in bags.

Cabbage (Green and Red).—Wash and shred finely. Blanch 1½ minutes and pack in bags. Do not use raw for salads.

Carrots.—Wash and scrape very young carrots and leave whole. Blanch 3 minutes and pack in bags.

Cauliflower.—Wash and break into small sprigs. Add lemon to blanching water and blanch 3 minutes. Pack into bags.

Celery.—Scrub crisp young stalks, cut in 1 in. lengths and blanch 3 minutes. Pack in bags, or in rigid containers, covering with blanching water. Do not use raw, but only in cooked dishes.

Corn on the Cob.—Use fresh young cobs and blanch 4–8 minutes, according to size. Pack individually in freezer paper or foil. Kernels can be scraped from blanched cobs and packed in cartons.

Herbs.—Wash herbs and cut very finely. Pack into ice-cube trays and freeze, then wrap frozen cubes in foil and pack in bags for storage. Parsley, mint and chives freeze most successfully.

Kale.—Use young tender, tightly curled kale, remove stems from leaves, and blanch 1 minute. Pack tightly into bags.

Mushrooms.—Wipe very fresh mushrooms, but do not peel. Blanch 1½ minutes, adding lemon juice to water. Pack cups down in containers, leaving headspace.

Onions.—Peel and chop or slice onions, blanch 2 minutes and pack, overwrapping to prevent smells escaping. Use for cooked dishes.

Parsnips.—Peel young parsnips and cut into 1½ ins. dice. Blanch 2 minutes and pack in polythene bags.

Peas.—Shell young sweet peas, blanch 1 minute and pack in bags.

Potatoes.—Scrape new potatoes, blanch 4 minutes and pack in polythene bags. Mash old potatoes with butter and hot milk and freeze in bags or cartons. Chips should be cooked in clean odour-free fat, drained on paper, cooled and packed in bags.

Spinach.—Use young tender spinach and remove stems. Wash very well and blanch 2 minutes. Press out excess moisture and freeze in bags or containers.

Tomatoes.—Wipe small whole tomatoes and pack in bags. Use only for cooking. Tomatoes simmered in their own juice may be pulped and sieved and packed in small containers.

Turnips.—Cut small, young, mild turnips in ½ in. dice and blanch 2½ minutes before packing in containers.

FRUIT

Fruit should be frozen on the day it is picked. It should be of top quality in peak condition. Fruit is usually packed dry without sweetening, dry with sugar, or in syrup. Ripe fruit may also be used raw or cooked as a purée. Fruit syrups made to standard recipes freeze very well. Citrus and other shop-bought fruit may also be frozen when prices are low.

Apples.—Use firm crisp apples for slices; freeze fluffy apples as purée or apple sauce. Pack apple slices in sugar, allowing 8 oz. sugar to 2 lbs. fruit, in containers or bags.

Apricots.—Cut apricots in half and remove stones. Pack in cold syrup made from 8 oz. sugar to 1 pint water.

Blackberries.—Pack dry in bags, or add 8 oz. sugar to 2 lbs. fruit.

Blueberries.—Pack dry in bags, or add 8 oz. sugar to 2 lbs. fruit.

Cherries.—Pack in plastic containers (cherry juice leaks through waxed boxes in the freezer) in syrup made from 8 oz. sugar to 1 pint water.

Currants.—Pack dry in bags, or add 8 oz. sugar to 1 lb. fruit, or pack in syrup made from 8 oz. sugar to 1 lb. fruit. Black-currants freeze very well as purée.

Damsons, plums and greengages.—Cut fruit in half, remove stones and pack in syrup made from 8 oz. sugar to 1 lb. fruit (a little extra sugar may be needed for damsons).

Gooseberries.—Pack dry in bags after topping and tailing. Fruit may also be frozen as purée.

Grapefruit.—Remove all pith and cut segments away from pith. Pack dry in sugar, allowing 8 oz. sugar to 2 breakfast-cups of segments, or pack in syrup made from 9 oz. sugar to 1 pint water.

Grapes.—Pack seedless varieties whole, or skin, pip and cut in half, and pack in syrup made from 6 oz. sugar to 1 pint water.

Melons.—Cut flesh in cubes or balls, toss in lemon juice and pack in syrup made from 6 oz. sugar to 1 pint water.

Oranges.—Prepare in segments or slices and pack in dry sugar, allowing 8 oz. sugar to 3 breakfastcups of orange pieces. Fruit may be packed in syrup made from 6 oz. sugar to 1 pint water.

Peaches.—Peel, halve and slice, and brush fruit with lemon juice. Pack in syrup made from 8 oz. sugar to 1 pint water.

Pears.—Peel and quarter fruit, remove cores, and dip pieces in lemon juice. Poach pears in syrup made from 6 oz. sugar to 1 pint water for 1½ minutes, drain and cool, and pack in cold syrup.

Pineapple.—Peel fruit and cut into slices or chunks. Pack unsweetened, or allow 4 oz. sugar to 2 breakfastcups crushed pineapple, or pack slices or cubes in syrup made from 6 oz. sugar to 1 pint water.

Raspberries.—Pack dry in bags, or add 4 oz. sugar to 1 lb. fruit. Fruit may be packed in syrup made from 6 oz. sugar to 1 pint water, or fruit may be packed as sweetened purée.

Rhubarb.—Wash sticks and trim to required length. Blanch 1 minute, and wrap in foil or put in bags. Cut-up rhubarb can be packed in syrup made from 8 oz. sugar to 1 pint water, or stewed sweetened rhubarb can be packed in containers or made into purée for freezing.

Strawberries.—Pack dry in bags, or add 4 oz. sugar to 1 lb. fruit, or pack in syrup made from 8 oz. sugar to 1 pint water. Strawberries are best packed dry without sweetening.

FISH

Fish should never be more than 24 hours old when frozen. Freshly caught fish should be cleaned and scaled. Flat fish and herrings are best gutted, and flat fish are easier to cook later if skinned and filleted. Fatty fish should be washed in fresh water but other fish can be washed in salt water, removing all blood and membranes. There are many different ways of packing fish for the freezer, but it is easiest to separate portions by a double thickness of Cellophane, then wrap in freezer paper, foil or polythene, pressing out all air, and freezing quickly.

White Fish.—Clean and pack fish and freeze quickly. Cod, plaice, sole and whiting will store for six months.

Fatty Fish.—Clean and pack fish, avoiding any salt in the preparation. Haddock, halibut, mackerel, salmon, trout and turbot will store for four months.

Smoked Fish.—Wrap fish very well in foil, freezer paper or polythene, and overwrap. Bloaters, kippers, smoked haddock and trout will store for 12 months.

Shellfish.—Cook and cool thoroughly. Pack tightly in cartons or bags. Crabs, lobster, crayfish, shrimps and prawns will store for one month. Oysters and scallops should be packed raw after washing in salt water, and they should then be packed in water, being stored no longer than one month.

MEAT, POULTRY AND GAME

All meat, poultry and game freeze extremely well. They should be hung for the required time before freezing, as meat hung after freezing deteriorates rapidly. Joints and birds should be trimmed and packed ready for cooking, and poultry and game should not be packed containing giblets or stuffing. Cooked meat and poultry dishes also freeze well.

Joints.—Remove bones if possible, trim surplus fat, and tie joints into shape. Wipe meat and pad sharp bones, and wrap in freezer paper, foil or polythene. Meat is best overwrapped.

Steaks and Chops.—Trim meat and separate individual pieces with Cellophane or greaseproof paper before wrapping.

Minced and Cubed Meat.—Pack in usable quantities in bags, excluding as much fat as possible. Do not add salt to mince. Mince may be shaped into hamburgers, separated by greaseproof paper before packing.

Offal.—Wash and dry well, and remove blood vessels and pipes. Wrap in Cellophane or polythene and pack in cartons or bags.

Sausages and Sausage Meat.—If possible, do not season highly or add much salt. Pack tightly in freezer paper, foil or polythene.

Ham and Bacon.—Store in the piece rather than sliced. Pack in freezer paper, foil or polythene, and overwrap. Do not store longer than three weeks if meat is sliced, three months in the piece.

Cooked Cold Meat.—Cut in slices and separate with Cellophane or greaseproof paper, and pack tightly to avoid drying. Slices may be packed in gravy or sauce. Do not store longer than one month.

Cooked Meat Dishes.—Prepare as for normal use, but do not season highly or overcook vegetables. Pack in containers after cooling quickly. Stews and casseroles, meat loaves and meat balls and cottage pie all freeze very well. Thicken gravy with cornflour.

Poultry.—Truss whole birds or joint neatly. Pad bones with greaseproof paper and divide joints with Cellophane or greaseproof paper. Omit giblets, liver and stuffing. Remove oil glands from geese and ducks. Pack in polythene bags, removing all air.

Game.—Hang and prepare for use, making sure shot wounds are well cleaned. Pluck and truss and draw if necessary (do not draw plover, quail, snipe and woodcock). Pack in bags, excluding all air.

Hares and Rabbits.—Bleed, hang and clean as for immediate use. Cut in joints and separate each piece with Cellophane or greaseproof paper, and pack in bags.

Venison.—Clean thoroughly, bleed and hang. Cut in joints and pack in bags. Use trimmings for minced or cubed meat for freezing.

Cooked Poultry and Game.—Prepare as for immediate use, undercooking vegetables and thickening sauces by reduction, or with cornflour. Pack in bags or boxes.

DAIRY PRODUCE

Butter.—Freeze in original wrappings, putting packages in bags for easy storage. Salted butter stores for three months, unsalted butter for six months.

Milk.—Milk should be pasteurised and homogenised and packed in cartons leaving 1 in. headspace. Only small quantities should be frozen which can be used quickly at one time.

Cream.—Cream should be pasteurised and cooled rapidly and packed in waxed containers leaving 1 in. headspace. 1 tablespoon sugar to each pint of cream will improve keeping time. Cream must contain 40% butterfat.

Cheese.—Freeze in small quantities (i.e. 8 oz. or less). Divide pieces with Cellophane and wrap in foil or freezer paper. Hard cheeses freeze best; blue cheeses, Camembert and Port Salut tend to crumble. All cheeses should be carefully wrapped and sealed to avoid drying-out and cross-flavouring.

Cream and Cottage Cheese.—Soft cheeses tend to separate on thawing. Cream cheese is best blended with heavy cream to be used as a cocktail dip, and should be packed in rigid containers. Cottage cheese must be frozen quickly to prevent water separation on thawing.

Eggs.—Eggs cannot be frozen in the shells. Whole eggs should be lightly mixed together and frozen in cartons in small quantities, adding $\frac{1}{2}$ teaspoon salt or $\frac{1}{2}$ tablespoon sugar to 5 eggs. Yolks should be lightly mixed and seasoned with $\frac{1}{2}$ teaspoon salt or $\frac{1}{2}$ tablespoon sugar to 6 yolks. Whites need no special preparation. Label eggs for the freezer very carefully, with details of seasoning.

Ice Cream.—Make ice cream to standard recipes and see it is smooth and well-beaten before packing. Pack in small usable quantities in cartons, and cover surface with foil to prevent ice crystals forming.

PUDDINGS, BREAD AND CAKES

All items made with flour freeze very well. It is usually easiest to freeze them when baked, but some items may be prepared and frozen raw to be cooked immediately before a meal.

Steamed and Baked Puddings.—Make standard sponge pudding or cake mixture recipes and steam or bake in foil containers. Cool and cover with foil, or put into bags. Sponge mixtures may be poured over sweetened fruit such as gooseberries, and may be frozen raw or cooked.

Fruit Crumbles.—Fresh sugared fruit may be packed in a foil container and covered with crumble topping, then topped with foil or put into a polythene bag. Pudding may also be cooked before freezing.

Gelatine Puddings.—Clear jellies do not freeze well. Mousses and cold soufflés which contain gelatine as well as eggs and cream, and sometimes fruit and egg whites, freeze well. They are best prepared in the containers in which they will be served.

Pastry and Pies.—Slab pastry may be packed in usable quantities and frozen raw in foil or polythene. Cooked pastry cases should be packed in boxes to avoid breakage. Pies may be frozen baked or unbaked, and if containing fruit, the filling need not be cooked before freezing. Freeze pies unwrapped, then pack in foil or polythene, or in boxes if likely to break.

Bread and Buns.—Pack in polythene bags in required quantities. Do not overbake fruit and nut breads, and cool quickly before packing.

Scones.—Pack in usable quantities in polythene bags, labelling if fruit or cheese have been added.

Pancakes, Griddlecakes and Drop Scones.—Cool thoroughly after cooking. Pack large thin pancakes with layers of Cellophane or greaseproof paper like a cake, and wrap in foil or polythene. Pack griddlecakes and drop scones in boxes, foil or polythene bags.

Sponge Cakes and Iced Cakes.—The same treatment applies to cakes with and without fat, to iced and un-iced cakes, to plain cake mixtures, and to those flavoured with chocolate and coffee. Delicate cakes are best packed in boxes to avoid crushing. Other cakes can be wrapped in foil or polythene. Spongecakes should not be filled with jam or fresh cream before freezing, but a butter icing filling and topping will freeze well. If freezing iced cake, freeze before wrapping in foil or polythene.

Fruit Cakes.—Wrap in foil or polythene. Store Dundee, sultana and other light fruit cakes, but do not waste space on rich fruit cakes which store well in tins.

Small Cakes.—Freeze small plain, fruit or iced cakes in bags, or pack iced cakes in boxes to avoid damage.

Choux Pastry Cases.—Pack baked eclair and cream bun cases in bags or boxes without filling or icing. Fill and ice after thawing at room temperature for two hours.

Biscuits.—Make biscuits to standard recipes, form into cylinder shapes about 2 ins. diameter and wrap in foil or polythene. Slice before baking. Baked biscuits may be frozen, but keep well in tins.

MISCELLANEOUS

Soups and Sauces.—Thicken by reduction, or with cornflour, and pack in small or large quantities according to end use.

Stock.—Freeze meat, poultry or fish stock in containers, allowing 1 in. headspace for expansion.

Sandwiches.—Prepare sandwiches with well-buttered bread, avoiding cooked egg whites, raw vegetables, salad cream or mayonnaise, and jam from fillings. Pack in groups of six or eight, with an extra slice or crust of bread at each end to prevent drying out. Keep sandwiches large and with crusts on, and wrap in foil or polythene and freeze a few inches from freezer wall.

Spaghetti, Macaroni and Rice.—Slightly undercook, drain thoroughly and pack in bags.

READERS' RECIPES 1967–71

EASY MACARONI CHEESE

½lb. quick macaroni.
½ lb. grated cheddar cheese.
1 thick slice stale bread.
1½ oz. margarine.

A small amount of milk.
Salt and pepper.
Tomatoes (if available).

COOK the macaroni as directed on the packet. Grease a large ovenproof dish, and cover the bottom with a layer of macaroni. Season and sprinkle with a generous layer of cheese and a few breadcrumbs. Continue with alternate layers, ending with cheese and breadcrumbs. Dot the top with margarine and pour on a little milk. Garnish with sliced tomatoes and bake in a moderate oven for 20–25 minutes. This dish is ideal for high tea or supper.

From Mrs. D. M. Stephenson, Yorkshire.

PHEASANT IN WINE

1 pheasant, ready for the oven
5 oz. tin tomato purée
¼ pint white wine.
¾ lb. onions.

½ lb. parsnips
1 lb. carrots.
Seasoning.

SLICE all the vegetables and place in a large casserole. Put in the pheasant. Mix together the tomato purée and wine. Season well and pour over vegetables and pheasant. Cook in slow to moderate oven, turning and basting the pheasant for 2–2½ hours until tender.

From Mrs. M. C. Rose, Salop.

APPLE CRUNCHIE

1 lb. cooking apples.
Lemon juice.
2 oz. margarine.

3 heaped dessertspoons soft brown
   sugar.
Quick porridge oats.

PEEL and cut up cooking apples and put in pie dish. Sprinkle with lemon juice. Mix together margarine and sugar, and enough oats to make a firm mixture. Spread over the apples and bake in a moderate oven for 20 minutes. Serve with cream.

From Mrs. J. Walker, Hampshire.

END-OF-WEEK PUDDING

4 oz. self-raising flour.	Milk.
4 oz. breadcrumbs.	Salt.
4 oz. suet.	Mixed herbs, chives or onions.
1 egg.	Leftover cooked meat or bacon.

MIX together flour, breadcrumbs, suet, egg and enough milk to make a stiff dough, and season with salt and herbs, chives or onions to taste. Add cooked meat, bacon or sausages, chopped small, and steam for three hours.

If there is no bread available, all flour can be used, but the pudding will not be so light. If there is no meat, the pudding can be served with a good thick gravy and plenty of fried onions. If there is any left, it is very good fried with bacon for breakfast next morning.

From Mrs. S. Davies, Somerset.

BARA BRITH

3 lbs. plain flour.	1 lb. currants.
¾ lb. brown sugar.	¼ lb. candied peel.
¾ lb. lard or butter (or mixed).	1 oz. yeast.
2 large eggs.	½ teaspoonful mixed spice.
1 lb. raisins.	1 teaspoonful salt.
	Milk to mix.

MIX yeast with a little warm milk. Rub the fat into the flour and mix the dry ingredients. Make a well in the middle and add the yeast. Mix into a soft dough, then cover and leave in a warm place for 1½ hours to rise, till twice its original size. Turn on to a floured board, place in greased tins and bake in a moderately quick oven for 1–2 hours. When cold, cut and butter as for ordinary loaf—thin slices with plenty of butter.

From Mrs. D. I. Wigley, Montgomeryshire.

QUICK FRUIT CAKE

12 ozs. mixed dried fruit.	¼ pint water.
1 egg.	4 ozs. brown sugar.
4 ozs. margarine.	8 ozs. self-raising flour.

PUT fruit, margarine, water and sugar in a saucepan and simmer slowly for 20 minutes. Take off stove and cool. Add beaten egg and flour. Put in greased oblong loaf tin (1 lb. size) and bake at 325°F (Gas Mark 3) for 1½ hours. The oblong shape makes for easy slicing for picnic packing and tea in the harvest field.

From Mrs. S. Cranwell, Bedfordshire.

CHOCOLATE SWISS ROLL

3 ozs. plain flour.
3 ozs. chocolate powder.
½ gill milk.
2 eggs.

3 ozs. caster sugar.
½ teaspoon baking powder.
2 ozs. magarine.
Vanilla essence.

Filling

4 ozs. icing sugar.
2 ozs. butter.

Vanilla essence.

GREASE Swiss roll tin and line with greaseproof paper. Dissolve chocolate powder in the milk and mix to a smooth paste. Sieve the flour and baking powder, and beat sugar and margarine to a cream. Add 1 egg, stir in briskly and beat for 5 minutes, then add the other egg and beat as before. Mix in the chocolate and milk, flavour with vanilla, fold in the flour and baking powder. Spread evenly over the prepared tin and bake at 425°F (Gas Mark 7) for 8–10 minutes, until the mixture feels spongy.

Prepare a damp tea towel with sugared greaseproof paper on top. Turn the sponge out on to this and roll it up after cutting off the outside edge. Leave until thoroughly cold. Make up butter icing for the filling. When the sponge is quite cold, unroll it. Spread with filling, then roll up evenly.

From Mrs. M. E. Sanders, Cornwall.

LORD CREWE'S CAKE

1 lb. butter.
1 lb. caster sugar.
2 lbs. plain flour.
2 teaspoonfuls baking powder
2 teaspoonfuls nutmeg.

1½ lbs. sultanas.
¼ lb. whole almonds.
¼ lb. citron peel.
4 eggs.
2 cups of milk.

THIS can be mixed either by creaming the fat and sugar, adding the dry ingredients, then the eggs and milk; or by rubbing the fat into the flour and adding dry and wet ingredients. Bake in a moderate oven (350°F or Gas Mark 4) for 2 hours. This quantity makes three loaves. We find that the addition of a few ground almonds adds to the keeping quality.

From Mrs. D. Freeman, Essex.

AFTERNOON TEA JUMBLES

1 oz. butter.
1 egg.
2 ozs. caster sugar.
1 oz. cornflour.

Grated rind from ½ lemon.
2 dessertspoonfuls milk.
Flour.

PUT the butter and sugar into a mixing bowl and work it with a spoon until creamy. Add the well beaten egg, the cornflour and grated lemon rind, and beat well. Add the milk and enough flour to make a soft dough. Roll out on a floured board or surface and cut into 3 ins. lengths, roll these lightly with the palm of the hand, and then form them into a letter "S" and bake for approximately 15 minutes in a moderate oven (350°F or Gas Mark 4).

From Mrs. Waghorn, Kent.

COCONUT COOKIES

2 egg whites.   6 ozs. desiccated coconut.
4 ozs. caster sugar.

WHISK egg whites to a stiff foam. Fold in sugar and coconut. Drop spoonfuls on to rice paper or a greased baking sheet. Bake at 335°F (Gas Mark 3) for 15 minutes. Cool before removing from tin.

From Mrs. Butcher, Yorkshire.

FLAT CURRANT CAKES

¾ lbs. self-raising flour.   3 tablespoonfuls currants
½ lb. lard and margarine mixed.   2 eggs.
½ lb. sugar.   Milk and water.

RUB fat into flour, add sugar and currants, then eggs. Mix with milk and water to a dropping consistency. Put into three greased sandwich tins and bake in a moderate oven. Butter on the top and cut into wedges.

From Mrs. Shucksmith, Goole.

BANANA NUT BREAD

1 cup sugar.   2 cups self-raising flour.
4 ozs. butter.   2 very ripe bananas.
2 eggs.   Vanilla essence.
3 tablespoonfuls sour milk.   1 cup chopped walnuts.
1 teaspoonful bicarbonate of soda

CREAM the butter and sugar, add the well-beaten eggs. Mash the bananas then add together with the flour and the bicarbonate of soda mixed with the milk. Add vanilla essence and finally the chopped nuts. Bake in a greased loaf tin, at 350°F Gas (Mark 4) for 1 hour. Slice and butter.

From Mrs. Moore, Yorkshire.

TIPSY CAKE

1 sponge cake.
1 wineglass sherry.
1 wineglass raisin wine.
1 quart cup custard
Almond essence.

Cup Custard
1 pint cream
1 pint new milk.
6 eggs well beaten.
1 cinnamon stick.
4 ozs. lump sugar.
10 ozs. blanched almonds.
A little rum and sherry.

PUT sponge cake in bowl and sprinkle with sherry and raisin wine. Leave for one hour. Pour over cup custard flavoured with almond essence. Make the cup custard by placing cream, milk, eggs and cinnamon in a bowl over boiling water and stirring carefully all one way until it becomes quite thick. Add sugar. When nearly cold, add blanched almonds, rum and sherry.

From Mrs. Dale, Staffordshire.

YORKSHIRE CURD CAKES

1 quart beastings (first milk of a newly calved cow)
Shortcrust pastry.
3 ozs. sugar.
1 beaten egg.
Pinch of nutmeg.

Handful of currants.
Finely grated lemon rind.
1 teaspoonful baking powder.
1 scant oz. melted butter.

PUT beastings into a heavy based pan and stand it over a gentle heat. Do not let it burn (it quickly becomes almost solid in the pan). When it is solid, turn it out into a large basin, straining it through a sieve. Before the curd is quite cold, break it up with a fork, not too finely.

Line a deep saucepan or tin with a good shortcrust pastry, and fill it with $\frac{1}{2}$ lb. curds and the remaining ingredients mixed together. Bake at 400°F (Gas Mark 6) for 30 minutes.

From Mrs. Shuttleworth, Hampshire.

APPLE CHUTNEY

3 lbs. sliced cooking apples.
$1\frac{1}{2}$ lbs. chopped onions.
$1\frac{1}{2}$ lbs. demerara sugar.
1 tablespoonful salt.
1 teaspoonful ground ginger.

1 teaspoonful mixed spice.
$\frac{1}{2}$ teaspoonful white pepper.
1 lb. sultanas.
1 pint vinegar.

BOIL all ingredients together for one hour.

From Mrs. Haynes, Isle of Man.

MARROW AND APPLE CHUTNEY

2 lbs. well-ripened marrow.	1½ oz. salt.
4 lbs. Bramley apples.	Cayenne pepper.
6 lbs. sugar.	Ground ginger.
8 ozs. onions or shallots.	1 oz. citric or tartaric acid.
8 ozs. seedless raisins.	¾ pint vinegar.

THIS is a very sweet chutney, very similar to mango chutney. Boil apples, chopped onions, raisins and sugar until apples are nearly pulped, stirring continuously. Add marrow cut into 1 in. cubes, and continue to simmer until marrow is quite transparent and apples are thoroughly pulped. Add salt, pepper and ginger to taste, citric acid and vinegar and continue to simmer for further 15 minutes. On no account should iron or chipped enamel pans be used. Let mixture cool slightly, stir and pour into hot jars. Tie down when cold.

From Mrs. Wilson, Suffolk.

PICKLED BEETS

Uncooked beetroot.	¼ oz. whole allspice.
1 quart vinegar.	¼ oz. cloves.
¼ oz. mace.	A few pepercorns.
¼ oz. cinnamon stick.	

WASH and peel the uncooked beetroot, shred finely using a grater. Pack into clean glass-topped preserving jars and cover with cold spiced vinegar. Make this by tying spices in a muslin bag and adding to the vinegar. Bring to boiling point and leave to stand for 2 hours. Use a saucepan with a tight fitting lid. Remove the spice bag and the vinegar is ready for use.

From Mrs. G. Edwards, Denbighshire.

PICKLED MUSHROOMS

Button mushrooms.	Vinegar.
Salted water.	Pickling spice.

CLEAN mushrooms with a cloth dipped in salt and water, and boil them in salted water for 5 minutes. Put on a cloth to cool. Pack into jars and fill with cold vinegar which has been boiled with pickling spice. A spoonful of olive oil poured on the surface will preserve them, but don't use them for a few days.

From Miss R. Roberts, Merionethshire.

319

SWEET PEAR PICKLE

3½ lbs. pears.
1½ lbs. sugar.

¼ oz. cloves.
½ pint vinegar.

PEEL and cut up pears into small pieces. Cook in the vinegar with cloves and sugar until tender and slightly thick. Pot and tie down. Ready for use immediately. Use a little more vinegar if pears are not ripe. Delicious with any kind of cold meat or game.

From Mrs. Codling, Lincolnshire.

MARROW JAM

4 lbs. marrow
5 lbs. sugar.

1 pint apple juice

Make apple juice from windfalls stewed with cores and skins included. Dice marrow, put in a large bowl and cover with 4 lbs. sugar. Leave overnight. Next morning, add apple juice and remaining sugar. Boil until marrow is cooked and slightly transparent (about ¾ hour). This jam sets very well.

From Mrs. J. Poole, Devonshire.

APRICOT AND RHUBARB JAM

8 ozs. dried apricots.
½ pint water.

1½ lbs. rhubarb.
3½ lbs. sugar.

MINCE apricots and soak overnight in water. Next day, simmer gently for 20 minutes, add rhubarb and simmer until rhubarb has softened. Add sugar, stir until sugar has dissolved, and boil rapidly until setting point is reached. This makes approximately 5 lbs. of delicious golden jam.

From Mrs. Cooper, Hampshire.

JELLY FROM LEFTOVERS

Gooseberries.
Redcurrants.
Blackcurrants.

Raspberries.
Sugar.

USE a mixture of fruit for this, just a few of each kind left in the garden. Put into a pan, cover with water and simmer until skins are tender. Drip through muslin overnight. Measure the juice and allow 1 lb. sugar to each pint of juice. Boil together for 20 minutes and it will set into a lovely jelly.

From Mrs. Q. Newcombe, Devonshire.

SIMPLE MARMALADE

2 lbs. Seville oranges.   4 lbs. sugar.
3 pints water.

TAKE oranges and boil with water until liquid is reduced to 1½ pints. Remove oranges and cut in half. Scoop out all fleshy part and sieve this into liquid, throwing away remains. Cut up peel and add to liquid. Add sugar and boil until set is obtained in 10 to 15 minutes.

From Mrs. M. Willies, Worcestershire.

CHEAP LEMONADE

1 orange   ½ oz. tartaric acid.
2 lemons.   ½ oz. citric acid.
2 lbs. sugar.   ½ oz. Epsom salts.

GRATE rind of orange and lemons and squeeze juice. Put all ingredients in china bowl and add 1 quart boiling water. Bottle when cold. Dilute to taste.

From Mrs. D. Harris, Dorset.

LEMON SQUASH (or ORANGE SQUASH)

2 lemons (or oranges).   3 cupfuls sugar.
1 oz. citric acid.   2 pints boiling water.

PEEL lemons or oranges thinly with a potato peeler. Put peel in a bowl with the juice, discarding the bitter white pith. Add acid, sugar and water and stir until sugar is dissolved. Leave until cold, strain and bottle.

From Mrs. K. Richards, Gloucestershire.

EASY ELDERFLOWER WINE

2 elderflower heads.   1 gallon cold water.
2 lbs. loaf sugar.   2 good sized lemons.
2 tablespoons white vinegar.

WASH the flower heads and place in a large china jug or earthenware jar, wash the lemons and slice them thinly. Add the sugar, white vinegar and finally the cold water. Leave to stand for 24 hours, then strain and bottle.

It is important to use bottles with screw tops. (Empty lemonade bottles are excellent). It is ready to drink in ten days time.

From Mrs. G. Edwards, Denbighshire.

CLOTTED CREAM

USE new milk and strain at once, as soon as milked, into shallow pans. In winter let the milk stand 24 hours, in the summer 12 hours at least. Then put the milk pan on a hot hearth if you have one; if not, set it in a wide brass kettle of water, large enough to receive the pan. It must remain on the fire till quite hot, but on no account boil or there will be a skin instead of a cream upon the milk. You will know when done enough by the undulations on the surface looking thick, and having a ring round the pan the size of the bottom. The time required to scald cream depends on the size of the pan and the heat of the fire; the slower the better.

Clotted cream is best done over a stick fire. Remove the pan into the dairy when done. Great care must be taken in moving the pans so that the cream is not broken both in putting on the fire and taking off. In cold weather it may stand 36 hours, and never less than two meals. When required, skim off the cream in layers into a glass dish for the table, taking care to have a good crust on the top.

From Mrs. G. Edwards, Denbighshire.

INDEX

323

325